CONCENTRATE Q&A
LAND LAW

FREE online study and revision support available at **www.oup.com/lawrevision**

Take your learning further with:

- Multiple-choice questions with instant feedback
- Interactive glossaries and flashcards of key cases
- Tips, tricks and audio advice
- Annotated outline answers
- Diagnostic tests show you where to concentrate
- Extra questions, key facts checklists, and topic overviews

unique features

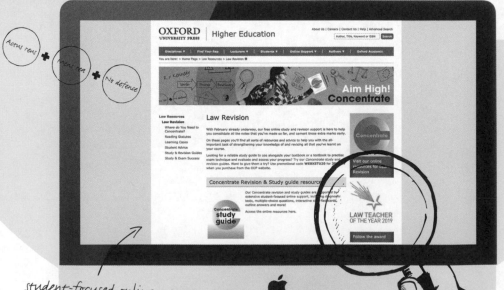

Actus reus + *mens rea* + *No defence*

student-focused online support

CONCENTRATE Q&A LAND LAW

Rosalind Malcolm

Barrister, Professor of Law, University of Surrey

THIRD EDITION

OXFORD
UNIVERSITY PRESS

OXFORD
UNIVERSITY PRESS

Great Clarendon Street, Oxford, OX2 6DP,
United Kingdom

Oxford University Press is a department of the University of Oxford.
It furthers the University's objective of excellence in research, scholarship,
and education by publishing worldwide. Oxford is a registered trade mark of
Oxford University Press in the UK and in certain other countries

© Rosalind Malcolm 2020

The moral rights of the author have been asserted

First edition 2016
Second edition 2018

Impression: 2

Public sector information reproduced under Open Government Licence v3.0
(http://www.nationalarchives.gov.uk/doc/open-government-licence/open-government-licence.htm)

Published in the United States of America by Oxford University Press
198 Madison Avenue, New York, NY 10016, United States of America

British Library Cataloguing in Publication Data

Data available

Library of Congress Control Number: 2020935472

ISBN 978–0–19–885320–6

Printed in Great Britain by
Bell & Bain Ltd., Glasgow

In memory of Margaret Wilkie who created
this series of Q & A books

Contents

Guide to the Book

Every book in the Concentrate Q&A series contains the following features:

Are you ready to face the exam? This box at the start of each chapter identifies the key topics and cases that you need to have learned, revised, and understood before tackling the questions in each chapter.

Not sure where to begin? Clear diagram answer plans at the start of each question help you see how to structure your answer at a glance and take you through each point step by step.

Demonstrating your knowledge of the crucial debates is a sure-fire way to impress examiners. These at-a-glance boxes help remind you of the key debates relevant to each topic, which you should discuss in your answers to get the highest marks.

What makes a great answer great? Our authors show you the thought process behind their own answers, and how you can do the same in your exam. Key sentences are highlighted and advice is given on how to structure your answer well and develop your arguments.

Each question represents a typical essay or problem question so that you know exactly what to expect in your exam.

Don't settle for a good answer—make it great! This feature gives you extra points to include in the exam if you want to gain more marks and make your answer stand out.

Don't fall into any traps! This feature points out common mistakes that students make, and which you need to avoid when answering each question.

Really push yourself and impress your examiner by going beyond what is expected. Focused further reading suggestions allow you to develop in-depth knowledge of the subject for when you are looking for the highest marks.

Guide to the Online Resources

Every book in the Concentrate Q&A series is supported by additional online materials to aid your study and revision: www.oup.com/uk/qanda/

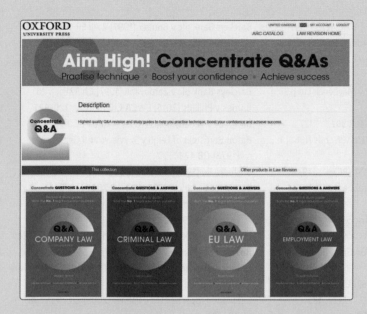

- Extra essay and problem questions with guidance on how to approach them.
- Video guidance on how to put an answer plan together.
- Audio advice on revision and exam technique from Nigel Foster.

Table of Cases

Table of Legislation

UK secondary legislation

International legislation

Exam Skills for Success in Land Law

1

During the Module

● Be sure to attend all your lectures and tutorials and engage fully in them. Make sure you prepare the work for tutorials and then speak up and play a full role—that is a sure-fire way to learn.

● Do go to the revision lecture if your tutor offers one. It will help you prepare for your revision time and will give you a broad overview of what you have done during the module, helping you to reflect on the coverage of topics.

The Revision Period

● Use previous papers to help you structure your revision. Your exam is likely to follow the same pattern and structure as in previous papers unless your tutor or your module has changed.

● Check the length of your paper and the number of questions you are required to complete during that time. This enables you to be able to practise under exam conditions. Basic arithmetic applies here: divide the length of the paper by the number of questions you have to do and then you know how long on average you have to write each question. Then sit in your room with a timer on and tackle questions from past papers.

● Practise writing some answers by hand rather than by word processing, especially if you are out of practice at handwriting. There are two points to be made here: is your handwriting legible and can you actually write fast enough to complete what is necessary within the time allowed for the exam? If legibility is your problem, then get a copy book and practise handwriting. And do those test exam questions in the privacy of your study under exam conditions until you have had enough practice at simply writing, so that is not a barrier in the exam.

● Avoid question spotting, which can leave you completely up the creek without a paddle. Do not limit your chances of success in this way. Basic arithmetic again applies. If you have to answer three questions and only one or two are what you have worked for, your chances of succeeding well (or at all) are tragically limited. Further, some students revise a topic on the basis that they will only answer an essay question on that topic. And then, horror of horrors, a problem question crops up for the first time in five years. Revise a topic from all angles. Be ready to answer either a problem or an essay question on it.

In the Exam Room

- READ THE QUESTION, THEN ANSWER THE QUESTION THAT HAS BEEN SET (not the one you wish had been set).

- You will be marked on whether you have spotted all the issues. So, in a problem question read it slowly and carefully. List the issues in your plan. There is unlikely to be anything in the question that is not important, so you need to ask yourself, 'What is that point about? Why is that fact included?'

- In a problem question, are you asked to advise purchasers or a named person? Write your answer on that basis: 'the purchasers are advised that they will be bound by this interest . . . '.

- In an essay, what is the instruction? Are you asked to comment or to compare or discuss? For example, if you are asked to discuss whether the law relating to overriding interests is in a fair and rational state, you are being asked to critique this area of law. So, if you set out to explain it you will only achieve so many marks (if you are accurate), but if you use that knowledge to critique this area of law, then you will be doing what the examiner wants and your mark will improve. Throughout the essay you will need to comment as you go along, and then your conclusion will address this precise point: 'In conclusion, this area of law is in a fair and rational state because, while the mirror principle in respect of registered title is the underpinning factor, nevertheless it is important to permit some interests to bind a purchaser even where they are not reflected on the register.' It means you have to think yourself into the question. You might have revised and practised questions on this topic, but this particular angle might be new. Don't be fazed by it, but think yourself into it. Use your knowledge and turn it round to address the question.

- You already know how long you have and how many questions you need to answer, so you know how long you have for each one. Make sure you have a working watch with you and that it is synchronised with the exam room clock. Give yourself time to read the paper and choose your questions, then set yourself a time limit for each answer. Don't be caught out at the end by running out of time and having to write sad billets-doux to your examiner— 'Sorry, out of time.' No marks for that.

● Don't worry about saving the planet when writing your answers. The answer book is all yours to use, so write on one side only and start each answer on a new page. That way, when you have last-moment inspiration you will have room to go back and add it in without sending your examiner on a hunt for that tiny asterisk.

● Write the question number clearly at the beginning of each answer and also write numbers clearly for subsections within each answer. Leave a space between subsections.

● Don't be afraid to use headings and underline them as you go along.

● Underline cases and statutes as you go along. Rulers are not required—just draw a freehand line under the relevant name.

● Remember, if you are allowed, to bring your statute book with you to the exam. Observe the rules as to what you are permitted to write or highlight in it. There is nothing more distressing than to have your statute book removed by the invigilator, plus the possible penalty of breaking the rules. Make sure that you have read the statutes in this book during lectures and as part of your preparation for tutorials. You want to have it as a comfort blanket with you, so it needs to be familiar to you.

● Always include the date of a statute, which is no problem if you have your statute book with you. If you can, do the same for cases, but that is less of a demand than for statutes.

● Don't quote big chunks verbatim from a statute—reference the section, subsection etc. to pinpoint it.

● Memory matters. Learn the case names. Use memory techniques that work for you—sticky notes around the house; card indexes; fancy software packages, whatever works best. And if, despite all that, in the exam room your mind goes blank, then identify a case by giving a few of its key facts: 'In a case where the young man was befriended by the gentleman farmer who made promises to him that if he worked for him then the estate would be his . . .'.

The Structure and Approach to Problem Questions

● All the books in this series have adopted the IRAC structure (Identify the issues, Relevant law, Apply the law, and Conclusions). This has the advantage of imposing a clearly remembered structure on you. The 'I' (the facts or factual issues) is the issue-spotting bit. You need to pick up all the issues to earn all the marks that are going. Miss one and you miss earning marks. The 'R' is the law. In land law, this is usually a mix of statute and case law. The 'A' is really the core of getting top marks—the trick with a problem question is applying the law to the problem. Stating the law is one thing—the clever bit is to do what lawyers do—apply it to the problem and become a problem solver. The 'C' is (obviously) the conclusion. A word of warning about the IRAC approach: it helps to get a structure into your answer—or more importantly into your thoughts in the first place. But in the answer plans we have often summarised the points quite extensively—so you will find that the suggested answers do go into quite a bit more detail than the answer plans. It is probably fair to say that the answer plan gives you the basics. But if you want to do better than that and get into the heady and utterly desirable upper-second and first-class answers, then study the suggested answers, where we have attempted to give you the full monty.

Last Word

● Do you write well? Lawyers are wordsmiths. Words are our tools and we must use them precisely to convey what we mean. Writing well is an essential requirement and if you have been pulled up about this in formative coursework, or, if you know that this is not your strong point, then do something about it. It may be that your university offers classes in writing skills. Go to them. Practise writing. Write letters to friends and relatives. Write a short story and ask someone to read it over and critique it. Learn basic grammar from an English grammar book. Read how others write. Read a judgment and see how judges construct their sentences. I would like to urge you to write beautifully—but clarity will suffice. Clarity comes from writing grammatically and coherently. You will not be marked on whether you have good knowledge of grammar. But you will be marked on whether you have made clear what you are arguing. That comes from good writing skills.

Definition of Land and Finders' Titles

2

ARE YOU READY?

In order to attempt the two questions in this chapter, you will need to have covered the following topics:

- the definition of land;
- the meaning and application of the Latin maxims: *cuius est solum eius est usque ad coelum et ad inferos* ('the owner of the land owns everything up to the sky and down to the centre of the earth') and *quicquid plantatur solo, solo cedit* ('whatever is attached to the land becomes part of the land');
- the law relating to fixtures and fittings;
- nature of property rights at common law;
- relative nature of property rights;
- possession as font of title for finders;
- title to registered land;
- the **Treasure Act 1996** and related Code of Practice and Order.

KEY DEBATES

Debate: property rights

These rights are complex and the ancient maxims regarding underground space may require modernisation given modern technology and current issues such as 'fracking', which takes place underground (see *Star Energy Weald Basin Limited and another v Bocardo SA*).

⊙
Debate: finders' title

Title at common law is itself a relative concept so a key debate is how the title of a finder of a chattel relates to other titles (ie weaker than that of the true owner, but—depending on the circumstances—perhaps a stronger title than that of anyone else). Part of this debate is that at common law the relative strength of property rights in a chattel depends largely upon the time at which they are acquired: titles acquired earlier in time generally have priority over those acquired later. So, the chimney sweep's boy in *Armory v Delamirie* **(1722) 5 Stra 505** succeeded in his claim against the jeweller; but he could not have resisted a claim brought by the true owner, and the case did not decide whether the boy could have successfully defended a claim brought by his master, or by the owner of the house in which the jewel had been found.

QUESTION   **1**

Cuius est solum eius est usque ad coelum et ad inferos ('The owner of the land owns everything up to the sky and down to the centre of the earth').

Discuss.

! CAUTION!

■ This question is either a dream or a nightmare! There is a vast amount of material to be covered and it is unlikely that you can deal with it all. You may be guided by what you have covered in lectures.

■ The usual advice not to regurgitate all you know holds good. Discuss the maxim critically: what are its limitations? Don't just dismiss it—consider to what extent it holds true.

■ Utilise the Point, Evidence, and Analysis (PEA) method to ensure that your answer is logically structured and contains sufficient analysis.

DIAGRAM ANSWER PLAN

Explain the meaning of the maxim.

▼

Show the limitations on the rights of fee simple owners to use their land.

▼

Deal in turn with the following items showing how the ownership of each is limited:

■ airspace;

■ water;

■ subterranean minerals;

■ wild animals.

▼

Turn next to the discussion of chattels (items of personal property—so not part of the land) and discuss the distinction between chattels and fixtures (items of real property—so part of the land). Mention the exception of treasure.

▼

Conclusion—briefly summarise the application of the maxim.

(A) **SUGGESTED ANSWER**

Introduction

This maxim, which was coined by Accursius, a professor at the University of Bologna in the thirteenth century, relates to the extent of the ownership enjoyed by the fee simple owner. There is, in fact, a number of limitations on the ownership of the fee simple owner.[1] Some are statutory, others are founded in the common law.

[1] This sets out what is coming next in terms of the discussion of the limitations of the maxim.

Limitation of Rights[2]

[2] The broad heading 'Limitation of Rights' is then sub-divided for clarity into the different areas.

Airspace

The first aspect to be considered is the extent of the fee simple owner's rights in the airspace above the property. The owner's rights extend to such a height as is reasonably necessary for the ordinary use and enjoyment of the land. In *Baron Bernstein of Leigh v Skyviews and General Ltd* **[1978] QB 479**, Griffith J stated that it was necessary to balance the rights of an owner to enjoy the land against the rights of the general public to take advantage of all that 'science now offers in the use of airspace'. Thus, the rights of the owner were limited to such a height as is necessary for the ordinary use and enjoyment of the land, and above that height the fee simple owner has no greater rights than any other member of the public.

Where there is an interference with the legitimate rights of the fee simple owner, then these rights may be maintained by an action for nuisance or trespass.[3] In *Kelsen v Imperial Tobacco Co (of Great Britain and Ireland) Ltd* **[1957] 2 QB 334**, the action of the defendant in allowing an advertisement to overhang the plaintiff's premises amounted to a trespass, as was the action of the defendant in *Woollerton and Wilson Ltd v Richard Costain Ltd* **[1970] 1 WLR 411**, in allowing the jib of a crane to swing over the plaintiff's property. It follows from this that normally the grant of a lease will include the right to the airspace above the land, unless there is a contrary intention demonstrated.

Two decisions show that use of the presumption that the owner of land owns the airspace above it can be complex and highly dependent on the particular facts.[4] In *Rosebery Ltd v Rocklee Ltd* **[2011] EWHC B1 (Ch)**, it was held that there is no such presumption where the lease is of, or includes, a roof and use of the airspace above the roof that could interfere with fellow lessees. The presumption in that decision was not applicable to part of a building which had been horizontally divided where good reasons for the demise to be limited to a stratum[5] so as not to include airspace (or subsoil) were applicable. By contrast, in *H Waites Limited v Hambledon Court Ltd* **[2014] EWHC 615 (Ch)**, the presumption was applicable in respect of the airspace above demised garages where there was a vertical division and the parties must have intended the demise to apply to the airspace above.

Under the **Civil Aviation Act 1982**, it is a defence to an action in trespass or nuisance for aircraft to fly at such a height that is reasonable under the circumstances.

Water

Water is incapable of ownership, and the rights which a landowner has over and in respect of it depend on whether the water flows[6] through a defined channel or percolates on or under land in an undefined channel. In the case of the former, the landowner may receive the water in an unpolluted state but may not diminish its flow downstream (*John Young & Co v Bankier Distillery Co* **[1893] AC 691**). Where water percolates in an undefined channel on land, although it is not subject to ownership the landowner can appropriate all of it to the detriment of the downstream landowner (*Ballard v Tomlinson* **(1885) 29 ChD 115**; *Bradford Corp v Pickles* **[1895] AC 587**; *Cambridge Water Co v Eastern Counties Leather plc* **[1994] 2 AC 264**).

[3] This demonstrates your knowledge of the actions which protect property rights.

[4] The two cases that follow flag this point nicely.

[5] The reference to stratum refers to the level—flats are divided into horizontal strata, so you do not normally get rights over the airspace above your flat.

[6] There is much statutory law controlling who can abstract water, which is sometimes termed 'regulatory property'. It is unlikely that your module will cover this important new area. Unless your lecturer has covered this, then you should address here just the traditional property-owning aspects rather than rights (and duties) conferred by statute.

Minerals

The maxim also states that the landowner owns everything down to the centre of the earth. With the exception of silver and gold, which are vested in the Crown by virtue, originally, of the *Case of Mines* **[1568] 1 Plowd 310**, at common law all minerals are owned by the landowner. However, ownership is, in fact, vested by various statutes in the Crown or other public bodies. For example, petroleum in its natural state is vested in the Crown by virtue of the **Petroleum Act 1998** and coal is vested in the Coal Authority by the **Coal Industry Act 1994**.

[7] This paragraph details a discussion of this case, which is topical on underground space.

In *Star Energy Weald Basin Ltd v Bocardo SA* (2010),[7] Star Energy, which had a licence under statute to search for and extract petroleum, had drilled wells that went directly under Bocardo's land at a minimum depth of 800 feet, and which reached depths of up to 2,900 feet in order to reach the natural reservoir of petroleum and gas. The drilling under Bocardo's land was done without its consent, and (for many years) without its knowledge. Bocardo claimed damages for trespass from Star Energy; in order to succeed it needed to show that it had title to the subterranean land at the depths at which the drilling took place. Lord Hope (with whose judgment the other members of the Supreme Court agreed) concluded that, in relation to what lies below the surface, the maxim is still good law. He admitted that at great depths, where there is enormous pressure and molten rock, it is impractical to seek to apply the maxim; but that was not the case here. Although the drilling was at such depths that it did not interfere with Bocardo's own use of its land, the fact that the petroleum could be reached by human activity raised the question of who owned the strata in which it was found. Although the Crown owned the petroleum, it did not own the surrounding strata; the only possible owner was therefore Bocardo, the drilling was held to be an actionable trespass, and Bocardo was awarded damages. No injunction was claimed in the case, and it seems unlikely that an injunction would be awarded in these sorts of circumstances, where the trespass is technical and does not cause the claimant any loss or inconvenience.

Wild animals on land

Wild animals are not subject to ownership (*The Case of Swans* **(1592) 7 Co Rep 156**), but they may be hunted by the fee simple owner on whose land they run. There is, however, a number of limitations to this right in respect of protected species (**Wildlife and Countryside Act 1981** (as amended) and the **Protection of Badgers Act 1992**, for example).

[8] This short paragraph introduces the subject of chattels and sets out the basic law of ownership.

[9] The exception is set out here.

Ownership of chattels[8] (items of personal property) found on land

The fee simple owner is *prima facie* entitled to all chattels found in or on the land, in the absence of a legitimate claim from the owner of the chattel, unless (where the object is found on the land) the finder acquires a prior right. Treasure (as defined in the **Treasure Act 1996**) is an exception to this:[9] it vests in the Crown, subject to prior rights and interests.

Distinguishing between fixtures and chattels

Land is defined in the **Law of Property Act (LPA) 1925, s 205(1)(ix)** as including 'the surface, buildings or parts of buildings' and whatever is attached to the land becomes part of the land under another Latin maxim, *quicquid plantatur solo, solo cedit*.[10] This raises, in practice, an important problem relating to ownership of those items which, but for the fact that they are attached to the land, would constitute chattels. The distinction needs to be drawn between those items which are fixtures, and therefore part of the realty (real property), and those which are not, and therefore personalty (personal property).

[10] The discussion of another maxim opens the analysis of the distinction between 'fixtures and fittings'.

There are two tests for determining whether an object is a fixture or a chattel. The first test relates to the degree of annexation. If the object is annexed to the land then it is, *prima facie*, a fixture. So, in *Holland v Hodgson* **(1872) LR 7 CP 328**, spinning looms bolted to the floor of a factory were attached other than by their own weight and were fixtures. In *Hulme v Brigham* **[1943] KB 152**, however, heavy printing presses, which stood on the floor without any attachment other than the force of gravity, were chattels. In *Chelsea Yacht & Boat Co v Pope* **[2000] 1 WLR 1941**, a houseboat, which was moored to the bank and which moved up and down with the tide, was held to be a chattel.

The paramount test, however, was foreshadowed by Blackburn J in *Holland v Hodgson* and relates to the purpose of annexation. Under this test, the question to be asked is whether the chattel has been affixed to the land for the better enjoyment of the object as a chattel, or for the more convenient use of the land. This leads to the result that the same object may constitute a fixture in one case, but a chattel in another. For example, in *Leigh v Taylor* **[1902] AC 157**, tapestries nailed to a wall were held not to be fixtures, but in *Re Whaley* **[1908] 1 Ch 615**, similar objects were held to be fixtures because the object of their annexation was to enhance the room. Lord Halsbury LC in *Leigh v Taylor* confirmed that the key test was the purpose of annexation, and this was confirmed in *Hamp v Bygrave* **(1982) 266 EG 720**, where garden ornaments that formed part of a landscape display were held to be fixtures, despite the fact that they rested on the ground simply by their own weight.

In *Elitestone Ltd v Morris* **[1997] 1 WLR 687**, the House of Lords held that what is of primary importance is the intention involved. It was indicated that this is an objective test to determine whether the object was intended for the use or enjoyment of the land, or for the more convenient use of the object itself. Clearly, the courts are prepared to apply a common-sense approach to this issue (*Botham v TSB Bank plc* **(1997) 73 P & CR D1**).

There are some exceptional cases where there is a right to remove fixtures. A tenant may remove trade fixtures that have been attached to the land for the purpose of carrying out his trade; ornamental and domestic fixtures, provided their removal will cause no substantial damage to the property; and agricultural fixtures in accordance with the procedure set out in the **Agricultural Holdings Act 1986** (tenancies of agricultural holdings) and **Agricultural Tenancies Act 1995** (farm business tenancies). In *Peel Land and Property (Ports No 3) Ltd v TS Sheerness Steel Ltd* **[2013] EWHC 1658 (Ch)**, the judge held that the fact that an item is bulky and awkward, and the exercise of severance is complex, does not necessarily mean that the item cannot be a removable tenant's fixture.

11 The conclusion rounds off the answer, bringing it back to the question set.

Conclusion[11]

The maxim is a starting point for the analysis of the rights that a property owner acquires in the land which is the subject of their freehold ownership. But there is a series of limitations, discussed above, which arise either as a result of statutory intervention or through judicial law making. Notably, the maxim is most alive in relation to the rights over subterranean soil. The topic remains of extreme current importance, given the development of modern technology to tunnel, quarry, mine, or conduct hydraulic fracturing under one's own land and neighbouring land. The development of unmanned aircraft may well give rise to further limitations to (or protection of) the right discussed above to airspace in the future.

➕ LOOKING FOR EXTRA MARKS?

- Make sure that your answer follows a logical structure—use headings to help you.
- Write critically about the Supreme Court decision and reference the debate about the implications of hydraulic fracturing (this is the technique commonly known as 'fracking', where drilling underground takes place for oil and gas).
- Consider raising the issue of other new technology and its impact on the ownership of land (eg unmanned aircraft vehicles, or 'drones'). This will demonstrate your grasp of the modern application of the maxim.

QUESTION | 2

Abel has entered into a contract to sell his house to Baal.

He consults you as to whether the following items (which were not mentioned in the contract of sale) are to be included in the sale:

(a) a replica of the 'Three Graces' which is standing in the garden;

(b) a stained-glass lampshade, attached to the ceiling by a chain, which was given to him by friends when he got married;

(c) the fitted kitchen, which Abel installed himself (he wants to dismantle it and adapt it for his new house);

(d) adjustable bookshelves, which slot into strips of metal screwed into the wall; and

(e) an ornamental fireplace, which is on hire-purchase from Quickfire Ltd.

CAUTION!

■ In order to answer this question, you should be able to distinguish between fixtures and fittings (items of personal property).

■ This is a single-topic question, so you should not answer it if you cannot explain the test of the purpose of annexation, which is critical to the distinction between fixtures and fittings.

■ Remember to distinguish between the *degree* of annexation (ie how securely the item is fixed to the land) and the *reason* for the annexation (why it is fixed to the land).

■ Many of the cases you will need to use to answer this question vary according to their facts, so it is important to be able to distinguish principles of law in this area from issues of fact.

DIAGRAM ANSWER PLAN

| Identify the issues | ▪ Explain the distinction between fixtures and chattels. |

| Relevant law | ▪ Use *Berkley v Poulet* (1976); *Chelsea Yacht & Boat Co v Pope* [2000]; *Mew v Tristmire Ltd* [2011]; *Elitestone Ltd v Morris* [1997] and related case law. |

| Apply the law | ▪ Explain the purpose of distinguishing between fixtures and chattels.
▪ Set out the tests to distinguish between fixtures and chattels.
▪ Discuss the development of tests through case law.
▪ Initial test—discuss the degree of annexation.
▪ Discuss the case law and its application to each of the scenarios in (a), (b), (c), (d), and (e). |

| Conclude | ▪ Advise Abel. |

A **SUGGESTED ANSWER**

[1] Grasp the nettle right from the start and state simply and clearly the key issue.

[2] This introduces the critical point that factual differences are relevant.

There are two tests[1] to determine whether an item has become part of the freehold:

(i) the method and degree of annexation;

(ii) the object and purpose of the annexation.

The earlier law emphasised the first test, while later cases introduced the second test to alleviate the injustice where limited owners had affixed items of value to the land. The second test is now dominant, so if the item is physically annexed to the land, this does not necessarily resolve the matter anymore. Nevertheless, the degree of annexation remains a relevant question.[2]

According to Scarman LJ in *Berkley v Poulet* (1976) 242 EG 39, if there is such a degree of physical annexation that an object cannot be removed without serious damage to, or some destruction of, the realty, then there is a strong case for the item to be classified as a fixture. In *Chelsea Yacht & Boat Co v Pope* [2000] 1 WLR 1941, a houseboat, which was moored by ropes, chain, and an anchor was held to be a chattel, and a similar result was reached in *Mew v*

Tristmire Ltd **[2011] EWCA Civ 912**, where landing craft had been converted and rested on wooden platforms in a harbour.

[3] Now start applying the law to each of the problems set.

[4] As is frequently the case in an exam question, not all the facts are set out. This is often deliberate, in order to prompt you to consider two sides of the question.

(a) Thus, the determination of the question whether the 'Three Graces' is a fixture[3] will depend on an application of the two tests. It is not clear[4] whether the statue is physically fixed to the land, although it would seem from the question that it is merely 'standing' on the land. If that is the case, then, *prima facie*, the statue is not a fixture. In the case of *Berkley v Poulet* itself, a white marble statue of a Greek athlete weighing half a ton and standing on a plinth was considered not to be a fixture. Similarly, a printing machine secured by its own weight and weighing several tons was held not to be a fixture (*Hulme v Brigham* **[1943] KB 152**).

[5] You have started by stating the general rule. Now go on to show how it can be displaced.

However, the general rule can be displaced[5] where the object of annexation is that the chattels should become part of the land. Thus, a drystone wall which was constructed of blocks of stone placed one on top of another was held to have been intended to become part of the realty (*Holland v Hodgson* **(1872) LR 7 CP 328**). Intention refers to the purpose which the object serves,[6] not to the purpose of the person who put the object in place: *Elitestone Ltd v Morris* **[1997] 1 WLR 687 (HL)**.

[6] Intention is often a thorny issue. Make sure you make this point about what intention means in this context.

The fact that the 'Three Graces' is an ornamental object may not be a conclusive indication that it is not intended to become part of the land. In *Lord Chesterfield's Settled Estates* **[1911] 1 Ch 237**, Grinling Gibbons carvings were held to be fixtures; and in *Re Whaley* **[1908] 1 Ch 615**, chattels, which were placed in the room in order to create a beautiful room as a whole, were held to be capable of being fixtures. In *D'Eyncourt v Gregory* **(1866) LR 3 Eq 382**, statues which were part of the architectural design of a property were held to be fixtures, and, likewise, in *Kennedy v Secretary of State for Wales* **[1996] EGCS 17**, a carillon clock resting on its own weight was held to be part of the design of the historic house.

[7] Note that this is the concluding paragraph in this section, coming to a viewpoint on the application of the law to the problem.

[8] Without the full facts, it is reasonable to suggest the answer in terms of probability rather than being absolute.

However, in this problem,[7] regardless of the question of whether the 'Three Graces' are in fact physically affixed to the ground, it would seem probable[8] that the statue remains a chattel unless, as in *Hamp v Bygrave* **(1982) 266 EG 720**, it can be objectively viewed as a feature of, and part and parcel of, the garden, or, as in *D'Eyncourt v Gregory* and *Kennedy v Secretary of State for Wales*, as a part of the architectural or historic design of the house.

[9] You can start the second problem within this question by going straight to the application, as you have set out the law at the start.

(b) The stained-glass lampshade would not seem to pose the same difficulties.[9] It is an object that is essentially a chattel and it is unlikely that any evidence could be adduced to change its character into a fixture. If the first test were to be applied alone, then there is a degree of physical annexation, which might suggest that the lampshade was a fixture. This test is no longer decisive. In *Leigh v*

Taylor **[1902] AC 157**, tapestries were fixed to the wall. The House of Lords held that the purpose of their annexation to the realty was for their better enjoyment as tapestries. Annexation on its own was not enough to make them fixtures. This decision was followed in the case of *Spyer v Phillipson* **[1931] 2 Ch 183**, where oak and pine panelling and a chimney piece had been erected, and, in *Berkley v Poulet* **(1976) 242 EG 39**, in relation to pictures which were hung in recesses in a panelled room. Thus, it is likely that the lampshade will be a chattel.

(c) The fitted kitchen poses a different problem. In the first place it is clearly annexed so it raises the general rule that it constitutes a fixture. Second, it would seem to be unarguable that the object of its annexation was for any other purpose than to create a room which could be used as a kitchen. While the fitted furniture may have been aesthetically pleasing, its primary purpose was for use as a kitchen.

In *Re Whaley* **[1908] 1 Ch 615**, the design of a beautiful room, 'an Elizabethan Room', by the installation of chattels of beauty, meant that those chattels became part of the room—they were fixtures. The unity of design of the room meant that the objects were part of the realty. The result in *Lord Chesterfield's Settled Estates* (mentioned earlier) was similar.

In *Botham v TSB Bank plc* **(1997) 73 P & CR D1**, the Court of Appeal decided that bathroom and kitchen units were fixtures, whereas kitchen white goods, such as refrigerators, were still chattels.

It is likely that the fitted kitchen in this problem will be a fixture.

(d) Similar arguments might prevail in respect of the bookshelves. They are annexed, although they could be easily removed with little damage. The object of their annexation is to make the room useful as a library (*Re Whaley*).

In fact, there would seem to be no question as to their intrinsic merit as chattels. The bookshelves have been installed for the more convenient use of the property, not for their use as chattels.

In *Vaudeville Electric Cinema Ltd v Muriset* **[1923] 2 Ch 74**, seats secured to the floor of a cinema hall were fixtures. Normally, free-standing seats would be considered chattels. Here, however, they were affixed to make the hall more convenient as a cinema and were held to be fixtures.

On these grounds, therefore, it is arguable that the shelves become fixtures.

(e) Here, the fireplace is annexed to the room. It is described as ornamental and might, therefore, fall into the category of the tapestries in *Leigh v Taylor* which, although affixed, were deemed to be chattels because the object of their annexation was for their better enjoyment as such.

[10] This point is tricky and requires knowledge of the cases referenced here (see McCormack (1990)).

However, there is a further complication[10] in that the fireplace is being purchased as part of a hire-purchase scheme. If the fireplace has been annexed to the land of the hirer, then it becomes annexed to the realty and the original owner (Quickfire Ltd) loses its title. It will be necessary to consider the contract of hire purchase to see whether Quickfire Ltd has reserved to itself the right to remove the fireplace in the event of default in the payment of the hire-purchase instalments. If there is such a right of removal, then this confers on Quickfire Ltd an equitable interest in the land, which is a right of entry (*Re Morrison, Jones & Taylor* [1914] 1 Ch 50).

The extent to which this right of entry is binding on Baal will depend on whether the land is registered or unregistered.

[11] Again, the question (as is common) does not specify, so you must consider both options—that the land is registered and that it is unregistered.

If unregistered,[11] then the equitable doctrine of notice prevails, and Baal will be bound unless he is a *bona fide* purchaser of a legal estate for value without notice (*Poster v Slough Estates Ltd* [1969] 1 Ch 495; *Shiloh Spinners v Harding* [1973] AC 691).

If the land is registered, the equitable right of entry can be protected by registration of notice by Quickfire Ltd under **s 32(1)** of the **Land Registration Act 2002**. If it is not protected by notice, then it will not bind a purchaser, as it is not an overriding interest.

+ LOOKING FOR EXTRA MARKS?

- Use the IRAC (Identification of the issues, Relevant law, Application of the law, and Conclusions) technique for answering this question within each section.

- This is a case law area where small distinctions of fact can change the outcome. Use cases clearly to demonstrate this important point.

Q QUESTION 3

Lord Blandish, the freehold owner of Brandy Towers, decided two years ago to open his home and its grounds to the public. In order to make the premises ready, he hired the firm of Dogget & Co to construct a Visitors' Centre. One morning, Noggs, an employee of the firm, had just entered the main driveway of Brandy Towers while on his way to work when he found a bag containing £500 in notes lying next to the driveway. All attempts to trace the owner of the bag and contents failed.

Shortly after this, Brandy Towers threw its gates open to the public. Victor, a member of the public, while visiting the grounds with his dog, Columbus, found Columbus digging in one of the flower beds. When Victor went to investigate, he found that Columbus had unearthed a bronze bracelet. Victor handed the bracelet to the receptionist at the Brandy Towers Visitors' Centre; but, despite the

④

efforts of the staff, the owner of the bracelet (which was discovered to have been made in 1932) could not be found.

Lord Blandish had purchased Brandy Towers from Viscount Willow in 1980, who had himself purchased it in 1930. Expert evidence suggests that the bracelet had lain in the ground for at least thirty years.

Consider the relative strengths of the claims that may be made to the bag of notes and to the bracelet.

! CAUTION!

- Note carefully what is asked: to consider the relative strengths of the claims to the bag of notes and to the bracelet. This means that you need to identify who may have a claim to these items, and then discuss the strengths of the claims relative to each other. Remember that it is not meaningful to attempt to state definitely who will be entitled to the items found, since this will depend upon who puts in a claim.

- As in every problem question, you should apply the law to the facts from the outset. The suggested answer, it will be seen, begins merely by setting out the basic principle in one short sentence, and then immediately seeks to apply such principle to the given facts. There then follows a discussion of the relative position of possible claimants to the bag: Lord Blandish, Noggs, and Dogget & Co. Lord Blandish's claim is discussed first: this is logical, because his claim depends upon his having a title to the bag and its contents before they were found, in which case his title, being prior in time, would be better than those of the other potential claimants (with the exception, of course, of the true owner).

- Remember that the person who can establish prior possession to a chattel has a better claim than another whose possession is later in time.

- By the way, in case you are wondering what became of the prehistoric boat in *Elwes v Brigg Gas Co* **(1886) 33 ChD 562**, and whether you can go and see it, alas no! After the decision in that case, the lord of the manor exhibited the boat in a special building near Brigg Railway Station until 1909, when he donated it to a public museum in Hull. Unfortunately, it was destroyed in an air raid on the museum in 1943: see Nash (1987 at p 119).

DIAGRAM ANSWER PLAN

Identify the issues	■ There is better title by prior possession.
Relevant law	■ The case law includes *Armory v Delamirie* (1722); *Waverley Borough Council v Fletcher* [1995]; and *Costello v Derbyshire Chief Constable* [2001].

Apply the law	**The bag of notes (object lying on the land)**
	■ Discuss the relative claims of:
	  ● Lord Blandish (present owner of the land);
	  ● Dogget & Co (finder's employers);
	  ● Noggs (finder).
	
	The bronze bracelet (object found in the land)
	■ Discuss the possible claim of the Crown (treasure).
	■ Discuss the relative claims of:
	  ● Victor (finder, but as trespasser);
	  ● Lord Blandish (present owner of the land);
	  ● Viscount Willow (previous owner of the land).

Conclude	■ Consider the relative strengths of the claims that may be made to the bag of notes and to the bracelet.

A SUGGESTED ANSWER

[1] By establishing the possible claimants at the outset, you can then focus on their relative claims.

[2] State the fundamental principle.

[3] No need to do more than reference these cases here as it is such a well-established principle.

[4] Here is the specific issue.

Possible claimants[1] to the bag of notes are Noggs, as the finder; Dogget & Co, as his employer; and Lord Blandish, as the owner of the land upon which it was found.

In English law,[2] the person who can establish a prior possession to a chattel has a better claim than another whose possession is later in time: *Armory v Delamirie* (1722) 5 Stra 505 and *Costello v Derbyshire Chief Constable* [2001] 1 WLR 1437.[3] In this problem, the issue[4] is whether Lord Blandish, the owner of the land on which the bag was found, can be considered to have possession of it before it was found. If he can, he has a right to it better than

[5] Don't forget to make this point—easily missed.

[6] Don't forget the exception—extra marks here for including it, plus the references to statute and case law that follow it.

[7] Nice sentence—extra marks here.

[8] Why not include the Latin phrase if you remember (and can spell) it? All the old cases, which are plentiful, use it.

[9] And now follows a discussion of the relevant cases.

[10] This is an extra marks section, where you discuss the various permutations of the facts which might have occurred.

[11] Concluding remarks on the bag of money round up the points.

[12] Now discuss the relative claims of the workers.

[13] Extra marks here for referencing this source.

everyone other than the true owner.[5] The only exception[6] to this common law position is where the found property represents the proceeds of crime, in which circumstance an innocent finder will be required to relinquish his find to the Crown (**Proceeds of Crime Act 2002, s 298(2)(b)**; *Fletcher v Chief Constable of Leicestershire* **[2013] EWHC 3357 (Admin))**. In the absence of any evidence to that effect, the common law position will prevail.[7] It is possible for Lord Blandish to have possession of a chattel lying upon his land, even without his knowing it is there, but only if he can show that he manifested an intention to exercise control over the land and the things upon it, ie an *animus possidendi*.[8] This may be difficult to establish if the land upon which the chattel is found is open to the public. Thus, in *Bridges v Hawkesworth* **(1851) 21 LJQB 75**,[9] a travelling salesman who found a bag of money lying on the customer side of a shop was held to have a better title to it than the owner of the shop. In *Parker v British Airways Board* **[1982] 1 QB 1004**, the Court of Appeal held that an air passenger who found a gold bracelet in the international executive lounge of an airport had a better claim to it than the occupiers, the British Airways Board, because it was found that the Board did not have a policy of searching for lost articles.

If the bag had been found inside Brandy Towers itself,[10] the requisite intention to possess would have been readily inferred: see Donaldson LJ in *Parker v British Airways Board* at p 1020. Such intention might, however, be more difficult to establish in respect of the grounds. On the other hand, at the time the bag was found, the grounds were not open to the public. The answer will depend, therefore, upon an analysis of all the facts, including evidence as to the range of persons who commonly used the driveway, the frequency of its use, and whether it was barred by a gate.

If Lord Blandish[11] was in possession of the bag of money when it was found, he will have a better title to it than the finder. Even if he was not in possession of it at that time, however, he may still have a better claim than the finder. Where an item is found by an employee[12] in the course of his employment, his employer has a better right to it than the employee: see dicta in *City of London Corporation v Appleyard* **[1963] 2 All ER 834** at p 839; and *South Staffs Water Co v Sharman* **[1896] 2 QB 44**, as explained by Harris (1961).[13] This principle extends (as in the *Appleyard* case itself), to independent contractors. As Dogget & Co were hired by Lord Blandish, anything that they or their own employees find on the land while constructing the Visitors' Centre, they find on Lord Blandish's behalf. The finder would therefore have merely custody of the bag and its contents, legal possession of which would pass to Lord Blandish. On either of these grounds, therefore, Lord Blandish is likely to have a better title than that of either Dogget & Co or Noggs.

It might be difficult for Noggs to assert a better title than either Lord Blandish or Dogget & Co, since, even in the absence of a claim by Lord Blandish, Noggs's find might be treated as made on behalf of his employer, Dogget & Co. Noggs might argue that he did not find the bag in the course of his employment, since it is arguable that his employment did not start until he reached that part of the grounds where the Visitors' Centre was being built. Against this, there is a stronger counter-argument that he was lawfully on the grounds only as an employee of Dogget & Co, which was there only as an independent contractor hired by Lord Blandish. It is therefore only in the unlikely event that neither Lord Blandish nor Dogget & Co claims that Noggs could assert a claim as finder.

[14] Extra marks to show that the **Treasure Act 1996** does not apply (and why).

As the bracelet is modern and made of bronze, it cannot be treasure within the **Treasure Act 1996**,[14] so ownership would not vest in the Crown. Possible claimants to the bracelet might therefore include Victor, as the finder; Lord Blandish, as the present owner of the grounds; and, possibly, Viscount Willow, as the owner of the land at the time when the bracelet was deposited in it.

Where, as here, the chattel is attached to the land, the freehold owner of the land can generally establish possession to it prior to that of the finder. Where the chattel is affixed to or buried in the land, the freehold owner's *animus possidendi* is presumed, so he will have rights to the chattel superior to those of the finder: *Parker v British Airways Board* at pp 1017–18. Thus, in *Elwes v Brigg Gas Co* (1886) 33 ChD 562, the life tenant was held to have a better title to the prehistoric boat contained in the soil than the finder, who was also a lessee. Lord Blandish's claim is even stronger in the present case because, unlike the finder of the prehistoric boat, Victor has no interest in the land.

[15] Remember the legal status of a visitor.

Furthermore, although Victor is a lawful visitor[15] to the grounds, his licence will almost certainly not extend to digging on the land: *Waverley Borough Council v Fletcher* [1995] 4 All ER 756 (CA). Since he finds the bracelet only by the excavations of his dog, he finds it as a trespasser. Whilst a trespasser may have some limited rights of possession, the court is even more likely in such circumstances to hold that Lord Blandish has a prior claim to possession (*Hibbert v McKiernan* [1948] 2 KB 142).

[16] Cover the issues one by one, as here.

The final issue[16] is therefore the relative strengths of the claims of Lord Blandish and his predecessor in title to the land, Viscount Willow. If Willow (or his estate) could establish that he was the true owner of the bracelet, and that he had lost (and not abandoned) it, he (or his estate) would have the prior claim (*Moffatt v Kazana* [1968] 3 All ER 271).

Apart from this, his claim to it would be merely as predecessor in title to the land. Fixtures, being part of the freehold, would have passed to Lord Blandish when Brandy Towers was conveyed to him; but the bracelet, even though it was apparently buried in the earth before the conveyance, is unlikely to be treated as a fixture (*Elwes v Brigg Gas Co* (1886) 33 ChD 562). Furthermore, it seems that the **LPA 1925, s 62**, will not operate to pass title to the bracelet on the conveyance (*Moffatt v Kazana* at p 275).

[17] Extra marks here—you have to go on and argue by analogy.

None of the reported cases has decided the rights of a previous freehold owner.[17] The Viscount's claim might, however, be based upon two lines of argument. First, an analogy might be drawn with the law relating to items concealed in goods after they have been sold. In *Merry v Green* (1841) 7 M & W 623, a sum of money was found in a secret compartment of a bureau after it had been sold at auction. It was held that the seller of the bureau, even though not the true owner of the money, had a better title to it than the current owner of the bureau, who had discovered the money. Second, it might be contended that the rights of a previous freehold owner were akin to the rights of the life tenant in *Elwes v Brigg Gas Co*. In that case, the life tenant was held to have a prior claim to the boat, even though it was discovered by lessees in possession under a ninety-nine-year lease.

However, whilst a lessor ceases to occupy the land upon the commencement of the term, he retains a reversionary interest in the land, unlike a vendor who conveys the freehold. The second argument is therefore a weaker one. Furthermore, it has been pointed out that there could be, in theory at least, 'an indefinite chain of claims from previous occupiers or their personal representatives' (*Hoath* [1990] **Conv 348**, at p 352). There is no fear of this in the problem, since the bracelet was deposited in the ground no earlier than 1932. Nevertheless, the courts might prefer to adopt the principle that the rights to the bracelet would have passed to Lord Blandish 'as an ordinary common law incident of land ownership' (*Hoath* [1990] **Conv 348**, at p 350).[18]

[18] Extra marks if you include this reference.

In the case of both the bag of money and the bracelet, the true owner of the item in question will have six years from the time of the find before his rights are barred (**Limitation Act 1980, ss 2, 4,** and **32**).[19] Time does not, however, run against a dishonest finder, ie one who does not attempt to trace the true owner. It has also been argued[20] that time does not in any event run against a true owner until he makes a demand (*Marshall* (1949) 2 CLP 68, referring to *Spackman v Foster* (1883) 11 QBD 99).

[19] It is easy to forget to add this limitation point.

[20] Note code for tricky point—many extra marks accruing here!

✚ LOOKING FOR EXTRA MARKS?

The comments indicate the following extra marks opportunities:

- using secondary sources;
- **Limitation Act 1980** point and case;
- argument by analogy where no reported case.

Q   QUESTION | 4

Julian and Julia were joint tenants both at law and in equity of a plot of land in Sevenoaks in Kent, which comprises a dwelling-house and an area of woodland. In 1985, they leased the plot to Noel for a term of ninety-nine years. Julian died in 1987, leaving all his personal property to charity. Julia died in 1988, leaving her entire estate to their daughter, Dorothy, who is now the owner of the freehold reversion on the lease.

A number of trees in the wood fell in the Great Storm of 1987; but Noel, a keen environmentalist, decided to leave them as they were, and ever since he has used the trunk of one of them, an ancient oak, as a seat. Three months ago, however, while Noel was attempting to sit on the trunk, it gave way. Noel discovered inside it a clay pot, which contained a solid gold locket and some coins. Noel contacted his local museum, which identified the locket and coins as dating from the early sixteenth century. The latter were found to be made of an alloy of silver and base metal. The silver content of some of the coins was 20 per cent; of others, only 5 per cent.

Crafty read about the find in a report in the local newspaper the following week and entered the wood at the dead of night with a metal detector. By this means, he uncovered, beneath the roots of a birch tree, a silver ashtray that had been made in 1900. Crafty took the ashtray home and hid it in a cupboard. His nocturnal activities have now come to light.

Last week, Noel found an old deed box under the floorboards of the attic. It contained £20,000 in bank notes. Evidence has revealed that the deed box and its contents belonged either to Julian or to Julia, or to both of them; but more precise evidence of ownership is lacking.

Consider who is entitled to the items found.

CAUTION!

- The mere length of such a question would deter many candidates from answering it. The length of a question on the examination paper, however, is no guide to its difficulty. This problem, though relatively long, is not particularly difficult; indeed, some of the information given is used to create an atmosphere, rather than to convey facts of legal significance.

■ In the context of treasure, objects may qualify as treasure if they are at least 200 years old when found and belong to a class designated by the Secretary of State as being of outstanding historical, archaeological, or cultural importance: the **Treasure Act 1996, s 2(1)**. As the answer indicates, however, the sole designation order made to date applies only to metal objects from the Iron Age. The reason for the making of this Order is explained in the Code of Practice. It is apparently to deal primarily with Bronze Age gold-covered perannular rings whose surface is gold over a base-metal core. The main aim is to remove the need for invasive and possibly harmful scientific analysis of such rings that would be necessary to determine the percentage of precious metal. See *The Treasure Act 1996 Code of Practice (Revised) England and Wales* (2002 edn), at p 10 (para 12).

■ Although not divided into sections by letters or numbers, the question naturally divides into several parts. The question setter has been fairly kind, because each part is broadly contained in a separate paragraph. Watch out though, because one possibly vital piece of information relating to the money in the deed box is contained in the opening paragraph.

DIAGRAM ANSWER PLAN

Identify the issues

■ These are the possible claims to gold locket, coins, clay pot, ashtray, and deed box and contents.

Relevant law

■ This is the **Treasure Act 1996**.

Apply the law

Discuss the possible claims to gold locket, coins, and clay pot:

■ the Crown (if items are treasure);
  ● payment and division of reward;
  ● Noel (the finder, lessee, and occupier);
  ● Dorothy (the freehold owner).

Discuss the possible claims to the ashtray:

■ the Crown (if item is treasure);
■ Crafty (the finder, but a trespasser and dishonest);
■ Noel (the lessee and occupier of the land; consider the terms of lease?);
■ Dorothy (does she have prior title as freehold owner?).

Discuss the possible claims to the deed box and contents:

■ Dorothy (as successor to Julia):
  ● presumption from ownership of the land containing the chattel.

Conclude

■ Who is entitled to the property found?

SUGGESTED ANSWER

[1] This is another example where you should waste no words, but go straight into the application of the law to the problem. The issues and the law will emerge straightaway.

[2] State the precise subsection.

Since the items found[1] by Noel and Crafty were found very recently, they may belong to the Crown as treasure under the **Treasure Act 1996**, subject to prior interests and rights: **s 4(1)**. Prior interests and rights include any (or those which derive from any) which were held when the treasure was left where it was found: **s 4(2)**.[2] The successor in title to the owner of the property at the time it was left or deposited in the ground would have a prior interest and right, but if the clay pot and its contents have been in the earth for hundreds of years it is highly unlikely that there will be any person able to make such a claim to them. There may be a slightly better chance of a claim by the successor in title to the true owner of the ashtray.

Subject to this, the Crown's claim depends upon the items comprising treasure, which is defined in **s 1**.[3] An object which is at least 300 years old when found and which is not a coin ranks as treasure if it has a metallic content of at least 10 per cent by weight of precious metal (which means gold or silver: **s 3(3)**). The solid gold locket therefore qualifies as treasure. Since the coins are at least 300 years old, they will all rank as treasure, whatever their metal content, if there are at least ten of them in the same find; if there are fewer than ten, each will rank as treasure (under **para (a)** of **s 1(1)**) only if it has a precious metal content of at least 10 per cent by weight. If, therefore, there are only four coins, the two at 20 per cent qualify under this criterion, but not those of merely 5 per cent. Each of the latter may still qualify as treasure under **para (d)**, however, as being an object which, when found, was part of the same find as an object which was treasure (ie the locket and the 20 per cent silver coins). Objects which are found together are part of the same find: **s 3(4)(a)**. The clay pot may also qualify on this basis. An object may also qualify as treasure if (being an object at least 200 years old when found) it belongs to a class designated by the Secretary of State as being of outstanding historical, archaeological, or cultural importance: **s 2(1)**. The only order made to date under this paragraph, however, is the **Treasure (Designation) Order 2002, SI 2002/2666**, which designates only metal objects (whether of gold or silver or a base metal) that date from the Iron Age or earlier (excluding coins). Even if the pot was to date from the Iron Age (which seems unlikely on the facts), it falls outside the designation, since it is made not of metal, but of clay.

A person who finds an object, or who acquires property in an object, which he believes, or has reasonable grounds to believe, is treasure must notify the Coroner for Treasure (established under the **Coroners and Justice Act 2009**). The notification must be within

[3] This paragraph deals in some detail with the definitions. Do this precisely, with reference to subsections as appropriate.

fourteen days of the day after the find (in the case of a finder) or of the day after the object is acquired (in the case of an acquirer). In each case, however, the fourteen days will not start to run until the finder or acquirer first believes and has reason to believe that the object is treasure. Failure to report[4] in time is a criminal offence punishable by imprisonment or a fine, or both: **Treasure Act 1996, ss 8, 8A**.

The Coroner for Treasure must investigate whether the object is treasure, and may hold an inquest: **Coroners and Justice Act 2009, ss 26, 27**. Before conducting an investigation, the Coroner for Treasure must notify the appropriate national museum (which in the case of an object found in England is the British Museum) and must take reasonable steps to notify the finder and the occupier of the land where the object was found: **Treasure Act 1996, s 9**.

If treasure has vested in the Crown and is to be transferred to a museum, the Secretary of State must determine whether a reward is to be paid by the museum before the transfer and (if so) the amount of the reward (which must not exceed the treasure's market value) and to whom it should be paid. If it is payable to more than one person, he must also determine how much each is to receive. The reward may be payable to the finder or later acquirer, to the occupier of the land at the time of the find, and to any person who had an interest in the land at that time, or who has had such an interest at any time since: **s 10**. The determination of the Secretary of State must be in accordance with a code of practice which he is required to prepare (**s 11**), the latest being the Code of Practice 2002. Any reward is likely to be divided between Noel (assuming that he has reported the find in time), as both finder and leaseholder, and Dorothy, as owner of the freehold reversion.

Assuming that the ashtray found by Crafty is not itself part of the same find as an object which is treasure,[5] it is unlikely to be treasure. Whatever its silver content, it was made too recently to satisfy any of the previously mentioned criteria. The **Treasure Act 1996** does, however, provide that any object which would have been treasure trove had it been found before the Act came into force is treasure within the meaning of the Act. Under the law of treasure trove, even a relatively modern object can comprise treasure trove provided it is substantially of gold or silver (which appears to mean at least 50 per cent: *A-G for the Duchy of Lancaster v G E Overton (Farms) Ltd* **[1982] Ch 277**). It must also be impossible to identify the true owner, and the object must not have been lost or abandoned; rather, it must have been hidden by the true owner with the intention of retrieving it at some later date. The court may draw an inference[6] from surrounding circumstances: *Overton (Farms)* case. The unusual location of the ashtray may suggest that it was hidden with a view to being retrieved. The Crown's title to treasure may, however, be disclaimed at any time, in which case the treasure may be delivered to any person in accordance with the Code of Practice: s 6. Even if the ashtray ranks as treasure trove at common law, and therefore as treasure under the Act, as it is a modern object, the Crown's title to it is likely to be disclaimed. Since Crafty was both a trespasser and a dishonest finder, it is unlikely that the ashtray, following a disclaimer, would be delivered to him.

[7] Another assumption to be made, taking you through all the possible issues.

Assuming that[7] the ashtray is not treasure, the next issue is to identify who has the best title to it. Crafty was a trespasser on the land and, since he took no steps to trace the true owner, was also dishonest. He will not therefore be able to assert a prior title: *Hibbert v McKiernan* [1948] 2 KB 142. Indeed, he may be subject to a criminal prosecution for theft. Noel will have a claim to the ashtray as lessee and occupier of the land on which it was found.

Dorothy may argue that she has a prior title as freehold owner. In *Elwes v Brigg Gas Co* (1886) 33 ChD 562, the tenant for life was held to have a prior title to the prehistoric boat found by his lessees. The boat had been in the land before the lease had been granted; the property granted by the lease did not extend to the boat; and the lease itself was for a particular purpose only, namely, for the exploration and extraction of gas.

[8] Show an opposite view, then argue it out.

By contrast,[8] in *City of London Corporation v Appleyard* [1963] 2 All ER 834, contractors, hired by lessees in possession to demolish a building, found a wall safe containing a large sum of money in bank notes. The court held that the lessors were not in possession of the notes before they were found; however, on the facts, they were able to assert, as against the lessees, at least a (superior) equitable title because of an express clause in the lease which reserved articles of value to the lessors. But for this clause, the lessees, as the persons in possession of the premises, and so in de facto possession of the notes, would have had the better claim. In regard to the general principle, *Appleyard* might be distinguished from *Elwes* either on the timing of the deposition (which, in *Appleyard*, must have occurred during the lease) or on the degree of annexation (on the principle that an object buried in the ground is more deeply embedded than one merely lodged in a safe).

Noel's lease will need to be scrutinised for restrictions or reservations such as were contained in the leases in *Elwes* or *Appleyard*. In the absence of any clear term or of any evidence as to the date of the ashtray's deposition, it will be difficult to ascertain which of Noel or Dorothy has the better right to it.

⁹ State the presumption.

In the absence of any further evidence as to the ownership of the deed box and its contents, the court will apply the presumption that the ownership of land carries with it ownership of the chattels it contains.[9] This principle was applied (to somewhat similar facts) in *Re Cohen* **[1953] Ch 88**, where Vaisey J said (at p 94) that the principle was 'a straw to be grasped at by the swimmer in this sea of ambiguity'.

¹⁰ Easy to forget this little twist in the facts, but you would lose marks if you did.

Since, by virtue of the right of survivorship, Julia acquired the sole legal title to the reversion on Julian's death, she will also be treated as the sole owner of the deed box and its contents. Therefore, upon her death, the box and the money it contains will pass under her will to Dorothy. The charity will receive nothing.[10]

✚ LOOKING FOR EXTRA MARKS?

- Note the points made in the comments: state any presumptions; work through the various possibilities one by one.

TAKING THINGS FURTHER

- Battersby, G, 'Acquiring Title by Theft' (2002) 65 *MLR* 603.
  An interesting and useful comment on **Costello v Derbyshire Chief Constable**.
- Bray, J, 'The Law of Treasure from a Land Lawyer's Perspective' (2013) 77 *Conv* 265–79.
  A good discussion on the meaning of treasure.
- Gray, K, 'Property in Thin Air' (1991) 50 *Camb LJ* 252.
  Discusses different aspects of the ownership rights which come with the fee simple.
- Harris, D R, 'The Concept of Possession in English Law', in A Guest (ed), *Oxford Essays in Jurisprudence (First Series)* (OUP 1961) 69–106.
  An erudite discussion of the importance and meaning of possession in relation to title.
- Howell, J, '"Subterranean Land Law": Rights below the Surface of Land' (2002) 53 *NI Legal Q* 268.
  Considers the rights below the soil and argues that even above the notional height at which the landowner's usable rights stop, there is not a free-for-all in the airspace above.
- Luther, P, 'The Foundations of *Elitestone*' (2008) 28(4) *Legal Stud* 574–90.
  Comments on the implications of the threefold classification of objects brought onto land put forward by the House of Lords, judgment in **Elitestone Ltd v Morris**: *chattels, fixtures, and items that are 'part and parcel of the land itself'.*

- McCormack, G, 'Hire-purchase, Reservation of Title and Fixtures' (1990) 54 *Conveyancer and Property Lawyer* 275.

  Considers whether goods supplied subject to a hire-purchase or reservation of title agreement may have become so attached to land as to form part of the land.

- Morgan, J, 'Digging Deep: Property Rights in Subterranean Space and the Challenge of Carbon Capture and Storage' (2013) 62(4) *ICLQ* 813–37.

  Considers the ancient maxims regarding underground space in the context of modern technology.

- Nash, M L, 'Are Finders Keepers? One Hundred Years since *Elwes* v *Brigg Gas Co*' (1987) 137 *NLJ* 118.

  *A concise run-through of case law since the **Elwes** case. Obviously not completely up to date, but still quite useful bearing in mind that limitation.*

Online Resources   www.oup.com/uk/qanda/

For extra essay and problem questions on this topic, as well as advice on revision and exam technique, please visit the online resources.

Adverse Possession

3

ARE YOU READY?

In order to attempt questions in this chapter, you will need to have covered:

- adverse possession in registered land;
- adverse possession in unregistered land.

KEY DEBATES

Debate: have the rules of adverse possession now tipped too far in favour of the registered proprietor?

For quite a number of years, there had been concern at the way the doctrine of adverse possession had operated, and there was particular concern following several cases in which squatters managed to bar the titles of local authorities to valuable properties, with a consequent loss of public assets (*Ellis v Lambeth LBC* (1999) *The Times*, 28 September 1999; *Lambeth LBC v Blackburn* (2001) 82 P & CR 494). Some considered this to be effectively legalised theft, and there was pressure to change the law of adverse possession. Reform proposals were put forward by the Law Commission in its report, *Land Registration for the Twenty-First Century: A Conveyancing Revolution*, Law Com No 271 (2001), and were enacted in the **Land Registry Act (LRA) 2002**.

The **2002 Act** effectively drew the teeth on the doctrine of adverse possession in registered titles by permitting the squatter to apply for an initial registration after ten years, which application will succeed (unless the registered owner fails to serve a counter-notice) only if one of three conditions (set out in **Schedule 6, para 5, LRA 2002**) is met. There has been some case law, such as *Zarb v Parry* [2011] EWCA Civ 1306 and *IAM Group plc v Chowdrey* [2012] EWCA Civ 505, on the interpretation of these conditions, and First-Tier Tribunal cases such as *Souaissi v Tingle* [2017] UKFTT 637 (PC) demonstrate the way in which this area of law may now be seen to be working.

(▶)

◁

Rashid v Nasrullah [2018] EWCA Civ 268 raises the interesting question of whether a registered proprietor who acquired title by fraud can be an adverse possessor (yes, said the Court of Appeal where the true owner delayed in bringing the claim).

The hammer blow to adverse possession lies in the fact that, on the squatter's first application for registration, the Land Registry will notify the registered owner and anyone else affected; the result is to wake up the registered owner to the need to act to prevent the squatter gaining title by adverse possession, and the registered owner has two years in which to do so.

Q QUESTION 1

In 1989, Len leased a plot of land in Lancaster called Greenacre (the title to which is unregistered) to Tim for a term of thirty-nine years at a premium of £50,000. The lease contains (*inter alia*) covenants by Tim as follows:

(a) to pay an annual ground rent of £20;

(b) not to part with possession of Greenacre; and

(c) not to build any dwelling-house on Greenacre.

In 1994, Adrian entered into adverse possession of Greenacre. He was, however, dispossessed in 2004, by Sue, who has remained in possession of Greenacre since that date. Tim continued to pay the ground rent under the lease until last year, but the rent is presently £20 in arrears. Sue intends to build a house on Greenacre and has already obtained planning permission for this purpose.

Len wishes, if possible, to regain possession of Greenacre in order to grant a fresh lease of it to Tim. If he cannot achieve that, he wishes at least to prevent Sue from building the dwelling-house. Adrian cannot, at present, be traced.

(a) **Advise Len.**

(b) **How (if at all) would your advice differ if the leasehold title to Greenacre were registered? You should assume that the relevant provisions of LRA 2002 have been in force at all relevant times.**

! CAUTION!

■ This question involves an analysis of the legal position where an adverse possessor is squatting upon land subject to a lease, both where the title is unregistered and where it is registered. Whilst this may appear to be a somewhat narrow point, it does in fact involve a discussion of fundamental principles of property law. The central case to be discussed in part (a) is *Fairweather v St Marylebone Property Co Ltd* [1963] AC 510.

■ It is to be noted that, although the question is one on adverse possession, it also demands some knowledge of other areas: a basic knowledge of leases, some particular knowledge of restrictive covenants, and an understanding of the application of the principles of registered land. All these topics throw additional light on the problem. So, a word of warning here: if you miss out a topic which you have been taught, you reduce your basic understanding of land law as a whole, and this could reduce (even if only slightly) your ability to produce a good answer to a question on a topic which you have revised.

■ Remember that a restrictive covenant in a lease is not registrable as a land charge under the **Land Charges Act (LCA) 1972**. The doctrine of the *bona fide* purchaser therefore applies; and a squatter (such as Sue) will be bound by such a covenant, since a squatter acquires title not by purchase (in the technical legal sense) but by operation of law.

■ Similarly, an adverse possessor of *freehold* land, not being a 'purchaser' within the **LCA 1972, s 4(6)**, will take subject to a restrictive covenant, even if it is not protected by registration.

■ Part (b) calls for a comparison with the position in registered land. Before the **2002 Act** came into force, upon the completion of the period of adverse possession against him, the registered owner held the estate in trust for the squatter until the latter was registered (by having the title transferred into his name). This meant that if the tenant in the meantime surrendered the lease to the landlord, the landlord would itself merely hold the registered leasehold estate in trust for the squatter. The **2002 Act** has abolished the mechanism of the trust in this context. It therefore seems that the landlord and tenant can now collusively defeat the squatter by the tenant's surrendering the lease before the squatter has secured registration. In this respect, the **2002 Act** produces a result similar to that which was held to apply to unregistered titles in the *Fairweather* case.

■ Finally, note carefully where a question (as here) states that you are to treat the land as registered but then adds the rider, like a sting in the tail, requiring you to then address the question on the basis of unregistered land. You would be surprised how many students get caught out by that and lose marks as a result.

DIAGRAM ANSWER PLAN

Identify the issues
- The legal issues are adverse possession in registered and unregistered land.

Relevant law
- This includes the **Limitation Act 1980**; *Fairweather v St Marylebone Property Co Ltd* [1963]; and the **Land Registration Act 2002**.

Apply the law

Discuss the following:

(a) **Unregistered title**
- Adrian and Sue's adverse possession is added together.
- Only Tim's title is barred, not Len's.
- Discuss Len's right to forfeit for breach of covenant.
- Sue has no right to relief from forfeiture (*Tickner v Buzzacott* [1965]).
- Discuss the effect of a surrender by Tim (*Fairweather*).
- The restrictive covenant binds Sue.

(b) **Registered title**
- Sue may apply for registration after ten years.
- Sue's application is likely to be refused.
- Tim receives notice of application.
- Sue cannot make a final application for a further two years.
- In that period, Tim can regain possession or surrender the lease.
- Adrian's title is barred by twelve years' adverse possession by Sue.

Conclude
- Advise Len.

A · SUGGESTED ANSWER

[1] Start with a clear statement of the key legal point, showing its link to the question.

(a) Where, as in this problem, land which is adversely possessed is subject to a lease, the **Limitation Act 1980, s 15(1)**, operates, at the end of twelve years, to bar the title of the tenant.[1] It would appear that the leasehold estate in Greenacre has been adversely possessed for such a period, because in unregistered titles an adverse possessor is permitted to add the period of adverse possession of the person whom he dispossesses (*Willis v Earl Howe* [1893] 2 Ch 545). Thus, the period of adverse possession, which was begun by Adrian in 1994, was continued by Sue, so that Tim's title was barred in 2006. If Adrian were to be traced, he would be able to bring an action for possession against Sue, since, although his period of adverse possession was merely ten years, his possession was prior in time to hers (*Asher v Whitlock* (1865) **LR 1 QB 1**). This would not, however, avail Tim, since his title, once barred in 2006, cannot be subsequently revived. Any action by Adrian would itself be barred twelve years after his dispossession by Sue, ie in 2016.[2]

[2] You need to be good at sums.

[3] Now deal with Len (the landlord).

The title of the landlord, Len, is not barred,[3] however, unless the adverse possession continues for twelve years after the expiration of the lease (**Limitation Act 1980, Schedule 1, para 4**), which has not yet occurred. By the same token, however, until Tim's lease comes to an end, Len is not entitled to bring an action for possession against Sue. This is because the statute bars the tenant's title only as regards the adverse possessor; vis-à-vis the landlord, the tenant's lease continues.

Thus, it would seem that Sue has acquired, through twelve years' adverse possession, a legal freehold estate in Greenacre, despite the possibility of its being brought to an end by Len's exercise of any right of re-entry contained in Tim's lease (**Law of Property Act (LPA) 1925, s 7**). If, therefore, Len is to gain possession of Greenacre immediately, he must seek to terminate the lease. If (as will usually be the case) the lease contains a right of re-entry for breach of covenant, Len may be able to forfeit the lease for existing breaches. He will not, however, be able to effect a forfeiture for the breach of the covenant against parting with possession for two reasons: first, by accepting rent from Tim after Adrian went into adverse possession, he has waived the right to forfeit for that breach; second, since the breach occurred more than twelve years ago, the statute has itself barred any right of action based on that breach (**Limitation Act 1980, s 15(1)**, and **Schedule 1, Pt I, para 7(1)**).

[4] Len's right to forfeit for breach of covenant.

Len may, however, bring an action for forfeiture[4] against Tim for breach of the covenant to pay rent. Since Tim's title has already been barred by Sue, there is no reason for him to defend the action: on the contrary, the termination of the lease will be to his advantage in ending his own continuing liability under it. Although there seems to be no reason why the adverse possessor should not be entitled to pay the rent on the tenant's behalf (see Wade 1962), the rent in the problem is already in arrears. Len may therefore be able to forfeit on this ground. It has been held, moreover, that an adverse possessor of a leasehold title, lacking privity of estate with the landlord, is not entitled to claim relief from forfeiture (*Tickner v Buzzacott* [1965] Ch 426). Thus, relief is not available to a squatter under the **Common Law Procedure Act 1852, ss 210–12**, since the squatter cannot claim under the lease.

[5] Landlord's right to accept surrender.

If, however, the lease in the question contains no such proviso for re-entry, Len may still be able to terminate the lease by accepting a surrender[5] from Tim. The House of Lords has held that a surrender by the tenant gives the landlord the right to immediate possession, thereby accelerating his right of action against the adverse possessor (*Fairweather v St Marylebone Property Co Ltd* **[1963] AC 510** (criticised, however, by Wade, discussed earlier, on the ground that it offends the maxim, nemo dat quod non habet)).[6]

[6] You can't give what you don't have.

An alternative possibility would be for Tim to purchase Len's reversion, and thereby bring the lease to an end through the doctrine of merger.

If Len cannot use any of these methods to terminate the lease, he will be unable to gain possession of Greenacre from Sue. Furthermore, since the statute does not transfer Tim's title to Sue, who has her own independent title to Greenacre, there is no privity of estate between Len and Sue. Therefore, Len cannot bring an action against Sue for the rent. Len can, however, sue Tim, who remains liable to pay the rent and to observe and perform the leasehold covenants even after his title is barred in 2006.

[7] Sue is bound by restrictive covenant.

Sue, however, will be subject to the leasehold covenant against building.[7] Such a covenant, being restrictive in nature, is enforceable in equity against anyone coming to the land other than a *bona fide* purchaser of the legal estate without notice. Sue cannot establish this defence, since an adverse possessor does not take by purchase (*Re Nisbet and Potts' Contract* **[1905] 1 Ch 391**). Len can, therefore, obtain injunctive relief to restrain Sue from building.

(b) If the title to the land were registered, the position would be different. The period of limitation under the **Limitation Act 1980, s 15**, does not run against a person in respect of an estate in land the title to which is registered: **LRA 2002, s 96(1)**. At the end of ten years' adverse possession, Sue may apply to be registered[8] as proprietor of Tim's lease: **LRA 2002, Schedule 6, para 1(1)**. The registrar must give notice of such application to both Tim and (if the freehold title is also registered) Len: **LRA 2002, Schedule 6, para. 2**. Unless Tim and Len fail to serve a counter-notice, Sue's application must satisfy any of the conditions set out in **para 5**.[9] The first condition applies only where there is an estoppel, and the third only where there is a boundary dispute, neither of which is relevant to Sue. It is also difficult to see how Sue could rely on the second condition, namely that she is 'for some other reason entitled to be registered' (*Crosdil v Hodder* **(Adjudicator's decision), 7 March 2011, unreported**; noted by Martin Dixon, 'At the Sharper End: Adverse Possession before the Adjudicator' [2011] *Conveyancer & Property Lawyer* 335). Assuming that none of these conditions is satisfied, Sue's application will be rejected.

[8] Sue's right to apply.

[9] Deal with conditions here and argue that Sue's application is likely to fail.

[10] Deal here with the next steps in the procedure.

If Sue remains in adverse possession,[10] she will be entitled to make a further application, two years after such rejection (**para 6(1)**). In practice, however, it is likely that Tim, having been notified by the

Land Registry of Sue's initial application, will bring an action for possession before Sue can remain in adverse possession for the additional two-year period.

If Sue remains in adverse possession for a further two years after the rejection of her initial application, she becomes entitled to be registered as proprietor on making such further application (**para 7**). The onus is on Sue to apply for registration. If Tim brings an action for possession against her before she has applied for registration, she cannot make such application during the proceedings (**para 6(2)(a)**). Alternatively, there would be nothing to stop Tim from surrendering his lease to Len before Sue makes such application, thereby enabling Len to bring an action for possession.

The foregoing presupposes, however, that Sue can establish an initial period of ten years' adverse possession in order to make a first application. **LRA 2002** enables a squatter who is a successor in title to add her predecessor's period of adverse possession to her own for this purpose (**para 11(2)(a)**). This does not, however, enable Sue to add the prior period of adverse possession of Adrian, since she is not his successor in title, but rather is in adverse possession against his title. This is different from the position in unregistered titles (*Willis v Earl Howe*). Sue's ten-year period against Tim therefore runs only from 2004, not from 1994. Sue cannot therefore make her first application for registration until 2014. Moreover, even if Sue were to apply in 2014, her application would probably be rejected, so Tim would still be able to obtain possession against her for the following two years (or even during any longer period if she has not by then made a further application for registration).

Since Adrian does not have a registered title, Sue will bar Adrian's title after twelve years' adverse possession against Adrian (ie in 2016).

✚ LOOKING FOR EXTRA MARKS?

■ This is a question for a careful, lawyerly progression through the stages. As in the suggested answer, go through it step by step.

Ⓠ QUESTION | 2

In November 1991, Squirrel, whose garden adjoined a plot of waste land, decided to make use of it for his own benefit. By the end of that year, he had levelled the plot, made a path across it, constructed flower beds, laid a lawn, and put up a child's swing. From that time, Squirrel and his family

⊙

used the plot as part of their own garden. In 1993, Squirrel fenced the plot off from the surrounding land on all sides, except where it adjoined his garden.

The fee simple owner of the plot, the title to which was unregistered, was Nutkin Ltd (Nutkin). The company soon became aware of Squirrel's use of the plot, but took no steps to remove him, because it intended to develop the plot in due course as a housing estate, when the requisite planning permission could be obtained, and it therefore had no use for the plot at the time. In 2002, Nutkin wrote to Squirrel indicating that it was treating Squirrel as a licensee of the plot, and inviting him to enter into a licence agreement. Squirrel did not reply. Last year, Nutkin, who had just obtained planning permission to build, again wrote to Squirrel stating that it was terminating the licence agreement. Squirrel wrote back saying: 'Tough luck—I'm claiming squatter's rights.' Following receipt of this letter, Nutkin brought proceedings against Squirrel for possession of the plot.

(a) **Advise Squirrel.**

(b) **How would your advice differ if the title to the plot had been registered?**

! CAUTION!

■ When the court is determining whether a title has been barred by adverse possession, it is generally engaged in an application of the legal principles to a complex set of facts. A range of different acts may have been performed on the land, and whether they amount to acts of adverse possession depends on their combined impact. Since law and fact are here intertwined, it is probable that your lectures on this topic will go through the facts of some of the cases in a fair amount of detail. Do watch out for the point that the cases turn on their own particular facts, and that a holding that a specified act in a given set of circumstances comprises an act of adverse possession does not mean that such an act will inevitably be held to have the same effect in a later case.

■ At each stage of the answer, the law is related to the facts of the problem. There is a tentative conclusion based on an application of the law to the facts. No definite answer is, however, possible, since too much turns on the interpretation of the facts and the inferences which may be drawn from them. The examiner will expect a clear statement of the relevant law and an application of the law to the facts given. It is, however, quite likely that the facts of an examination problem on adverse possession will be capable of more than one interpretation. If this is so, you should point this out, and not try to suggest that there is only one possible answer. To do so may indicate a failure to appreciate a basic principle—the difference between law and fact.

■ In *J A Pye (Oxford) Ltd v UK* **(2008) 46 EHRR 45**, the Grand Chamber of the European Court of Human Rights (ECtHR) was asked to determine whether the English law of adverse possession under **LRA 1925** breached **Article 1** of the **First Protocol to the European Convention on Human Rights (ECHR)**. As Lord Neuberger explained in the House of

Lords in *Ofulue v Bossert* (2009) (at **para 68**), the Grand Chamber decided that, whilst **Article 1** was engaged, the statute fell within the margin of appreciation afforded to the UK government. The decision of the House of Lords in *J A Pye (Oxford) Ltd v Graham* [2003] **1 AC 419** on the meaning of adverse possession is therefore good law, and was applied by the House of Lords in the *Ofulue* case. Although *Pye* involved adverse possession under the **LRA 1925**, there is no reason why the meaning of adverse possession laid down by the House of Lords in that case should not apply also to claims brought under **LRA 2002**.

■ If, in part (b) of the problem, Squirrel had completed twelve years' adverse possession before 13 October 2003, this being the date that **LRA 2002** came into force, he might have been able to claim under **LRA 1925**, which provides that, at the end of the period of adverse possession, the registered proprietor holds the title in trust for the squatter. On the facts, however, because twelve years' adverse possession had not been completed before that date, the applicable statute is **LRA 2002**. The new regime is so tough for squatters that few cases falling outside the three special circumstances set out in **para 5** to **Schedule 6** are likely to succeed. In practice, most well-advised squatters will prefer to sit tight, rather than risk eviction by serving an initial application for registration. What this means is that there will be cases in the future where adverse possessors will have been on land for decades without having acquired the title against which they are squatting. It might become increasingly difficult for courts to resist the conclusion that an action by the registered proprietor against such persons infringes **Article 8** of the **ECHR**. Alternatively, future courts might extend the doctrine of proprietary estoppel to these sorts of circumstances, although it is clear that the present requirements for an estoppel would not be met by long use alone.

DIAGRAM ANSWER PLAN

Identify the issues	■ The legal issues are adverse possession and human rights.
Relevant law	■ This includes the **European Convention on Human Rights (Articles 1, 8)**; *Leigh v Jack* **(1879)**; and related case law.

Apply the law	Discuss the following:
	
	(a) **Unregistered title**
	  ■ Act of adverse possession:
	    ● the status of *Leigh v Jack*;
	    ● the impact of **Article 1** to **First Protocol ECHR**: *Beaulane v Palmer* **[2006]**.
	  ■ Intention to possess (*animus*).
	  ■ Unilateral express licence:
	    ● the impact of **Article 1** to **First Protocol ECHR**: *Pye v UK* **[2003]**.
	  ■ The possible impact of **Article 8 ECHR**: *Connors v UK*; *Leeds CC v Price*.
	
	(b) **Registered title**
	  ■ The regime under **LRA 2002**.
	  ■ The possible impact of **Article 8** (as in (a)).

Conclude	■ Advise Squirrel.

A SUGGESTED ANSWER

[1] Start with a statement of the problem.

(a) Squirrel will be unable to resist Nutkin's action[1] unless he can establish that he has acquired title by adverse possession and Nutkin's right to possession has been barred by the **Limitation Act 1980**. The period of limitation cannot begin to run unless and until Nutkin was either dispossessed or discontinued possession of the plot, and Squirrel took adverse possession. For possession to be adverse, two elements must be present:

● Squirrel must have taken exclusive possession without Nutkin's consent;

● Squirrel must establish that he had the necessary intention to possess.

[2] Here comes the discussion of the differing factual bases for the cases.

The acts that are sufficient for adverse possession vary with the circumstances.[2] In *J A Pye (Oxford) Ltd v Graham* **[2003] 1 P & CR 10, 140**, Slade J's statement in *Powell v Macfarlane* **(1977) 38 P & CR 452**, pp 470–1, says that what has to be shown as constituting factual possession 'is that the alleged possessor has been dealing with the land in question as an occupying owner might have been expected to deal with it and that no-one else has done so'. What acts constitute adverse possession depend on the character and value of the property and the uses to which it can be put (*Lord Advocate v Lord Lovat* **(1880) 5 App Cas 273**). Thus, in *Red House Farms (Thorndon) Ltd v Catchpole* **(1976) 244 EG 295**, the mere act of shooting rabbits on marshy land (which could be used for little else) was held enough. However, in *Tecbild v Chamberlain* **(1969) 20 P & CR 633**, the playing of children and the tethering of ponies were held too trivial to amount to acts of adverse possession (similarly in *Williams v Raftery* **[1958] 1 QB 159** and *Boosey v Davis* **(1987) 55 P & CR 83**). Acts that change the nature or potential use of the land are likely to suffice (*Treloar v Nute* **[1976] 1 WLR 1295**—infilling of a gully; *Thorpe v Frank and another* **[2019] EWCA Civ 150**—repaving of the land) and in *Chambers v Havering LBC* **[2011] EWCA Civ 1576**, it was held that if the effect of fencing was in fact to exclude the paper owner, then that could be a relevant act.

Since the land is capable of being developed, it is unlikely that the placing of a removable swing, planting of flowers, or laying of a lawn, will be anything more than trivial acts. The levelling of the plot indicates some change in the nature of the land and this act may be more significant. Fencing off the land is generally considered the strongest act of adverse possession (*George Wimpey & Co Ltd v Sohn* **[1967] Ch 487**; *Williams v Usherwood* **(1983) 45 P & CR 235**; *Chambers v Havering LBC* **[2011] EWCA Civ 1576**).

The next issue is whether the fact that Nutkin had a future intention to develop the plot and had no present use for it prevents Squirrel's possession from being adverse. In *Beaulane Properties Ltd v Palmer* **[2006] Ch 79**, the judge interpreted the expression 'adverse possession' narrowly so as to revive the doctrine of *Leigh v Jack* **(1879) 5 Ex D 264**: namely, that there can be no dispossession of the paper owner unless the squatter's acts are inconsistent with the purpose for which the paper owner intends to use the land. That doctrine had been condemned[3] as wrong by the House of Lords in the *Pye* case (mentioned earlier); but when the *Pye* case was considered by the Lower Chamber of the ECtHR, it was held that the English law of adverse possession under **LRA 1925** was incompatible with **Article 1** to the **First Protocol: (2006) 43 EHRR 3**. In the light of this, the judge in the *Beaulane* case considered it appropriate to adopt (in accordance with **s 3, Human Rights Act 1998**)

[3] Here comes the discussion about the **ECHR**.

an **ECHR**-compatible interpretation of the statute by reviving *Leigh v Jack*. Shortly after *Beaulane*, however, the Grand Chamber of the ECtHR reversed the lower Chamber in *Pye*, holding that the English law of adverse possession in the case did not breach the Convention: **(2008) 46 EHRR 45**. This swept away the rationale for the interpretation of 'adverse possession' in *Beaulane*. As the English law of adverse possession is in this respect Convention-compliant, there is no reason for a court to apply *Beaulane* in future. It is therefore highly unlikely that *Beaulane* will be followed; indeed, it was disapproved of by the Court of Appeal in *Ofulue v Bossert* **[2009] Ch 1**, and no argument based on it was raised when *Ofulue* went on appeal to the House of Lords: **[2009] UKHL 16**. Nutkin's future intention to develop cannot therefore prevent Squirrel's possession from being adverse.

[4]Here is the discussion about the requirements to prove intention to possess.

The *animus* required[4] of an adverse possessor is merely an intention to possess. In *Pye*, the notion that the intention to possess must be to the exclusion of all others, including the true owner,[5] was rejected. The court will require clear evidence that the trespasser had not merely an intention to possess but has also made such intention clear to the whole world: *Powell v Macfarlane*. In most instances, the intention of the occupier will need to be inferred from his acts. In the problem, the act of fencing is probably sufficient to indicate the requisite *animus*.

[5]Laid down in *Littledale v Liverpool College* [1900] 1 Ch 19.

Nutkin might argue that there was no adverse possession at any time on the basis that it should be assumed, from the fact that it had a future intended use for the land and that Squirrel's occupation was not inconsistent with such intended use, that Squirrel was in occupation with its permission. Such doctrine of implied licence[6] emerged in *Wallis's Cayton Bay Holiday Camp Ltd v Shell-Mex & BP Ltd* **[1975] QB 94**, but the effect of this was reversed by **para 8(4)** of **Schedule 1** of the **Limitation Act 1980**, which provides that an implied licence is not to be assumed by implication of law from such circumstances alone. So, Nutkin could argue that permission is to be inferred from other evidence in the case such as the fact that Nutkin wrote to Squirrel in 2002 stating that it was treating him as a licensee.

[6]Discussion of licence.

Nutkin's writing to Squirrel looks more like an attempt to create an express licence. Had Squirrel accepted the offer of a licence, any adverse possession would have stopped immediately—but he did not do so. The issue is: can Nutkin unilaterally turn Squirrel into a licensee? This point was considered in *BP Properties Ltd v Buckler* **(1987) 55 P & CR 337**, where the Court of Appeal held that a unilateral licence communicated to the erstwhile adverse possessor had this effect. The court stated that the result might have been different if the adverse possessor had written back contesting the licence. Although the principle in the *Buckler* case has been criticised

(H Wallace, 'Limitation, Prescription, and Unsolicited Permission' [1994] *Conv* 196), it was treated as sound after a detailed analysis in *Colin Dawson Windows Ltd v King's Lynn, West Norfolk BC* [2005] 2 P & CR 19, and Hart J was happy to rely on it for additional support in *Clowes Developments (UK) Ltd v Walters* [2006] 1 P & CR 1.

If Squirrel were to fail to establish that he had barred Nutkin's title under the **Limitation Act**, he might still argue that, by enabling Nutkin to evict him without just cause after he has been in occupation for so many years, English domestic law breaches the right to respect for his home and family life under Article 8 of the **ECHR**.[7]

[7] Discussion of **Article 8**.

In *Connors v UK* (2004) 40 EHRR 189, the family had lived as licensees on a local authority gypsy site for sixteen years when, following allegations that their behaviour had breached the terms of the licence, they were given notice to quit. The local authority dropped the complaints, but brought proceedings for possession, then forcibly evicted the family from the site. Although the claim for possession had no defence under English law, the ECtHR held that **Article 8** had been breached. Although it was agreed that the interference had a legitimate aim, the court took account of the fact that no misbehaviour had been relied upon and that gypsies were a vulnerable minority. In *Leeds City Council v Price* [2006] UKHL 10, the House of Lords was able to distinguish *Connors* on the ground that the gypsies in their case had entered the land as trespassers and had been there only a few weeks before the local authority evicted them.

The decision in *Doherty v Birmingham City Council* [2008] UKHL 57 was also a case concerning the right of gypsies to remain on land occupied as their home. In *Doherty*, they had occupied the land under a licence for seventeen years when the council served notice to recover possession to carry out improvement works. The House of Lords considered that the statutory framework was defective in that it did not provide safeguards for the travellers and Doherty was granted leave to apply for judicial review. In *Manchester City Council v Pinnock* [2010] UKSC 45, the Supreme Court held that this test was too narrow and that if the claimant raises **Article 8**, the court must consider proportionality.

Squirrel's position in the problem seems to fall between that of the applicants in *Connors* and in *Price*. Squirrel initially entered the plot as a trespasser, but the registered proprietor purported to grant him a licence, and he has been occupying the plot for many years. Nevertheless, it seems unlikely that Squirrel would succeed under **Article 8**. First, it is doubtful whether the plot amounts to a 'home', because it has merely been an addition to Squirrel's garden. Second, **Article 8(2)** prohibits interference by a public authority with the exercise of the right, and it is arguable that the aim of **Article 8** is to protect a person against the arbitrary acts of a public authority: *Kroon v Netherlands* (1994) 9 ECHR 263. In seeking to evict Squirrel from its land, Nutkin is not acting as a public authority, so Article 8 would not appear to be engaged. On the other hand, the court is a public authority, and so the judge is obliged to abide by Convention rights. If this means that the courts must apply Article 8 where the person bringing the possession action is not a public authority, the Article would have horizontal effect. Surprisingly, it is still unclear under Strasbourg jurisprudence whether **Convention** rights can operate in this way. Third, unlike the gypsies in *Connors* and *Doherty*, Squirrel's status as occupier of the plot is not that of a member of a minority in need of special protection. An argument based on Article 8 on the facts is therefore probably one of last resort.

[8]The regime under **LRA 2002**.

(b) If the title to the waste ground had been registered,[8] Squirrel's position would be weaker. Even if the acts of adverse possession began at the earliest date, November 1991, Squirrel (assuming he has the necessary *animus possidendi*) cannot establish twelve years' adverse possession before 13 October 2003, when the LRA 2002 came into force. Any claim he has to adverse possession cannot, therefore, be based on the regime in LRA 1925, but only under the (for him) harsher regime of LRA 2002. Under the 2002 Act, an adverse possessor cannot bar the title of the registered owner unless he complies with the procedure under LRA 2002, ss 96–98 and Schedule 6. If Squirrel has completed ten years' adverse possession, he can apply to the Land Registry for registration. As he does not fall within one of the three exceptional circumstances in para 5 to Schedule 6, he will not obtain immediate registration. Instead, the Land Registry will inform the registered proprietor of the application. If, exceptionally, the registered proprietor does not object within the requisite period (approximately three months), the applicant will be registered in its place; when, in order to regain its legal estate, the former registered proprietor will have to establish a ground for rectification (*Baxter v Mannion* [2010] EWHC 573). However, assuming that it objects within that period, the registered proprietor will not lose its title at this stage; it has a further two years in which to evict the squatter. If the squatter has not been evicted within such additional period, he may apply a second time to be registered, when title will be transferred to the squatter. However, as Squirrel has not made even an initial application to the Land Registry to set the final two-year period rolling, he will be unable to rely on adverse possession to resist Nutkin's action for possession. As in part (a), a defence based on Article 8[9] is unlikely to succeed.

[9]Make the point re **Article 8** but no need to repeat it—cross-refer back to (a).

LOOKING FOR EXTRA MARKS?

- A careful discussion of the cases in part (a) showing the different and fine distinctions between them will gain extra marks as showing a sophisticated understanding of the way law and facts interact.

TAKING THINGS FURTHER

- HM Land Registry Practice Guide 5—*Adverse possession of (1) unregistered land (2) registered land where a right to be registered was acquired before 13 October 2003*, October 2011 (updated 18 May 2020).
  A very useful practical guide to the way adverse possession works.

- Wade, H W R, 'Landlord, Tenant and Squatter' (1962) 78 *LQR* 541.
  Demonstrates the point regarding leasehold land which is squatted.

Online Resources   www.oup.com/uk/qanda/

For extra essay and problem questions on this topic, as well as advice on revision and exam technique, please visit the online resources.

4 Transfer of Title and Third-Party Rights

ARE YOU READY?

In order to attempt the questions in this chapter, you will need to have covered the following topics:

- legal and equitable interests;
- registered land and the **Land Registration Act (LRA) 2002**;
- unregistered land and the **Land Charges Act (LCA) 1925**;
- protection of third-party rights.

KEY DEBATES

Debate: should the interests of third parties that are not entered on the register bind the purchaser?

The property legislation of 1925 laid the foundation of our present system of land law. The reforms effected by the legislation were sweeping; it envisaged the registration of title to all land and an entirely new system of conveyancing. The position of third-party interests over the land remains a controversial area. especially in relation to overriding interests. The **LRA 2002** extends registrable estates and interests considerably and reduces correspondingly the number and nature of overriding interests (as set out in **Schedule 3, para 2, LRA 2002**). Where an interest is capable of entry on the register, its registration is essential if it is to bind a purchaser of the land, and it will only be binding if it is so registered, unless it can be brought within one of the overriding interests listed in **Schedule 3, para 2**.

Q   QUESTION   1

The object of all property legislation is to ensure that a purchaser of land obtains a good title easily and cheaply, whilst at the same time providing protection for third-party rights in the land.

Consider how property legislation has sought to achieve this, and how successful it has been.

!   CAUTION!

- To answer the question well, you will need to show a very brief knowledge of certain aspects of property law before the legislation. However, most land law courses and textbooks will include some reference to these, which assist in understanding our present-day system.

☐   DIAGRAM ANSWER PLAN

The 1925 legislation established a structure to make land more freely alienable whilst also protecting any interests of third persons in the land.

▼

Section 1, LPA 1925.

▼

Equitable interests in unregistered land which attach to the land itself are registrable under **LCA 1925** (now **1972**), and registration, where applicable, replaces the doctrine of notice (**s 198, LPA**).

▼

The residual category of equitable interests is neither overreachable nor registrable.

▼

There is simplification of legal title in co-ownership. Fragmentation of title occurs only in equity.

▼

There are problems with registration of charges under **LCA** as it works as a 'names' register.

▼

Within the system of registration of title under **LRA 1925** (now **LRA 2002**) everything a purchaser needs to know is on the register. But this principle is distorted by overriding interests and rectification.

SUGGESTED ANSWER

[1] The first answer plan point: free alienability.

The main purpose[1] of the 1925 legislation was to make land more freely alienable and to avoid the necessity for a purchaser to investigate title every time the land changed hands, whilst at the same time affording protection to the owners of equitable interests in the land. The problem[2] is to achieve a balance between the interests of a purchaser and those of the owner of an equitable interest.

[2] Show what the key problem is.

[3] It is possible that you will not have covered unregistered land in your course. If so, then this sentence is an 'extra marks' section and you would not be prejudiced if you omitted it.

In unregistered land,[3] a purchaser was always bound by *legal* estates and interests in the land (rights '*in rem*'), but was not bound by equitable ones if he was a *bona fide* purchaser for value without notice of them (equity's darling). Because of the reduction in the number of estates[4] which *may* subsist at law to two (**LPA 1925, s 1(1)**), and the number of interests which *may* subsist at law to five (**s 1(2)**), there was a drastic reduction in the number of legal estates and interests by which a purchaser would be bound.

[4] This starts point two in the answer plan.

The effect of **s 1, LPA 1925** was inevitably to increase the number of estates and interests which became equitable. The reason for this was to remove these as far as possible from the title to the legal estate which the purchaser is buying. The legal estate is vested in an estate owner, who conveys it to a purchaser, leaving this unencumbered. Certain types of equitable interests which arose under a settlement or a trust for sale (now a trust of land) are overreached by a sale by two trustees. This means that they attach to the proceeds of sale of the land instead of to the land itself. Where this is not possible because the equitable interests are of the type which attach to the land itself (generally commercial interests), they are registrable and a purchaser can discover them by searching the register set up under **LCA 1925** (now **1972**). After 1925, therefore, most equitable interests in land became either overreachable or registrable.

[5] This is a discussion of overreaching in respect of the equitable interests created as a result of the impact of **LPA 1925,** as explained in question 1. Notice that there is a story unfolding here.

Overreachable interests are the old estates[5] which, because of **LPA 1925, s 1(1)**, became necessarily equitable. These include life estates, fee tails (largely extinct now), and fee simples that are not absolute, such as conditional and determinable fees, or that are not in possession, such as fee simple remainders and reversions. They all have the common feature that they give a right, at some time, to beneficial ownership and occupation of the land. After 1925, such interests could only take effect behind either a trust or a settlement. **LPA 1925, s 2(1)** provides that they are overreached on a sale of the land, which means that they no longer attach to the land itself but attach instead to the proceeds of sale. They are protected by the overreaching machinery of the trust of land and the settlement, namely, that a purchaser will not obtain a good title to the land unless he has a good receipt for the purchase money from two trustees. This same machinery protects the purchaser also, because if the purchaser complies with the requirement for a receipt, he obtains a good title to the legal estate, freed from the equitable interests.

The trusts of land and settlement allow considerable flexibility of ownership in land, but not at the expense of complicating the title to the legal estate. Wherever land is held on limited forms of ownership (for any estate less than a fee simple absolute in possession), then these now have to take effect behind a trust of land: **Trusts of Land and Appointment of Trustees Act (TLATA) 1996**. They are off the legal title and are of no concern to a purchaser, provided he has a good receipt from two trustees. **TLATA 1996** prohibited the creation of any future settlements under the **Settled Land Act (SLA) 1925** (although the few that do exist continue) and converted all existing trusts for sale under **LPA 1925** into trusts of land. The basic protection of interests under a trust of land and a settlement, and the protection given to a purchaser, remain, however, the overreaching provisions: **s 2(1), LPA 1925**.

The simplification of title to land[6] is illustrated also by the 1925 provisions for co-ownership. After 1925, only a joint tenancy may subsist at law (**s 34(2), LPA 1925**); and as the right of survivorship applies to this, there can be no fragmentation of the legal title. A purchaser therefore knows that he can take a conveyance of the legal title from the surviving joint tenants. Wherever there is co-ownership of land there is a trust of land, and the *equitable* interests of the co-owners may be either a joint tenancy or a tenancy in common, and so may either pass to the surviving co-owners (if a joint tenancy) or to their estates (if a tenancy in common). There were possible hazards for a purchaser in taking a conveyance from only one surviving joint tenant, however, as there could have been a hidden severance of the equitable joint tenancy before the death of the predeceasing joint tenant. The **Law of Property (Joint Tenants) Act 1964** therefore provides that a purchaser will get a good title from a single surviving joint tenant if the conveyance specifically states that the vendor is a beneficial owner, and there is no endorsement of a severance on the conveyance to the joint tenants. If the title to the land is registered, a restriction can be entered on the register to warn a purchaser that there is a tenancy in common in equity. The provision of a trust and the overreaching mechanism simplified the legal title to land as far as fragmentation of ownership was concerned, but did not solve the problem for a purchaser of interests in the land which a third party might have. These interests were necessarily equitable after 1925, with the exception of easements and profits and charges over land, which may be legal if they comply with the requirements of **s 1(2), LPA 1925**, but may also be equitable. Whether an equitable interest

[6] This section deals with the way in which co-ownership is handled. Notice again, that there is a story approach here, which helps keep the thread going.

was binding on a purchaser or not depended upon the equitable doctrine of notice, which could be hazardous for a purchaser. **LCA 1925** (now **1972**) made these equitable interests registrable.[7] They are protected, in unregistered title, by registration under **LCA**, and a purchaser may search the register to discover these. Registration, where applicable, replaces the old doctrine of notice (**s 198, LPA 1925**). Constructive notice was particularly hazardous for a purchaser, as he might find himself bound by an equitable interest which the court decided that he *should have* discovered, even though he had no actual knowledge of it at all. After 1925, the purchaser will be bound only by those registrable interests which are registered, irrespective of notice (*Midland Bank Trust Co v Green* [1981] AC 513).

Even in 1925, the legislation affecting unregistered titles did not cater for all equitable interests, and there was a residual class of equitable interests to which the old doctrine of notice still applied. It was obviously felt to be too onerous a task to register all the old restrictive covenants affecting land, and so **LCA 1925** provided for registration of only those restrictive covenants and equitable easements created after the legislation came into force on 1 January 1926. Those interests created before that date still depend upon the old doctrine of notice.

Moreover, a bare trust[8] is not protected by the overreaching machinery, which requires two trustees, and its binding effect on a purchaser is again determined by notice in unregistered titles.

Since 1925, the equitable doctrine of estoppel[9] has developed considerably, and now the courts recognise proprietary interests created by estoppel. These interests are not registrable as land charges, however (*E R Ives Investment Ltd v High* [1967] 2 QB 379), and so must depend for their validity against a purchaser of unregistered land upon the doctrine of notice. In registered land, **LRA 2002, s 116** states that, 'for the avoidance of doubt . . . an equity by estoppel . . . has effect from the time the equity arises as an interest capable of binding successors in title'. The estoppel would then require protection in the normal way under the **LRA**, that is, either by notice or as an overriding interest.

The main 'breach' of the 1925 scheme arose in hidden co-ownership.[10] Due to changing social circumstances, working wives and cohabitees frequently contribute to the high price of a home. The courts have recognised that such persons may acquire a beneficial equitable interest[11] in the home under a resulting or constructive trust, or both, even though their names do not appear on the legal title. However, it was decided in *Williams & Glyn's Bank Ltd v Boland* [1981] AC 487 that such interests were overriding under **s 70(1)(g), LRA 1925** (now subject to **Schedule 3, para 2, LRA 2002**). The underlying rationale is that occupation is usually notice of an interest in

[7] They include restrictive covenants, equitable easements, estate contracts, options to purchase, and general equitable charges.

[8] Where there is a schism of the legal and equitable ownership in land, arising, for example, from a resulting trust.

[9] This is an 'extra marks' point. It is a great example of the remaining importance of the doctrine of notice. Don't let anyone tell you that this is no longer relevant—unregistered land may be disappearing, but not yet!

[10] Here you go now, with the great modern example of gender equality being recognised by the courts.

[11] The Law Commission's Report on the implications of *Williams & Glyn's Bank Ltd v Boland* (Law Com No 115 (1982)) recommended that co-ownership interests should be made registrable, but this has not been implemented, and it is difficult to see how it could be when such interests are acquired informally, and may often be disputed by the owner of the legal title.

the land. The effect of this type of notice in registered land has influenced notice in the unregistered system and evidence of occupation was a relevant factor in *Kingsnorth Finance Co v Tizard* **[1986] 1 WLR 783**, so that the increased caution of conveyancers has reduced the potential hazards in this area for a purchaser.

However, if there is a sale (or mortgage or other dealing) by two co-owners and trustees of land, then any hidden beneficial interests in the land are overreached and attach instead to the proceeds of sale. They can then no longer be 'rights' or 'interests' in the *land* and so cannot be overriding and binding on the purchaser (*City of London Building Society v Flegg* **[1988] AC 54**). Moreover, **s 26, LRA 2002** provides that an owner's powers in respect of registered land are to be taken to be free of any limitation[12] unless such limitation is protected by a restriction on the register.

One of the difficulties of the registration of land charges in unregistered title is that they are registrable against the name of the estate owner[13] at the time of their creation. For such a system to work, it is necessary to have the full and correct name of the estate owner (*Oak Co-operative Building Society v Blackburn* **[1968] Ch 730** and *Diligent Finance Ltd v Alleyne* **(1972) 23 P & CR 346**).

In theory, a purchaser needs to search against all estate owners since 1 January 1926, when **LCA 1925** came into force. A purchaser was given only thirty years' title, however, and so, from 1956 onwards, could not know the names of all the persons against whom he had to search. The situation was further aggravated when the **Law of Property Act (LPA) 1969** reduced the period of title to fifteen years (**s 23**). The Act therefore made some allowances for this difficulty, and **s 24** provides that as regards a *purchaser* a land charge shall be binding only if he actually knows of it. It also provides for compensation to a purchaser adversely affected by not having a root of title[14] sufficiently old to disclose registered land charges (**s 25**).

Another criticism which may be made of the **LCA** system is that, because registration is the sole criterion of whether an interest is binding or not, it may operate unfairly. Its provisions may be used deliberately to evade interests of which a purchaser has actual knowledge. In *Midland Bank Trust Co v Green* **[1981] AC 513**, a collusive sale, not for value, was held to defeat an option to purchase which had not been registered. In *Hollington Bros v Rhodes* **[1951] 2 TLR 691**, a purchaser who bought the freehold reversion of an equitable lease was held not to be bound by it because it had not been registered, notwithstanding that he paid a discounted price because of the equitable lease. Given the development of constructive trusts[15] and the courts' willingness to apply the equitable maxim that 'equity will not allow a statute to be used as an engine of fraud', it is possible that these cases might be differently decided today.

[12] Such as a limitation under **s 8, TLATA** that the trustees shall not make any disposition of the land without the consent of certain persons.

[13] Point six of the answer plan.

[14] In practice, land charges searches are carefully kept by solicitors with the deeds, so that there is often a complete chain of them going back for many years, and very few claims for compensation have been made.

[15] See the concluding paragraphs of the suggested answer to question 3 in this chapter.

[16] This is a nice point to make.

The **LCA 1925** was only ever intended to be a stopgap measure.[16] **LRA 1925** extended the system of registered title to land, and when the title to land becomes registrable, **LCA 1972** (formerly **1925**) no longer applies. All those interests that, prior to registration of title, were registrable in the Land Charges Registry at Plymouth (under the **Acts of 1925** or **1972**) are then registrable at the Land Registry. In 1925, it was envisaged that the title to all land in the country would be registered very much more quickly than in fact has happened, so that the problems arising because of the length of title were not foreseen.

LRA 2002 (replacing **LRA 1925**) provides for the title to land to be registered at the Land Registry. There are three registers: property, proprietorship, and charges. The register is intended to be a 'mirror' of the title, and title is deduced by furnishing a purchaser's solicitor with official copy entries on the register. This avoids the necessity (in unregistered title) for a vendor to deduce fifteen years' title to a purchaser each time the land is sold. The title information document, issued by the Land Registry, contains a copy of the register entries and the date when it was last compared with the register, and this is the evidence of title to registered land. A purchaser takes subject to any minor interests which are noted on the register, and subject in any event to any overriding interests. Many of the overriding interests (although not all) are the same as the legal interests in unregistered title, and many of the minor interests are equitable interests in unregistered land.

[17] This Act came into force on 1 October 2003.

Some of the flaws in the system of registered titles contained in **LRA 1925** were dealt with by **LRA 2002**.[17] This made substantial changes to land law with the same underlying objective of making conveyancing easier and safer for a purchaser. It includes significant measures towards the ultimate goal of registration that the register should be a mirror of the title. More estates and interests are now registrable, and the overriding interests,[18] which are binding on a purchaser in any event, are much reduced. There are new requirements[19] for a person claiming title as an adverse possessor to first serve a notice on the registered proprietor, and this seems likely to reduce considerably claims to titles[20] by adverse possession, except for a few cases such as boundary disputes.

[18] **Chapter 5** deals with this, particularly **question 2**.

[19] The changes made to adverse possession are discussed in **Chapter 3**.

[20] It is possible, in certain circumstances, to rectify the register against a registered proprietor. For a question on this, see **Chapter 5, question 3**.

Most conveyancers would say that the system of registered titles is an easier system of conveyancing than unregistered, and it was finally introduced for the last area in the country in 1990.

Given the enormous social changes since 1925, which have caused problems for the scheme set up by the 1925 legislation, it is remarkable that much of the basic structure remains intact, and that the courts have largely been able to adapt it to our modern requirements.

Conveyancing practice has similarly adapted to an awareness of the overriding interests by which a purchaser will be bound, and conveyancers now make exhaustive enquiries of anyone in 'actual occupation' who might thereby have an overriding interest formerly under **s 70(1)(g), LRA 1925** and now under **Schedule 3, para 2, LRA 2002.**

✚ LOOKING FOR EXTRA MARKS?

- This is a very lengthy suggested answer and you will note in the comments suggestions where sections are 'extra marks' or where you might be writing this for coursework. This includes the following areas which have been included in the suggested answer:
  - unregistered land (you may not have covered it in your course). In particular, the sections which consider overreaching and then *Midland Bank v Green* and other cases would work very well for coursework. These could all be safely omitted in an exam answer;
  - proprietary estoppel;
  - hidden co-ownership.
- For coursework (or extra marks) you could add the commentary of J T Farrand, *Contract and Conveyance* (4th edn, Sweet & Maxwell 1983), who made scathing attacks on it. He commented on the claim that the register is a 'mirror of the title' (Theodore B T Ruoff, *An Englishman Looks at the Torrens System: Being Some Provocative Essays on the Operation of the System after One Hundred Years*, Law Book Company of Australasia 1957), and that 'The view may be taken by conveyancers that [overriding interests and rectification of the register] render the mirror image seriously and unacceptably incomplete . . .'.

Ⓠ QUESTION | 2

'In my opinion therefore, the law as to notice as it may affect purchasers of unregistered land, whether contained in decided cases, or in a statute . . . has no application even by analogy to registered land' (Lord Wilberforce in *Williams & Glyn's Bank Ltd v Boland* [1981] AC 487).

Explain and discuss this statement.

！ CAUTION!

- This question again addresses the central issue of any system of land law and conveyancing, namely the balance to be achieved between the desire of a purchaser for a clear title to land and the protection of a possible third party's rights and interests in the land. It is a favourite topic for examiners and might also appear as coursework.
- This issue is dealt with differently in the unregistered and registered systems of conveyancing, so take care to deal with that.

DIAGRAM ANSWER PLAN

> The aim of the 1925 legislation was to simplify conveyancing by removing equitable interests from the legal title.

▼

> There is a residual class of equitable interests for which registration would not be appropriate.

▼

> In registered title, minor interests will only bind a purchaser if they are protected by an entry on the register, but overriding interests are binding in any event.

▼

> The rationale for this is that in most cases (but not in all) occupation will give notice of a person's possible interest.

▼

> As to failure to protect minor interests on the register, the courts have been prepared to uphold them by imposing a constructive trust in appropriate cases.

▼

> Both **TLATA 1996** and **LRA 2002** refer to 'actual knowledge' in the context of determining whether rights are binding or not.

SUGGESTED ANSWER

The quotation expresses what may come to be seen as the high-water mark of the rejection of the doctrine of notice in registered land. As is discussed in this answer, the trend more recently has been tacitly to recognise that the doctrine has a limited role to play.

¹ This paragraph sets the scene and gives a potted explanation of the position in registered land.

² See question 1.

The main aim¹ of the 1925 legislation was to simplify conveyancing² for a purchaser. To this end, it provides that the legal fee simple estate shall be vested in an estate owner, who, on sale, deduces title and conveys it to a purchaser. If the title is registered, the estate owner is the registered proprietor and can transfer the title to a purchaser. Any equitable interests are 'off the title'. On sale, those that take effect behind a trust are overreached and attach to the proceeds of sale of the land; if not overreachable, many are registrable under **LCA 1972** (formerly **1925**) or on the register of title at the Land Registry, and so are discoverable by a purchaser who can search the register.

³ Watch out for this point—a lot of students assume that overreaching applies only to unregistered land.

The overreaching provisions of **LPA 1925** apply to both unregistered and registered title³ (*City of London Building Society v Flegg* **[1988] AC 54**). In registered land, the trustee estate owners are the registered proprietors, and a restriction in the proprietorship register alerts a purchaser to the existence of a trust and of the necessity to obtain a receipt for purchase money from two trustees. Those equitable interests registrable in unregistered land[4] under **LCA 1972** become registrable as minor interests in the register of the Land Registry (usually in the charges register).

One of the problems of pre-1926 conveyancing, which the 1925 legislation sought to solve, was the hazard to a purchaser of the doctrine of notice. In particular, it was recognised that constructive notice (the notice which a purchaser should have had if the proper enquiries had been made) was a haphazard affair, which could expose a purchaser to considerable risks. To avoid this, those equitable interests which attach to the land itself, and are not capable of satisfaction out of the proceeds of sale of the land, were made registrable (in unregistered titles) under **LCA 1925** (now **1972**). Moreover, **s 4, LCA 1972** provides that registrable land charges which are not registered are void against certain classes of purchaser. This means that, where applicable, registration is the sole determinant of whether a registrable interest will bind a purchaser of the land or not.

The overall decisiveness of registration under **LCA 1972**, even at the expense of justice,[5] is demonstrated by the case of *Midland Bank Trust Co v Green* [1981] AC 513. In that case, an unregistered option to purchase was void for want of registration even against someone who *actually* knew of it, had not given value, and was most certainly not *bona fide*. The case might be treated as an example of the adage that hard cases make good law. Lord Wilberforce recognised this,[6] but said 'The Act is clear and definite . . . it should not be read down or glossed; to do so would destroy the usefulness of the Act.' The decision is nevertheless open to criticism in that it permitted the destruction of an equitable interest by a fraudulent conveyance. Lord Denning MR, in the Court of Appeal in the same case, gave a dissenting judgment in which he said, 'No court in this land will allow a person to keep an advantage which he has obtained by fraud . . . Fraud unravels everything.'

Even in 1925, however,[7] it was conceded that the legislation could not cover all equitable interests. It was obviously too mammoth a task for the Land Charges Registrar to register all the old restrictive covenants on unregistered titles (many over a century old), and the binding effect of these and equitable easements was left dependent upon the old doctrine of notice. Since 1926, the doctrine has also been applied to beneficial interests arising under a resulting or constructive trust and estoppel interests. All these interests arise from informal arrangements, and this in itself presents a difficulty in registering them.

[4] If you can do this—compare registered with unregistered—then you have got it, and you should congratulate yourself.

[5] This is an 'extra marks' point. It appears as an aside but shows that you grasp the issue, which is the conflict between certainty and justice.

[6] Mentioning their Lordships by name alongside the quotation is worth extra marks. If you don't have it stored in your memory bank, then a paraphrase will do fine. This would be good in a coursework assignment.

[7] This next section is 'extra marks' in an exam question, but in coursework would be what was expected.

In registered title, interests are either overriding (binding in any event on the registered proprietor or a transferee from him) or minor, and binding only if protected by an entry on the register. It is a curious paradox, therefore, that at the same time as registration alone could make an interest binding in unregistered titles, **LRA 1925, s 70(1)(g)** introduced into registered titles what can only have been intended to be a limited and particular form of notice. This section made overriding 'the rights of every person in actual occupation of the land . . . save where enquiry is made of such person and the rights are not disclosed'. It is re-enacted in a modified and restricted form in **Schedule 3, para 2, LRA 2002.**

[8] This following discussion of **Hunt v Luck** is, again, 'extra marks'. Also, great to include it in coursework.

The section roughly corresponds with the old rule in **Hunt v Luck [1901] 1 Ch 45**, which was of general application to unregistered land before 1926, but which was largely superseded by **LCA 1925.**[8] The rule fixes a purchaser with notice of rights which he should have discovered by reason of persons in occupation of the land. The rule did not operate, however, to fix a person with notice of rights which were consistent with, and therefore not discoverable by reason of, the occupation (**Barnhart v Greenshields** (1853) **9 Moo PCC 18**).

This rationale was applied in **Caunce v Caunce [1969] 1 WLR 286**, a case involving unregistered title, where it was held that a wife's occupation of the matrimonial home with her husband did not give a mortgagee notice of the fact that she had a beneficial interest in the home. Stamp J said, 'She was there, ostensibly, because she was the wife, and her presence there was wholly consistent with the title offered by the husband to the bank.' This case was regarded as wrong in **Boland**, and in 1981 it would probably have been decided differently, as co-ownership by wives was by then much more common. It was, however, decided very much according to the application of the rule in **Hunt v Luck**.

The notice imposed by the rule in **Hunt v Luck** did not apply where an occupier had concealed his rights, and, in registered land, the saving in **LRA 1925, s 70(1)(g)** reflected this. Where a purchaser had enquired of *the person in actual occupation* (not merely of the vendor's solicitor or agent), he had a clean bill of health and took free from any interests which *that person* had failed to disclose.

[9] This discussion of the Court of Appeal decision is 'extra marks' in an exam answer. Showing knowledge of the judgments in a lower court, as here, is very impressive. Great also for coursework.

In **Lloyds Bank plc v Rosset [1989] Ch 350 (CA)**[9] (reversed on other grounds by the House of Lords, [1991] 1 AC 107), Mustill LJ said, '[E]ven if constructive notice no longer applies in this field, the old law still gives a flavour to the new words of [s 70(1)(g)].' Otherwise, he said, s 70(1)(g) would produce an unacceptable contrast with the workmanlike solution in **Caunce v Caunce**. The new **Schedule 3, para 2, LRA 2002** also provides that a person of whom enquiry is made who fails to disclose their interest will not be protected, but there is an additional requirement that such a person 'could reasonably have been expected' to disclose the interest. Presumably, therefore, an enquiry made of a person who is senile, or an infant of tender years (who could have an interest under a trust) would not allow a purchaser to take free of their interests. Conversely, if the criterion of competence of a person of whom enquiry should be made is that they can be expected to respond to the enquiry, then the paragraph may well reverse the decision in *Hypo-Mortgage Services Ltd v Robinson* [1997] 2 FLR 71 for a minor who has reached years of discretion. There are no decisions on this amended wording as yet (*Link Lending Ltd v Bustard* [2010] EWCA Civ 424 not actually having to deal with the point).

Regarding occupation as the sole determinant of whether a right is binding upon a purchaser or not has caused problems in the registered system of conveyancing, as it is not always apparent that an occupier has *rights*. The mortgagee in *Boland* did not expect the wife to have rights in the property, and the purchaser in *Hodgson v Marks* [1971] Ch 892 assumed that the lady he saw at the house was the housekeeper and not the beneficial owner of the property. These cases, where the inference that occupiers had rights could not necessarily be drawn, therefore involved an extension of the rule in *Hunt v Luck*.

Although in most cases occupation will give notice to a purchaser, it will not necessarily do so, as the rule in *Hunt v Luck* recognised. In *Williams & Glyn's Bank v Boland*, the House of Lords refused to limit the section by reference to the old rule of notice, and Lord Wilberforce said, 'In the case of registered land, it is the fact of occupation that matters.' The new **para 2**, however, appears to bring the 'occupation' section back close to the notice rule, as it exempts from its protection an interest of a person whose occupation would not have been apparent on a reasonably careful inspection (*Thomas v Clydesdale Bank plc* [2010] EWHC 2755) and of whose rights the purchaser did not have any actual knowledge (*Mehra v Mehra* [2008] 3 EGLR 153).

Happily, these problems have been largely overcome by improved conveyancing practice. The very whisper of an occupier, other than the vendor, sends shivers down the spine of any experienced conveyancer, and will produce a barrage of questions as to his status and rights. Such questions are now included in all forms of conveyancers' pre-contract enquiries.[10] A purchaser or mortgagee will require a person in occupation other than the vendor to sign a waiver of any rights they may have and to undertake to vacate the property on completion. Mortgagees require applicants to sign declarations as to

[10] Displaying such knowledge of conveyancing practice as here is worth 'extra marks'.

who will occupy the mortgaged property, thereby seeking to obtain an admission that only the mortgagor has rights in the property. There is much to be said for this improved practice, which takes account of **Schedule 3, para 2.**

11 As in the earlier comment, showing the ability to compare and contrast registered and unregistered land shows you have mastered this topic.

Moreover, there has been some cross-fertilisation from the registered to the unregistered system.[11] In *Kingsnorth Finance Co v Tizard* [1986] 1 WLR 783, the standards of enquiry as to occupation in registered land were applied to unregistered title. A mortgagee was found to have constructive notice of the rights of a wife whose occupation, although intermittent, should have been apparent, and whose existence was evident from the mortgage application form.

As regards the requirement for a minor interest to be protected by a notice on the register, the courts have been prepared to use a constructive trust in order to give effect to interests which were void for want of registration, but which would have been binding under the old equitable doctrine of notice. In *Lyus v Prowsa Developments Ltd* [1982] 1 WLR 1044, an estate contract which had not been registered as a minor interest in registered land, and was not overriding, was held to be binding on a subsequent purchaser who took expressly subject to it. The rationale for this was that 'equity will not allow a statute to be used as an instrument of fraud'. However, the case contrasts starkly with the earlier decision in unregistered title of *Hollington Bros v Rhodes* [1951] 2 TLR 691. There, a purchaser who paid less than the market price for property because of an equitable lease affecting it, nevertheless took free from the lease as it was not registered. In *Peffer v Rigg* [1977] 1 WLR 285, Graham J was prepared to find a constructive trust to protect a beneficial minor interest in registered land which had not been registered (although he also reached the same conclusion by ascribing requirements of good faith to **LRA 1925, s 59(6)**, and the decision has been strongly criticised). For the imposition of a constructive trust, there must be some element of unconscionability and unjust enrichment, which is of course more than mere notice.

In *Barclays Bank plc v O'Brien* [1994] 1 AC 180, the House of Lords applied notice as the criterion to determine whether a lender should be bound by any undue influence which a borrower might have over a surety or a co-borrower. It is not clear whether this case concerned registered or unregistered title, but presumably the principle is intended to apply to both. (This was queried by Professor Mark Thompson in his note on the case in [1994] *Conv* 140.[12]) In *Barclays Bank plc v Boulter* [1997] 2 All ER 1002, Mummery LJ in the Court of Appeal said that in cases like *O'Brien* it was irrelevant whether the land was registered or unregistered title.

12 A slightly abstruse point certainly worth extra marks, but no panic if you think you wouldn't have got it.

[13] This follows from the arguments made. But if you have a different conclusion then, as long as it is justified by your arguments, there is no cause for panic.

The reality, then, is that the courts appear to be ready, in some circumstances, to recognise the unjustness of a system depending entirely upon registration.[13] They are prepared to resort to the old doctrine of notice as offering a fair and just solution to the problem of whether a purchaser should be bound or not by an interest in the land. And in appropriate circumstances, they are prepared to impose a constructive trust to give effect to some of these interests.

Although clearly not countenancing constructive notice, recent statutes have referred to 'actual knowledge' as relevant in determining a person's rights. **Section 16, TLATA 1996**, which applies only to unregistered land, provides that a conveyance by trustees contrary to a limitation on their powers of disposition will not invalidate it as regards a purchaser unless he has 'actual knowledge' of the limitation. As mentioned earlier, **Schedule 3, para 2, LRA 2002** refers to a purchaser's 'actual knowledge' of a person's interest, and it seems that the legislation is prepared to recognise the significance of notice in some circumstances.

✚ LOOKING FOR EXTRA MARKS?

- Don't be put off by the length of this suggested answer. It is very lengthy and probably more than most students could manage in the exam room but has been included as it may well be useful for a coursework piece (it is a favourite topic for examiners). All the 'extra marks' points are flagged up in the comments for convenience.

Ⓠ QUESTION | 3

'The property statutes generally prescribe a very high degree of formality for transactions relating to land. It is a curious paradox therefore that wide-ranging exceptions to these general rules have been recognised.'

Explain and discuss this statement.

❗ CAUTION!

- This question is a very general one requiring a considerable overall knowledge of land law, both the statutes and the case law. It is one which is more likely to be set for course work rather than in an examination, as it requires wide reading and reflective thought. It is an interesting question, the answer to which demonstrates how the judges have applied principles of equity to prevent injustice from the strict application of statutory requirements.

DIAGRAM ANSWER PLAN

> Give an explanation of why formalities are required in transactions concerning land.

▼

> Sketch a brief overview of principal legislative requirements in land transactions.

▼

> Give the statutory exceptions where no formalities are required and reasons for them.

▼

> Provide case law exceptions arising from the application of equitable principles such as resulting and constructive trusts and estoppel.

▼

> Provide a conclusion.

A **SUGGESTED ANSWER**

[1] There are lots of ways to open this answer. Here the tone is set with a general introduction. You could easily cut this down for an exam answer.

Land was always of great importance in a feudal society[1] and was transferred publicly by handing over the title document in a ceremony known as 'livery with feoffment of seisin'. In our modern society, a house is likely to be the most expensive and important purchase that anyone makes. Most people live in their house for a number of years, so that their proof of ownership needs to be enduring. Often, they will need a mortgage to assist them in their purchase, and the building society or bank will require proof of ownership and notice of their charge to appear on the title to the property. There may be third-party rights, such as easements or restrictive covenants, which the property enjoys, or which are enjoyed over it, and these need to be properly created and recorded. There may be a fragmentation of ownership, as with co-owners or successive owners, and this also needs to be recorded in some way. The formalities for transactions with land are to ensure that all these matters are correctly created and recorded, and that third-party rights are protected by the appropriate registration.

[2] Next follows the description of the formalities required in the different contexts. This section would be required for a good exam answer.

[3] Shows knowledge to add in the exception, but you could safely omit it in the pressure of the exam room.

In order to create or to transfer a legal estate[2] or a legal interest in land, **s 52, LPA 1925** requires a deed to be executed. (The exception[3] to this is **s 54(2), LPA 1925**, which allows a lease not exceeding three years to be created by word of mouth.) The requirements for a document to constitute a deed are contained in **s 1, Law of Property (Miscellaneous Provisions) Act 1989**. A deed no longer has to be sealed, but it must be signed as a deed and delivered. Where the title is registered (as most titles are nowadays), there is a transfer of the title by deed, but the legal title is not completed until the purchaser registers the transfer (**s 27(1), LRA 2002**) and the purchaser's name then appears in the proprietorship register instead of the vendor's. **LRA 2002** envisages electronic deeds with electronic signatures eventually, although this provision in the Act will not be introduced for some years yet.

A trust of land must be evidenced in writing and signed by the person declaring it (**s 53(1)(b), LPA 1925**), and a disposition of a beneficial interest under a trust (of any property) has to be in writing and signed by the transferor or his agent (**s 53(1)(c), LPA 1925**). The **Wills Act 1837, s 9** (as amended by the **Administration of Justice Act 1982**), prescribes the formalities required for leaving any property (including land) by will. The will must be signed by the testator, whose signature must be attested by two witnesses, and, broadly speaking, all three must be present and sign at the same time.

Because of the enquiries which have to be made and the documentation required for the purchase of land, a conveyancing transaction is usually effected in two stages: a contract to sell and the actual transfer of the legal estate. The formalities for a contract for the sale are prescribed by **s 2(1), Law of Property (Miscellaneous Provisions) Act 1989**; they are that the contract must be in writing and signed by both parties, or in two parts, one part signed by each party, and the two parts exchanged. This is the usual procedure followed by solicitors in a conveyancing transaction.

In addition to the formality provisions for the actual transactions, the **LCA 1972** provides for the registration of certain interests in unregistered land in order to give notice of them to a purchaser and to protect them, and **LRA 2002** provides for the registration of many interests created. **LRA 2002** extends the registration of interests created in land with registered title and correspondingly reduces the number of overriding interests that are binding without registration on a purchaser.

[4] Now cover the exceptions. There are some statutory exceptions[4] to the general requirement of formality. The statutory exception contained in **s 54(2), LPA 1925** provides that a lease taking effect in possession for a term not exceeding three years at the best rent reasonably obtainable without taking a fine (ie a capital sum) can be created informally without a deed. This exception is one of pure convenience and a recognition that many people create periodic tenancies of a flat or a room quite informally. Registration of such leases is not necessary to give notice of them to a third party. Another statutory exception to the rule was the **Limitation Act 1980**, under which, for the same rationale of convenience, the law was prepared to recognise that a person who adversely possessed land extinguished the title of the true owner after twelve years and acquired a possessory title. Lord St Leonards described the purpose of the Limitation Acts as 'the prevention of the rearing up of claims at

great distances of time when evidences are lost' (*Dundee Harbour Trustees v Dougal* (1852) 1 Macq 317). It was undesirable that the true paper owner should be allowed to 'sleep' on his rights and the policy of land law has always been to keep property freely alienable. Some unfortunate cases involving local authorities (see, eg, *Ellis v Lambeth LBC* [1999] *The Times*, 28 September 1999) received public condemnation, however, and **LRA 2002** severely limits the application of the Limitation Acts to registered title. They are regarded as inconsistent with a system of registered title, and the Act introduces a new procedure involving the service of notices for extinguishing a paper title.

The main exceptions to the requirements for formalities, however, are to be found in the applications by the courts of the principles of equity. Implied, resulting, and constructive trusts are specifically exempted by **s 53(2), LPA 1925** from the formality requirements for the creation of a trust in **s 53(1), LPA 1925**, and these trusts are recognised by **s 1(2)(a), TLATA 1996** as trusts of land. Where property is purchased by one person but conveyed into the name of another, without any intention of gift, equity will infer a resulting trust of the beneficial equitable interest for the person who has provided the purchase price (see *Hodgson v Marks* [1971] Ch 892, where the freeholder owner of a house conveyed the legal title to someone else). Where someone provides part only of the purchase price, such as a one-third contribution, then their equitable interest under a resulting trust will be one-third of the beneficial ownership (*Bull v Bull* [1955] 1 QB 234). A constructive trust is one imposed by the court on the owner of the legal title to the property, requiring such person to hold the whole or part of the beneficial equitable interest for someone else. The courts have imposed constructive trusts in a variety of circumstances, but basically to divest a person of their beneficial ownership when they have obtained an unjust enrichment by unconscionable dealing. Thus, in *Bannister v Bannister* [1948] 2 All ER 133, the defendant had purchased two freehold cottages from his sister-in-law at below the market price on the oral understanding that she should be allowed to live in one of them for the rest of her life. The court gave effect to this arrangement by imposing on the defendant a constructive trust. Constructive trusts have been applied also to commercial transactions such as the case of *Lyus v Prowsa Developments Ltd* [1982] 1 WLR 1044. The principles of constructive trusts are still developing in recent case law to determine the extent of beneficial co-ownership between cohabitees such as in *Stack v Dowden* [2007] 2 AC 432, where Lady Hale expressed the view that a wide variety of social circumstances could also be relevant in establishing a constructive trust, and in *Jones v Kernott* [2011] UKSC 53.

The courts have also been prepared to recognise proprietary interests arising from an estoppel,[5] where a person acts to their detriment in reliance upon a statement made by someone as to their rights

[5] Estoppel is always a nice example of courts bypassing the formality requirements. In an exam (as opposed to coursework), you could safely omit the lengthy discussion which follows and summarise it in a sentence or two.

in property. The doctrine of proprietary estoppel, like constructive trusts, has been applied to a variety of widely differing circumstances. It was said in *Crabb v Arun District Council* **[1976] Ch 179** that the court should satisfy the estoppel by 'the minimum equity to do justice to the plaintiff' (*per* Scarman LJ), and a variety of interests has been awarded on the finding of an estoppel. In *Crabb v Arun DC*, the estoppel interest was one in the nature of an easement, in *Inwards v Baker* **[1965] 2 QB 29** and *Matharu v Matharu* **[1994] 2 FLR 597** a licence, in *Griffiths v Williams* **(1977) 248 EG 947** a long lease, and in *Pascoe v Turner* **[1979] 1 WLR 431** a conveyance of the fee simple absolute. In *Gillett v Holt* **[2001] Ch 210**, the Court of Appeal allowed an estoppel to limit the principle of testamentary freedom. An issue of continuing uncertainty is how the court should satisfy the estoppel. The maximum equity is the claimant's expectation, as in *Pascoe v Turner*. In other cases, the courts have regarded the equity as already satisfied (as by some countervailing benefit, eg *Sledmore v Dalby* **(1996) 72 P & CR 196**). It was suggested in *Jennings v Rice* **[2002] EWCA Civ 159** that where the extent of the expectation is uncertain, the court should lean towards merely compensating for the detriment. In *Thorner v Major* **[2009] 1 WLR 776**, by contrast, the expectation was certain, as there had been a mutual understanding that the claimant would inherit a farm that he had worked on unpaid for nearly thirty years; the House of Lords restored the decision of the trial judge, who had held that the minimum equity to do justice was to award the claimant the farm.

One of the time-honoured maxims of equity is that 'equity will not allow a statute to be used as an instrument of fraud'. This is a very general maxim with potential for a very wide application. It was the basis of the old doctrine of part performance, which provided an exception to the formality requirements of **s 40, LPA 1925**, and underpins the enforcement of secret trusts contrary to the formality requirements of the **Wills Act 1837**. A case such as *Midland Bank Trust Co v Green* **[1981] AC 513** demonstrates very clearly that an inflexible requirement of statutory compliance can be a fertile ground for fraud, and that a modification of the requirement with an application of equitable principles may be highly desirable. The applications of resulting and constructive trusts and estoppel show that the courts are ready to apply equitable principles to create exceptions to the formality requirements of the statutes where they believe that justice requires it. In *Lyus v Prowsa Developments Ltd* **[1982] 1 WLR 1044**, Dillon J refused to allow an express agreement to be rendered void by a failure to comply with the registration requirements of **LRA 1925**. In *Yaxley v Gotts* **[2000] Ch 162**, referring to the **Law of Property (Miscellaneous Provisions) Act 1989**, Robert Walker LJ said 'the doctrine of estoppel may operate to modify (and sometimes perhaps even counteract) the effect of **s 2** of the **1989 Act'**, and 'any general assertion of **s 2** as a no-go area for estoppel would be unsustainable'. He pointed out that **s 2(5)** expressly exempts the operation of resulting, implied, or constructive trusts from the section, and considered the analogies drawn in various cases between constructive trusts and estoppel.

Whilst formality in land transactions is desirable, there must necessarily be some temperance of the requirement to allow for circumstances where there are sound reasons for enforcing informal arrangements and undertakings between parties which do not comply with the statutory formalities.

✚ LOOKING FOR EXTRA MARKS?

■ This is a lengthy answer, which you could use for coursework. In the exam context, there are lots of points included which would be worth extra marks and which are flagged up in the comments: for instance, the discursive introduction and the lengthy discussion of the case law in proprietary estoppel.

Ⓠ QUESTION | 4

Peter is considering purchasing a freehold house from Vincent. The title is unregistered and Peter has discovered the following matters:

(a) There are two sets of restrictive covenants, one made in 1922 and one made in 1945.

(b) The next-door neighbour uses a track across the bottom of the garden as access to his garage, which he cannot reach in any other way. Vincent has told Peter that this is an informal arrangement which he made with the neighbour some years ago, before the garage was built.

(c) Although Vincent appears to be living alone in the property, there is a Class F land charge registered against his name at the Land Charges Registry.

Advise Peter how these matters may affect his title to the property.

How would your answer differ if the title to the house were registered?

❗ CAUTION!

■ This is a very common type of examination question. Even if the subject matter is not addressed as directly as it is here, it may feature in a more disguised form in other questions.

■ You need to consider the nature of the interests created (unless, as with the restrictive covenants, you have actually been told about them), and then to decide whether or not they will bind a purchaser of the legal estate in the land.

■ It has been usual to ask the question for both unregistered and registered titles, and the answers may be different. But some examiners may now be confining their question to registered title only—make sure you read the question carefully for this instruction.

DIAGRAM ANSWER PLAN

Identify the issues	The legal issues are: (a) third-party rights and restrictive covenants; (b) third-party rights and easements; (c) third-party rights and Class F land charges.
Relevant law	(a) *Wilkes v Spooner* [1911]; s 25, LPA 1969; and minor interests. (b) **Section 1(2), LPA 1925** and s 2, **Law of Property (Miscellaneous Provisions) Act 1989; Schedule 3, para 3, LRA 2002**; estoppel and s 116, **LRA 2002**. (c) **Family Law Act 1996; Civil Partnership Act 2004; LCA 1925 (now 1972); LRA 2002**.
Apply the law	(a) 1922 restrictive covenants are not registrable and whether they bind a purchaser such as Peter depends upon whether he has notice of them or not. If *bona fide* purchaser for value of the land without notice of the covenants at any time, then this will permanently destroy their binding effect (***Wilkes v Spooner** [1911]*). The 1945 covenants are registrable under **LCA 1925**; if registered, they are binding. If not registered, they are not binding. **Section 25, LPA 1969** allows Peter to claim compensation for a pre-root of title land charge of which he did not have actual knowledge (**s 24**). In registered title, restrictive covenants are minor interests, binding only if protected by a notice on the register. (b) Informal arrangement cannot create legal easement within s **1(2), LPA 1925** for which a deed is necessary, nor an equitable easement for which a document in writing complying with **s 2, Law of Property (Miscellaneous Provisions) Act 1989** would be required. Enjoyment of the right for twenty years 'next before action' would give the neighbour the right to an easement by prescription (legal easement). Legal easements are binding in unregistered land. In registered land, an easement acquired by prescription may be overriding under **Schedule 3, para 3, LRA 2002** if it complies with the requirements of that paragraph. If the easement is supported by an estoppel, it will be equitable. In unregistered land, estoppel interests are not registrable, and whether they bind a purchaser depends upon the doctrine of notice. In registered title, only legal easements can be overriding. **Section 116, LRA 2002** specifically states that interests arising by estoppel are capable of binding successors in title. (c) Class F land charge protects the spouse's right of occupation of the matrimonial home under the **Family Law Act 1996**, even if she is not in occupation at the time. The **Civil Partnership Act 2004** extends this right to a registered civil partner. Registration will give notice that there is a wife or registered civil partner around and, as such, a person may have an equitable interest in the home nowadays, Peter should make enquiries. A beneficial interest as such is not registrable under the **LCA 1972** and its validity against a purchaser depends upon the doctrine of notice. In registered title, a spouse's rights of occupation under the Act are minor interests only and cannot be overriding, even if the spouse is in actual occupation.
Conclude	■ Advise Peter.

[1] Go straight into the application of the law to the problem. In a problem question with several parts, don't spend time setting out lengthy introductions.

[2] Watch the dates—they are key.

(a)[1] Restrictive covenants entered into before 1926[2] are not registrable under **LCA 1972** (formerly **1925**). Their binding validity against a purchaser of the land therefore depends upon the doctrine of notice. If Peter were a *bona fide* purchaser for value of the land without notice of the covenants, he would take free from them. His investigation of the title appears to have revealed the covenants, however, so that he will take subject to them as he has actual notice of them. The only exception to this would be if, although Peter himself knew of the restrictive covenants, there were a purchaser in the chain of title who was a *bona fide* purchaser for value without notice of them for some reason (see *Wilkes v Spooner* [1911] 2 KB 473).

[3] And so a different answer for this set of covenants.

[4] Actual notice point shows practical understanding of different types of notice.

[5] And make the contrast between actual and no actual notice.

The 1945 restrictive covenants[3] were registrable under **LCA 1925** (now **1972**) and, if registered, will be binding on Peter. They will be registered against the name of the estate owner in 1945, which Peter is unlikely to have on his title as the period of title deduced to a purchaser was reduced to fifteen years, starting with a good root, by **LPA 1969**. However, there may well be an old search with the deeds showing the covenants and **s 24, LPA 1969** provides that *actual* notice[4] of a pre-root land charge determines its validity against a purchaser so that **s 198, LPA 1925**, which provides that registration constitutes notice, shall not apply. If Peter enters into the contract without *actual knowledge*[5] of the covenants, **LPA 1969, s 25** provides for compensation for a purchaser affected by the land charge.

If the title to the land were registered, the restrictive covenants would be registered in the charges register as minor interests. They are binding if so registered, but not binding if not registered. In practice, many old pre-1926 restrictive covenants are registered in the charges register of a registered title. They are evident from the title, as each subsequent conveyance of the land is made expressly subject to them, and the Registrar enters them on first registration.

[6] Don't start off by saying, 'This is an easement.' Explore the options.

(b) The neighbour is enjoying a right of access which is similar to an easement,[6] and Peter needs to investigate this situation. It cannot be a legal or equitable easement expressly granted, for which a deed or contract in writing would be necessary.

If the neighbour has used the track for twenty years, then he may have a *prima facie* right to a claim to an easement under the **Prescription Act 1832**, or possibly under the doctrine of lost modern grant. The right may be negatived (in either case) by permission having been granted to him, as one of the essentials of all forms of prescription is that the user upon which they are based must be as of right. It is possible that the 'informal arrangement' may amount to an oral permission at the start of the twenty-year period and it may be sufficient to defeat it if it refers to the continued user throughout the period. If the neighbour has acquired an easement by prescription, then it will be a legal one, which will be binding upon Peter.

If the right of access was informally granted before the garage was built, then it may be possible for the neighbour to claim a right of access supported by estoppel. In *E R Ives Investment Ltd v High* **[1967] 2 QB 379**, the facts were similar to this and a neighbour, relying upon an agreement for access, built a garage. The successor in title to the person who had agreed to the access was estopped from denying the right. There were, however, other considerations, as the doctrine of *Halsall v Brizell* **[1957] Ch 169** also applied. Nevertheless, the court also recognised a right of access supported by an estoppel in *Crabb v Arun District Council* **[1976] Ch 179**.

If the neighbour is therefore able to say that he built the garage in reliance upon the agreement for access, and so acted to his detriment, then it may well be binding on Vincent. As an unregistrable equitable interest, it would be binding upon Peter unless he was a *bona fide* purchaser for value without notice of it. As he clearly has notice, he would not appear to fall into that category.

[7] Now deal with the registered title point. In registered title,[7] a legal easement acquired by prescription may be an overriding interest under **Schedule 3, para 3, LRA 2002** if exercised within one year of Peter's purchase, or if Peter actually knows of it (which he appears to do), or it would have been discoverable on a reasonably careful inspection of the land.

An equitable easement is not an overriding interest under **Schedule 3, para 3, LRA 2002** and so will only bind a purchaser if protected by a notice on the register. **Section 116** states, however, that estoppel interests are capable of binding successors in title of registered land. This means that the estoppel will bind Peter if—assuming that it has not been protected by entry of a notice on the register of title—the neighbour is in actual occupation of the track (which seems unlikely to be established merely by walking along the track). If, however, Peter were to obtain registered title to the house, and the neighbour were later to establish that he had an estoppel protected as an overriding interest through actual occupation of the track, the neighbour might be able to obtain rectification of the register by the entry of an equitable easement against the registered title (assuming the equity was satisfied by the award of an equitable easement).

(c) A Class F land charge indicates that Vincent's wife (or registered civil partner under the **Civil Partnership Act 2004**) is claiming a right of occupation of the matrimonial home under the **Family Law Act 1996, Pt IV**. (The **Civil Partnership Act 2004** extends such rights of occupation to a civil partner where that partnership has been registered.) It is irrelevant that she has actually left the home. It was held in *Watts v Waller* **[1973] QB 153** that a wife not in occupation of the matrimonial home still had a conditional right of occupation capable of registration as a land charge under the forerunner of the **1996 Act**. Peter will have to insist that this charge is cleared off the title before he completes the purchase of the property.

As Peter is aware of the existence of such a person, he should also make enquiries as to whether they have any beneficial interest in the matrimonial or shared home. It is sufficiently usual nowadays for a wife to have contributed to the purchase of a matrimonial home so that a purchaser who is put on notice that there is a wife should make enquiries as to any beneficial interest she may have (*Kingsnorth Finance Co v Tizard* **[1986] 1 WLR 783**). So, although the Class F land charge will not protect any such beneficial interest and only protects a wife's right of occupation, it might well be held to give a purchaser notice that there is a wife who might have a beneficial interest.

[8] And the registered title point. You could make all the registered title points together. The key is to be clear.

In registered title,[8] the statutory right of occupation of a spouse or registered civil partner under the **Family Law Act 1996** is registrable as a minor interest and would be binding on Peter if so registered. **Section 31(10)(b)** of the **Act** provides that it will not become an overriding interest, even if they were in actual occupation within the meaning of **LRA 2002, Schedule 3, para 2**. Any beneficial interest, which would be a minor interest, would be binding on Peter if protected by a restriction on the register. It could not be an overriding interest under **para 2**, as the person is not in actual occupation. Under **LRA 2002**, rights under the **Family Law Act** remain minor interests.

✚ LOOKING FOR EXTRA MARKS?

- There are a lot of points to gain here and the answer plan is deliberately detailed. Copy that approach in the exam and then tick off the points as you deal with them.

- Dealing with the registered title point can involve a nice opportunity to make a contrast between the outcomes, so do that if possible.

Q QUESTION | 5

Petra has entered into a contract with Vera to purchase the freehold title in a bungalow, which was registered in 1960. An investigation of the property and its title has revealed the following transactions:

(a) in 1992, Vera's predecessor in title granted to a neighbour, Nell, a right of way across the back garden; and

(b) in 2000, Vera leased a garage at the side of the bungalow to her friend, Freda; and

(c) earlier this year, Vera made a declaration of trust in relation to the property in favour of her son Ben, who is aged sixteen.

Advise Petra whether she will take the land free from, or subject to, the interests of Nell, Ben, and Freda.

What difference would it make to your answer if the land were still unregistered?

! CAUTION!

■ This is another question which adapts well to the instruction to consider the situation in both registered and unregistered land. To make your answer clearer to follow for the marker, use subheadings to indicate 'registered land' and 'unregistered land' in each part of the answer.

■ Very often examination questions deal with the application or not of overreaching, as does part (c) of this question. You need to know the principles which apply in both registered and unregistered title and the relevant cases which establish these. Remember that overreaching occurs in exactly the same way in registered and unregistered land.

DIAGRAM ANSWER PLAN

Identify

The legal issues are:

(a) third-party rights and easements;

(b) third-party rights and leases;

(c) third-party rights and declaration of trust; doctrine of overreaching.

Relevant law

(a) **Section 1(2)(a), LPA 1925**; minor interest; and Class D land charge.

(b) **Schedule 3, para 2, LRA 2002**; class C(iv) land charge under **LCA 1972**.

(c) **Section 53(1)(b), LPA 1925**; **Schedule 3, para 2(b), LRA 2002**; **LCA 1972**.

Relevant law

(a) **Right of way**

- If granted by deed and it complies with **s 1(2)(a), LPA 1925**, this will be capable of being a legal easement. In order to 'operate at law', however, it must be completed by registration against the title of the burdened land.

- If an equitable easement, it can only be a minor interest, and will be binding if protected by a notice on the register.

- In unregistered land, a legal easement (granted by deed and complying with **s 1(2)(a), LPA**) is a right *in rem* binding on everyone. An equitable easement is a Class D land charge and only binding if entered on the register, even if (as here) the purchaser Petra actually knows of it.

(b) **Lease**

- A legal lease exceeding seven years is registrable substantively; leases not exceeding seven years (including periodic tenancies) are overriding interests under **Schedule 3, para 1**. An equitable lease is a minor interest capable of protection on the register. It may also be overridi g under **Schedule 3, para 2, LRA 2002** as Petra, who has been told of it, has 'actual knowledge' of it.

- In unregistered land, a legal lease is a right *in rem* and binding on everyone. An equitable lease is an estate contract and binding if registered as a class C(iv) land charge under **LCA 1972**, but not binding if not registered.

(c) **Declaration of trust**

- Assuming that the declaration of trust complies with the formality requirements of **s 53(1)(b), LPA 1925**, then it is an equitable interest, but is not overreachable, as there is only one trustee. It is a minor interest and may be protected by an entry on the register. If not so protected, if Ben is of mature years and may be expected to respond to enquiries, then his interest may be overriding under **Schedule 3, para 2(b), LRA 2002**.

- In unregistered title, Ben's equitable interest is neither overreachable nor registrable under **LCA 1972**. Its binding effect therefore depends upon notice, which presumably Petra has.

Conclude

- Advise Petra.

SUGGESTED ANSWER

(a) Right of Way

¹ State the relevant key fact.

² Now state the law.

Nell has a right of way across Vera's garden.[1] To be a legal easement,[2] this must comply with the definition contained in **LPA 1925, s 1(2) (a)**. Thus, it must be for a period equivalent to a fee simple or a term of years. The use of the word 'granted' implies that it was created by deed as required by **LPA, s 52**. If it was created by deed which complies with **s 1(2)(a), Law of Property (Miscellaneous Provisions) Act 1989**, then it will be a legal interest. If it was not created by deed, then it may be possible to argue that, provided the right of way has been exercised openly and without permission or the use of force and has been used without interruption since 1992, a legal easement has been created by prescription, although the 'grant' may prevent this.

³ Now deal with equitable option.

If the easement is not legal,[3] it may still be enforceable in equity. It will be necessary to show that there is an enforceable contract in respect of which equity would grant specific performance. Such a contract must comply with the rules in the **Law of Property (Miscellaneous Provisions) Act 1989, s 2**, which require that the contract must be made in writing and incorporate all the terms. If there is no such written contract, then it might have been possible to rely on the equitable doctrine of proprietary estoppel if there was an assurance on which Nell had relied to her detriment (*Whittaker v Kinnear* [2011] EWHC 1479). However, if Vera and Nell intended to rely on a formal agreement, as is suggested by the term 'grant' in the question, then they will not be able to rely on proprietary estoppel (*Herbert v Doyle* [2010] EWCA Civ 1095).

As an equitable easement, it can be protected in registered land as a minor interest by a notice on the register.

⁴ Now deal with registered title.

Under **LRA 2002**,[4] a legal easement expressly granted is a registrable disposition under **s 27(2)(d)** and will not operate at law until registered (**s 27(1)**). It will not be an overriding interest under **Schedule 3, para 3**. A legal easement acquired by prescription may be an overriding interest under the paragraph, however, if it was exercised within one year of the sale to Petra, or Petra actually knew about it, or its existence was discoverable on a reasonably careful inspection of the land.

Equitable easements are minor interests and are not binding on a purchaser unless they are protected by an entry on the register. Equitable easements do not fall within the scope of overriding interests in **LRA 2002, Schedule 3, para 3**. Nor would it be binding under **Schedule 3, para 2**, as the use of an easement in the form of a right of way does not amount to 'actual occupation' (*Chaudhary v Yavuz* [2011] EWCA Civ 1314).

[5] Now turn to unregistered title.

If the title to the bungalow is unregistered,[5] then, if the easement is legal, it binds Petra, since legal interests bind the whole world. The issue as to whether it is legal or equitable depends on the same arguments as in the first part of the answer.

If the right of way is equitable, then, as it was created after 1925, it must be registered as a Class D(iii) land charge under **LCA 1972, s 2(5)**. If it is not registered, as such it is unenforceable against Petra as the purchaser for money or money's worth of a legal estate. There is no equivalent category in unregistered land to the overriding interest, so, if the equitable interest is not registered it is unenforceable by Nell, regardless of the state of knowledge of the purchaser, Petra.

(b) Lease

The lease, if a legal lease for more than seven years, is an estate

[6] State the key issue.

which must be registered substantively[6] with its own title num-

[7] Deal with legal status.

ber. Where the lease is a legal lease[7] (created by deed or within **LPA 1925, s 54(2)** (discussed later)) for a period not exceeding seven years, it will be an overriding interest under **LRA 2002, Schedule 3, para 1**, and so binding on Petra. This would apply also to a periodic tenancy, which is legal under **s 54(2), LPA 1925**, even if created by word of mouth. In *City Permanent Building Society v Miller* [1952] **Ch 840**, it was held that the words 'leases granted' in **s 70(1) (k), LRA 1925** (the forerunner to **Schedule 3, para 1**) could mean only legal leases and not equitable leases, and similarly the word 'grant' in **para 1** would not include equitable leases. If the lease is an equitable lease, it will be a minor interest, and binding if noted on the register. However, if Freda could be said to be in actual occupation of the garage, then it may be possible for her to bring her lease, even if only equitable, within the protection of **LRA 2002, Schedule 3, para 2**. It has been held that the intermittent use of a garage can amount to actual occupation (*Kling v Keston Properties Ltd* (1983) **49 P & CR 212**).

[8] Key point in case law.

It is important to distinguish actual use from actual occupation[8] (*Ruoff & Roper on Registered Conveyancing*, at para 10.019), and while the use of land to park a car has been accepted as actual oc-

[9] Now set out case law briefly—not too much detail, as you won't have time in the exam.

cupation (*Saeed v Plustrade* [2012] EWCA Civ 2011),[9] use of a right of way has been held not to amount to actual occupation (*Chaudhary v Yavuz* [2011] EWCA Civ 1314). However, since the lease relates to a garage, which can clearly be subject to physical occupation (*Malory Enterprises v Cheshire Homes (UK) Ltd* [2002] **EWCA Civ 151**), it would seem that Freda's lease could be protected even where it is equitable as an overriding interest. However,

Schedule 3, para 2 is not as wide as the former **s 70(1)(g), LRA 1925**, and **para 2(c)** excludes the interest of a person whose occupation would not have been obvious on a reasonably careful inspection of the land if the purchaser does not have actual knowledge of it. It is quite likely that a reasonable inspection would not have discovered Freda's occupation, but Petra does seem to have 'actual knowledge' of the lease, so that it will still be overriding, even if only equitable.

In unregistered land, if the lease is legal, it will bind the whole world. To be legal, the lease must be for a term certain and must be created by deed in accordance with **LPA 1925, s 52**, except where **s 54(2)** applies. This subsection provides that leases taking effect in possession for a term not exceeding three years at the best rent which can reasonably be obtained without taking a fine can be created by parol. The section includes all periodic tenancies.

A valid contract complying with the requirements of the **Law of Property (Miscellaneous Provisions) Act 1989, s 2** will create an equitable lease, which is registrable as an estate contract under Class C(iv) of **LCA 1972, s 2(4)**. For the same reasons that prevailed in respect of an equitable easement, if it is not registered, it is unenforceable against Petra.

(c) Declaration of Trust

[10] This is a key starting point to address.

A preliminary point[10] raised by this question, which applies to both registered and unregistered titles, is whether the declaration of trust of land has complied with the formality requirements of **LPA 1925, s 53(1)(b)**. This requires a declaration of a trust of land to be evidenced in writing and signed by the person declaring it (Vera), and if this has not been done, then the trust is unenforceable by Ben, although not void. In *Hypo-Mortgage Services Ltd v Robinson* [1997] 2 FLR 71, it was argued that the creation of a trust for children by a co-owner would amount to a transfer of that co-owner's beneficial equitable interest, which would be caught by **s 53(1)(c)** rather than **s 53(1)(b)** and so require to be actually in writing and signed by the transferor or their agent, and whilst not actually deciding the point, Nourse LJ expressed the opinion that this might well be right.

As Vera is a sole trustee, the overreaching provisions of **LPA 1925, s 2(1)** will not apply, as Petra will not obtain a receipt for the purchase moneys from two trustees.

If the title were registered, then Ben's interest would be a minor interest and could be protected by a restriction on the register. It would then be binding upon Petra. If not so protected, had Ben been eighteen years of age and in actual occupation of the bungalow, then he would have had an overriding interest under **LRA 2002, Schedule 3,**

para 2, which would also have been binding upon Petra (*Williams & Glyn's Bank Ltd v Boland* [1981] AC 487).

Hypo-Mortgage Services Ltd v Robinson [1997] 2 FLR 71, which was a case on the now repealed **s 70(1)(g), LRA 1925**, held that a minor's interest cannot be overriding by reason of their occupation, which is merely as a shadow of their parents. There was some criticism of this decision (Roger Smith felt that a better rationale for the decision would have been that a minor might well not be able to respond to enquiries from a purchaser (R Smith, *Property Law* (5th edn, Pearson 2006)).

[11] Nice point to make, showing good knowledge of reforms.

These criticisms[11] have been taken into account in the wording of **Schedule 3, para 2**, where **para 2(b)** exempts from overriding status the interest of a person of whom enquiry was made who did not disclose their right when he could reasonably have been expected to do so. Ben, aged sixteen, might be such a person, so that he might have an overriding interest if no enquiry is made of him (*Link Lending Ltd v Bustard* [2010] EWCA Civ 424).

In unregistered title, Ben's interest would be a family-type beneficial equitable interest which is not registrable. Its binding effect on a purchaser therefore depends upon notice, and if Petra were a *bona fide* purchaser for value without notice of Ben's interest, then she would take free from it. Notice may be actual, imputed, or constructive (as in *Kingsnorth Finance Co. v Tizard* [1986] 2 All ER 54), but as Vera has actually told Petra, then she may well have actual notice.

LOOKING FOR EXTRA MARKS?

- There are a number of points to make, but if you can keep a cool head and deal with each in turn they are not as complicated as at first sight.
- Pick up criticisms and reforms reflecting those.

QUESTION | 6

Alan is the registered proprietor of a row of three cottages Nos 2, 4, and 6 Cowslip Lane. His friend, Betty, telephones him to ask if she can rent No 2 while she is looking for somewhere to buy. Alan agrees, and she moves in and starts paying rent on a monthly basis from 1 January.

Alan decides to put No 4 on the market and he receives two offers from Carl and Damien. Carl makes the higher offer, but wishes to defer completion of the contract until he returns from six

◀

months' employment abroad. Carl suggests to Alan's estate agent that the property should not be sold to Damien and that Carl will better any offer from Damien by £5,000 and will exchange contracts within a month, but with completion to be deferred until his (Carl's) return from abroad. The estate agent telephones Alan, who agrees to this proposal. The next day, however, Alan receives a draft contract from Damien, and Alan and Damien exchange contracts by the end of that week.

Alan is short of money and he approaches his bank for a loan. The bank agrees to lend him £10,000 but suggests that it should hold the land certificate of No 6 (which is in a safety deposit box at the bank) as security for the loan. Alan agrees.

Alan has now decided to emigrate and he agrees to sell Nos 2 and 6 to Edith. Edith moves into No 2, but is surprised when Betty, who has been away on holiday, lets herself into the cottage. Edith then receives a letter from the bank threatening to foreclose on the mortgage on No 6. Damien receives a letter from Carl, saying that he has an agreement with Alan which takes precedence over Damien's agreement.

Advise Edith and Damien whether Betty, the bank, and Carl have contracts which are enforceable against them.

! CAUTION!

- The question concerns the judicial interpretations of the **Law of Property (Miscellaneous Provisions) Act 1989, s 2**. As usual, the advice is to separate out the issues and to deal with each in turn. Some of the precedents are conflicting, so grasp the nettle and suggest what, in your view, would be the likely outcome.

- The part of the question dealing with leases is straightforward. The status of collateral agreements (which do not comply with the formality requirements of the section) and 'lockout' agreements has featured in a number of cases, some of which have received comment in Case Notes in *The Conveyancer* (see, eg *Pitt v PHH Asset Management*: Mark Thompson, 'The Enforceability of Mortgages' [1994] *Conveyancer and Property Lawyer* 140 and *Record v Bell*: Michael Harwood, 'Law of Property (Miscellaneous Provisions) Act 1989 s 2–s 40 Reincarnate?' [1991] *Conveyancer and Property Lawyer* 471.

- Since **LRA 2002** came into force, it is no longer possible to create a mortgage by depositing a land certificate.

DIAGRAM ANSWER PLAN

Identify the issues	■ The legal issue is the judicial interpretation of the **Law of Property (Miscellaneous Provisions) Act 1989, s 2.**
Relevant law	■ Section 2(5), Law of Property (Miscellaneous Provisions) Act 1989; s 54(2), LPA 1925; Schedule 3, para 1, LRA 2002; *United Bank of Kuwait plc v Sahib* (1997); and related case law.
Apply the law	■ There is an exception for leases not exceeding three years (s 2(5), **Law of Property (Miscellaneous Provisions) Act 1989; s 54(2), LPA 1925**). ■ Consider overriding interests: **Schedule 3, para 1, LRA 2002**. ■ Consider the creation of mortgage by deposit of title deeds. ■ Consider the effect of *United Bank of Kuwait plc v Sahib*. ■ Determine whether the contract is to exchange contracts or 'lock-out' agreement.
Conclude	■ Advise Edith and Damien.

A SUGGESTED ANSWER

[1] Set out the issues and itemise them. The question bundles them, so you are doing both yourself and the marker a favour by separating them.

[2] Take the actors in turn.

[3] Set out the law and remember to give a very precise reference to the statute—so don't forget your statute book for the exam.

[4] Hedging your bets here by use of this phraseology.

There are three issues[1] to be addressed in this problem: (i) whether Edith is bound by the agreement between Alan and Betty; (ii) whether Edith is bound by the agreement between Alan and the bank; and (iii) the effect of the agreement between Alan and Carl on Damien.

Betty[2]

Betty is occupying No 2 and is paying rent. Under the **Law of Property (Miscellaneous Provisions) Act 1989, s 2(1)**,[3] a contract in writing is required for the sale or other disposition of an interest in land. There is no suggestion of writing in Betty's case; the agreement appears to have been concluded[4] over the telephone. However, there is an exception in **s 2(5)** in respect of contracts to grant a lease for a term not exceeding three years to which **LPA, s 54(2)** applies. **Section 54(2)** applies to leases taking effect in possession for a term not exceeding three years at the best rent which can be reasonably obtained without taking a fine. The 'best rent' in the subsection means the 'market rent': *Fitzkriston LLP v Panayi* [2008] EWCA Civ 283; and see *Looe Fuels Ltd v Looe Harbour Commissioners* [2008] EWCA Civ 414. If the lease is a monthly periodic tenancy (which from the agreement it would appear to be),[5] and satisfies the other statutory requirements, then it falls within **s 54(2)** and, therefore, within the exception contained in **s 2(5)**. This means that there would be a valid contract, and, once Betty has taken possession, a legal lease is in existence. A legal lease not exceeding seven years is an overriding interest within **LRA 2002, Schedule 3, para 1**[6] and so is binding on Edith. Edith would have to give Betty one month's notice to quit.

The Bank[7]

The bank can only enforce its loan against No 6 if it has a property right binding on Edith. Alan did not grant the bank a legal mortgage, and the issue is therefore whether the bank has an equitable mortgage.[8] It was established in *Russel v Russel* (1783) Bro CC 269[9] that the deposit of title deeds as security for a loan creates an equitable charge over the land to which the deeds relate. The deeds had to be deposited for the purpose of securing the loan: *Thames Guaranty Ltd v Campbell* [1985] 1 QB 210. In registered land, the equivalent principle used to be the creation of an equitable lien over the land by the deposit of the land certificate with the lender as security, and this was expressly provided for by **LRA 1925, s 66**. Although the mere deposit with such purpose did not comply with the evidential requirements for a contract to create an interest in land laid down in **LPA 1925, s 40(1)**, the principle in *Russel v Russel* was based on the doctrine of part performance, which was expressly preserved by **LPA 1925, s 40(2)**. However, **s 40** was repealed and replaced by the formality requirements of **s 2 of the Law of Property (Miscellaneous Provisions) Act 1989**, under which there is now no valid contract unless there is compliance with **s 2**. The mere deposit of title deeds can no longer be treated as creating an equitable mortgage by virtue of part performance because, as there is now no contract, it cannot be partly performed. In *United Bank of Kuwait plc v Sahib* [1997] Ch 107, it was argued that the principle in *Russel v Russel* survived **s 2** on the basis that the creation of a mortgage by deposit of title deeds is *sui generis* and independent of contract; but the Court of Appeal rejected that argument.[10] After the decision in *Sahib*, there was no reason to preserve that method of creating equitable mortgages in registered land, so it was abandoned in **LRA 2002**.

Therefore, in the absence of a written contract complying with **s 2**, the bank will not have an equitable mortgage, and can have no property right binding on Edith; it has merely personal remedies against Alan. If there was a written contract satisfying **s 2**, the bank should have protected such contract by entry of a notice on the charges

[5] Again, hedge your bets—always wise not to state these issues categorically.

[6] Nice point—worth extra marks.

[7] Headings and plenty of space between sections are such small things to remember but make such a difference, enabling the marker to spot your brilliance.

[8] The preceding sentence explains how you get to this conclusion.

[9] From here, we get into a discussion of the case law and starting with this case enables you to demonstrate your knowledge of the development of the law in this area.

[10] This displays your knowledge of the case law and how the cases have developed. It demonstrates a real grasp of the topic and will appear as big ticks in the marker's head.

register; if it has not done so, its equitable mortgage will not be binding on Edith if she has taken a transfer of the legal estate.

Carl

The validity of Carl's agreement with Alan depends on whether it may be said to amount to a contract to exchange contracts, or a 'lockout' agreement.[11] If it can be construed so as to impose an obligation on Alan to exchange contracts with Carl, then it needs to be in writing in accordance with the requirements of the **Law of Property (Miscellaneous Provisions) Act 1989, s 2(1)**.[12] If it is a negative agreement simply preventing Alan from negotiating with anyone else, then it does not require formality.

In *Walford v Miles* **[1992] 2 WLR 174**, there was an agreement that, in consideration for the plaintiffs' agreeing not to withdraw from negotiations, the plaintiffs would terminate negotiations with any third party. This was held to be simply an agreement to negotiate and was not actionable (other than as a misrepresentation). Other types of agreement occurring at the point of exchange of contracts are sometimes classifiable as collateral contracts.[13] In *Record v Bell* **[1991] 1 WLR 853**, an oral warranty as to the state of the title was given as an inducement to exchange contracts. Again, it was held that such a warranty was outside the requirements of **s 2(1)**. Similarly, in *Pitt v PHH Asset Management Ltd* **[1994] 1 WLR 327**, an agreement whereby the vendor's agent agreed not to consider any further offers for the property on the basis that the plaintiff would exchange contracts within two weeks of the receipt of the draft contract constituted a lock-out agreement outside the ambit of **s 2(1)**. In *Grossman v Hooper* **(2001) 27 EG 135**, the Court of Appeal considered that it was inappropriate to describe separate agreements as 'collateral contracts'. They were either part of the contract for the transfer of the land or they were separate from it.

The agreement between Carl and Alan that Alan will not sell to Damien amounts to a lock-out agreement in that it prevents any further negotiations with Damien. In that respect, it is outside the ambit of **s 2(1)** (*Pitt v PHH Management*). However, the agreement also commits Carl to exchanging contracts within a month. It is arguable that such an agreement concerns an interest in land and requires formalities for it to be valid (*Dallia v Four Millbank Nominees* **[1978] Ch 231**). But it may instead fall into the category of collateral contracts, as in *Record v Bell*. Clearly, it is difficult to reconcile the authorities. However, on the basis of *Pitt v PHH Asset Management*, where the agreement did include an obligation to exchange within a month, and *Record v Bell*, where the warranty related to the title of the property, it would seem more likely that the courts would construe Carl's agreement with Alan not to sell to Damien as not subject to the requirements

[11] Start the section by setting out the issue.

[12] And now apply the law (this is IRAC at work).

[13] This sentence enables you to embark on a discussion of relevant cases which display your knowledge.

of **s 2(1)**. In that event, the agreement not to sell to Damien would be enforceable as a separate agreement between Carl and Alan.

If, therefore, pursuant to his contract with Damien, Alan conveys No 4 to Damien, Alan will be liable in damages to Carl for breach of the lock-out agreement. If, on the other hand,[14] Alan were to convey No 4 to Carl (with whom he has no valid contract of sale), he would be liable in damages to Damien for breach of contract; but Damien's contract will be binding upon Carl only if Damien had protected it by registration as a minor interest.

[14] Deal in this way with the various possibilities.

LOOKING FOR EXTRA MARKS?

- Discuss the cases thoroughly to show the different permutations of facts which can take place and the effect of those on the outcome.
- Separate out the facts using subheadings.

TAKING THINGS FURTHER

- Cavill, D, Wheeler, S, Dixon M, et al *Ruoff & Roper Registered Conveyancing* (Sweet & Maxwell 2020).

  Looseleaf encyclopaedia.

- Hayton, D, 'Equitable Rights of Cohabitees' [1990] *Conv* 370 and 'Constructive Trusts of Homes —A Bold Approach' (1993) 109 *LQR* 485, and the judgment of Robert Walker LJ in **Yaxley v Gotts [2000] 1 All ER 711** at 713 (albeit tempered by his comments in **Stack v Dowden**).

  For further reading on the topic of comparing constructive trusts and estoppel.

- Law Commission, *Land Registration for the Twenty-First Century: A Conveyancing Revolution* (Law Com No 271, 2001).

  The key report on the issue of land registration—you really need to know about it.

- Owen, G and Cahill, D, 'Overreaching—Getting the Right Balance' (2017) 1 *Conv* 26–44.

  For an interesting review of overreaching.

- Riddall, J G, 'Unwin Avenue and Reginald Road' (1977) *Conv* 405.

  For an amusing and lightly written comparison of the binding effect of certain interests in the two systems of registered and unregistered land—but remember that it was written before **LRA 2002** *came into force!*

Online Resources   www.oup.com/uk/qanda/

For extra essay and problem questions on this topic, as well as advice on revision and exam technique, please visit the online resources.

5 Registered Land

ARE YOU READY?

In order to attempt the three questions in this chapter, you will need to have covered the following topics:

- **Land Registration Act (LRA) 2002;**
- registrable, minor, and overriding interests.

KEY DEBATES

Debate: the underlying principle of registration of title was that the register at HM Land Registry should, so far as possible, reflect the title to the land. This 'mirror' principle is often missing, though.

The system of registration of title also recognises two categories of interests which, unlike the legal estates mentioned in earlier chapters, are not registrable substantively. The first of these is registrable interests that can be protected by the entry of a notice on the register (**s 32(1), LRA 2002**). Under the old law, these interests were known as minor interests and some commentators continue to adopt this nomenclature for ease of reference. The second of these is interests that override the register (usually referred to as overriding interests), which are set out in **LRA 2002, Schedule 1** (unregistered interests which override first registration), and **Schedule 3** (unregistered interests which override registered dispositions). Overriding interests are interests which, although not entered on the register, are nevertheless interests subject to which registered dispositions of the land take effect (**s 11(4)(b)** and **s 30(2)(ii), LRA 2002**). The overriding interests which are set out in **Schedule 3** to the Act are much reduced and modified, as part of the general policy of the Act to make the register a mirror of the title and so avoid the presence of any binding interests which do not appear on it. The existence of overriding interests is an important qualification to the basic principle that the register is an accurate reflection of the title to the land.

Q   QUESTION   1

Hector is the registered proprietor of a large Victorian house that he bought in the spring of 2014 with the aid of a loan of £50,000 from the Troy Building Society, which registered its legal charge a month later. His mother provided half the deposit and agreed to pay half the mortgage instalments. As she was recently widowed, Hector invited her to set up home with him. The house required some extensive redecoration and rewiring before it was habitable, and the vendor allowed Hector to have access for these purposes before completion. After completion, Hector's mother took a fort-night's holiday, and Hector had the work finished during this time. She moved in with her furniture and possessions on her return.

In the autumn of 2015, Hector converted the house into three flats. He now occupies the ground floor with his mother and he let the flat on the first floor to Ajax on a monthly tenancy in December 2015. Early in 2016, Hector's brother, Paris, took possession of the flat on the second floor under a seven-year lease at a rent of £3,000 per year. Paris had a friend, Helen, who had recently become unemployed, so he allowed her to share the flat free of charge. In September 2018, Paris accepted an offer of a two-year contract abroad. He decided to keep the flat on, however, and has continued to pay Hector the rent. Paris had told Helen she can remain there as long as she wants, provided she pays the electricity bills.

At the rear of the house, there is a large car-parking area. Hector entered into an agreement in October 2017 with his neighbour Odysseus that Odysseus could park his caravan there when not travelling abroad with it.

Hector, unbeknown to his mother, took out a second mortgage from the Sparta Bank in November 2017 to prop up his failing business. As he has not been making any repayments recently to either the Troy Building Society or the Sparta Bank, they are both seeking to recover their loans. Hector has now fled the country and his business is insolvent.

Discuss.

!   CAUTION!

- This is a question that mixes different issues relating to overriding interests. The major area of difficulty is without doubt that of **Schedule 3, para 2, LRA 2002** and the effect of the case law under the former provisions in **LRA 1925, s 70(1)(g)**. So, a knowledge of the case law on **s 70(1)(g)** is indispensable.

- Whilst many interests may become overriding under **Schedule 3**, such as the interest of Hector's mother, they may well be minor interests in their own right and you should not omit to say that, as such, they may be protected by an entry on the register. The question also includes some of the other interests which may override the register and those which require to be completed by registration.

- The question is written like a novel—don't answer it that way. Use headings, and deal with each person in turn.

DIAGRAM ANSWER PLAN

Identify the issues	■ The legal issues are minor and overriding interests.
Relevant law	■ This is the **LRA 2002**.
Apply the law	■ Consider what interest Hector's mother has, and whether it is minor or overriding. Then decide if it is binding on (i) the Troy Building Society; and (ii) the Sparta Bank.
	■ What interest has Ajax? Is it a minor or overriding interest? Is it binding on the building society and the bank?
	■ What interest has Paris? Is it a legal or equitable lease? (As the question does not specifically indicate, you should consider both.) In both cases, is it a minor or an overriding interest, and is it binding on the building society or the bank?
	■ What is the nature of Helen's occupation? Is this capable of being a minor or an overriding interest? Is it binding on the building society or the bank?
	■ What sort of interest may have been created by Hector's agreement with Odysseus? Would such an interest be a minor or an overriding interest and therefore binding or not?
Conclude	■ Include the nature of the various interests and their status.

A SUGGESTED ANSWER

[1]Establish headings and deal with each in turn.

[2]You need to state this to show she has an equitable interest at the outset.

[3]Don't just jump to a consideration of overriding interests. It is easy to forget the minor interest established here.

Hector's Mother[1]

Hector's mother has an equitable interest behind a resulting trust[2] in the house by virtue of her contribution to the purchase price. Can her interest override the interest of the legal mortgagees? A beneficial equitable interest under a trust is not specifically included in the list of overriding interests (**Schedule 3, LRA 2002**). It is, however, a proprietary interest and is therefore a minor interest,[3] which Hector's mother could have protected by an entry of a restriction in the proprietorship register of the title to which it relates (**LRA 2002, ss 40, 43**). The restriction would have prohibited a dealing with the registered estate unless the purchaser or mortgagee obtained a receipt from two trustees. This would not have given her protection against the Troy Building Society (for the same reasons given later as to why her overriding interest would be postponed to them), but would have prevented Hector from mortgaging to Sparta Bank without appointing a second trustee.

[4] Many students forget to make this point.

Even though Hector's mother did not enter a restriction,[4] under **LRA 2002, Schedule 3, para 2**, an interest belonging to a person in actual occupation of land at the time of the disposition is protected as an overriding interest. The effect of **LRA 2002, s 29(1)** and **Schedule 3, para 2** is to make it clear that such an interest must be of a proprietary, not a personal, nature. Two issues arise here: what is actual occupation and when must such occupation occur?

[5] Explain here why the 'old law' is relevant.

In answering this question, the case law decided under the old law[5] contained in **s 70(1)(g), LRA 1925** will continue to be relevant in many respects and until it is replaced and updated by case law under **Schedule 3, para 2**. A person claiming such an overriding interest must establish actual occupation at the time of the completion of the disposition, that is, in this case, the two mortgages. This is also now clear from the wording of **Schedule 3, para 2** and the decision in *Cook v The Mortgage Business plc* [2012] EWCA Civ 17, which confirmed the position established under the old law in *Abbey National Building Society v Cann* [1991] 1 AC 56. *Thompson v Foy* [2009] EWHC 1076 (Ch) also suggests (*obiter*) that occupation must be established both at the date of the disposition and at the date of registration, although this was not previously the position established by *Abbey National v Cann*. What is clearly established is that such a claim to an overriding interest is enforceable, provided that the *rights* remain subsisting at the date of registration. Thus, Hector's mother's claim to an overriding interest will depend upon her establishing that she was in actual occupation at the date of the completion in the spring of 2011. If, further to the *dicta* in *Thompson v Foy*, she is required to show actual occupation at the date of registration, then she will also have to show occupation at the date of registration of each of the mortgages.

[6] Now deal with the case law in some detail.

Actual occupation naturally includes the physical presence of the person claiming the interest[6] (*Hodgson v Marks* [1971] Ch 892). In *Williams & Glyn's Bank Ltd v Boland* [1981] AC 487, actual occupation was said to be a matter of fact to be construed in ordinary words of plain English. However, later cases found shades of meaning within this apparently literal interpretation of the section (*Abbey National Building Society v Cann*; *Link Lending Ltd v Bustard* [2010] EWCA Civ 424; *Lloyd v Dugdale* [2002] 2 P & CR 13). In *Lloyds Bank v Rosset* [1991] 1 AC 107, the presence of builders in occupation of the site of a semi-derelict farmhouse was held to be capable of satisfying the requirements of the section, but in Cann it was doubted whether acts in preparation for a future occupation, such as laying carpets and moving in furniture, were sufficient. Thus, the physical presence of the mother may not be necessary if it can be shown that the decorators were present in the property as her agents. They were, in fact, hired by Hector, not his mother, so there may be an argument that they were not acting as her agents for these purposes. It is a controversial question whether someone who is not physically present on the premises, but who is employing a builder who is on the site, can claim to be in actual occupation. Someone whose presence is merely fleeting, such as a prospective purchaser who enters to measure the premises for curtains, is not to be considered to be in actual occupation (*Abbey National Building Society v Cann*), nor is a builder who enters to carry out repairs and renovations, himself in actual occupation (*Canadian Imperial Bank of Commerce v Bello* (1992) 64 P & CR 48). A temporary absence may not destroy the absentee's continuing to be in actual occupation. In *Chhokar v Chhokar* [1984] FLR 313, a wife was held to remain in actual occupation during the period she was in hospital having a baby. Other cases such as *Thompson v Foy* [2009] EWHC 1076 (Ch) and *Link Lending Ltd v Bustard* [2010] EWCA Civ 424 demonstrate that distinctions of fact can alter the outcome significantly. In the problem, Hector's mother does not begin actual occupation until a fortnight after the completion of the transaction. This would seem to be distinguishable from a case where the continuity of occupation has been broken by a temporary absence. Thus, it would be necessary for the mother to establish vicarious occupation through the decorators; a task which may prove too difficult.

[7] Deal with each requirement in **Schedule 3, para 2(c)(i)** in turn.

A further requirement in **Schedule 3, para 2(c)(i)** is that the occupation would have been obvious on a reasonably careful inspection of the land at the time of the disposition.[7] Given that neither Hector's mother nor her possessions were present until a fortnight later, she clearly will not fulfil this requirement. However, **Schedule 3, para 2(c)(ii)** sets out the additional requirement that the person to whom the disposition was made must have been unaware of the interest. Although this point is not made clear in the question, it is quite possible that the Troy Building Society did know of her interest, since she provided part of the deposit and is paying half of the mortgage repayments. If this is the case, then the Troy Building Society would not be able to rely on this exception.

[8] An 'extra marks' point.

It might be argued, however, that Hector's mother has waived her right[8] as against the Troy Building Society, as she must have known of its charge over the property and must have impliedly consented to its taking priority over her interest (*Paddington Building Society v Mendelsohn* (1985) 50 P & CR 244). She had agreed to pay half the mortgage instalments. In any event, as the charge in favour of the

Troy Building Society was contemporaneous with the purchase, her trust was engrafted on an already encumbered title (*Abbey National Building Society v Cann*).

These arguments will not prevail against the Sparta Bank.[9] By the time the mortgage with the Sparta Bank had been entered into, Hector's mother was in occupation and it is likely that such occupation would have been obvious on a reasonably careful inspection of the land (**Schedule 3, para 2(c)(i)**). Not only is she, therefore, clearly in actual occupation at the time of the creation and registration of its charge, but she is also unaware of it and, therefore, cannot be taken to have waived her priority. Her beneficial interest will be, under **Schedule 3, para 2**, an overriding interest and binding on the bank.

In neither case will her interest have been overreached, since there is only one trustee[10]—Hector (*Williams & Glyn's Bank Ltd v Boland* **[1979] Ch 312; s 27, LPA 1925**).

Ajax

Ajax occupies a flat in the house under a monthly tenancy, which is presumably a legal periodic tenancy within the **Law of Property Act (LPA) 1925, s 54(2)**.[11] It is protected as an overriding interest under the **LRA 2002, Schedule 3, para 1**, as a legal lease granted for a term not exceeding seven years. Leases for more than seven years are registrable substantively under **LRA 2002**. Ajax's lease, being a proprietary interest, is also protected under **Schedule 3, para 2**, provided Ajax is in actual occupation. Overriding interests must be in existence before the date of the disposition and at the date of registration of the purchaser's interest. Thus, Ajax's interest will be enforceable against the Sparta Bank by virtue of its protection under **Schedule 3, para 1**, but not against the Troy Building Society, whose legal charge was created and registered before the lease was created.

Paris and Helen

Paris's lease is not registrable substantively as it is not for more than seven years and, as it was not created until after the acquisition of the property and the creation and registration of the charge in favour of the Troy Building Society, his interest will not be binding on that building society.

Paris is in occupation of the second-floor flat under a seven-year lease. If this is a legal lease, then it is protected under the **LRA, Schedule 3, para 1** and would be binding on the Sparta Bank. If it is equitable, that paragraph does not apply, and he would have to rely on **Schedule 3, para 2** unless it was protected by an entry of a notice on the charges register. However, he is no longer in actual occupation himself, so his occupation would not be discoverable on a

[9] Deal with the banks separately— they raise different points (which is why the examiner has included them).

[10] Don't forget that overreaching also applies to registered land.

[11] Include this for complete coverage of all the points, and then deal with substantive registration of leases for more than seven years.

reasonable inspection so as to satisfy **Schedule 3, para 2(c)(i)**. Helen is occupying the flat in his absence under an informal arrangement and her occupancy would constitute no more than a personal right to occupy as a bare licensee. As such, she does not satisfy the requirement of **Schedule 3, para 2** (*Strand Securities Ltd v Caswell* **[1965] Ch 958**). At the time of the second mortgage, Paris is no longer in occupation himself. Therefore, neither he nor Helen has any protection under **Schedule 3, para 2** against the Sparta Bank.

LOOKING FOR EXTRA MARKS?

■ Taking care to be thorough with your referencing of statutory authority is important to get the highest marks possible.

■ Discuss case law in detail where distinctions of facts are important.

■ Explain why the old law remains relevant.

■ Include the minor interest point.

QUESTION | 2

'. . . Overriding interests are an obstacle to achieving a conclusive register, which is one of the principal objectives of the Land Registration Act 2002 . . .' (C Harpum, S Bridge, and M Dixon, *Megarry and Wade: The Law of Real Property*, 8th edn, Sweet & Maxwell 2012).

(a) Discuss with regard to the overriding interests protected under **Schedule 3, LRA 2002**, indicating how these differ from the overriding interests formerly contained in **s 70(1), LRA 1925**.

(b) How has **LRA 2002** lessened the impact of overriding interests?

CAUTION!

■ This question requires, in the first instance, an account of the system of registered title in general, and overriding interests in particular. But don't simply list the different types of interests without more. What is required is a critical analysis of the problems to be encountered in the system of registered conveyancing brought about by a group of interests which, despite their non-appearance on the register, still bind the purchaser.

■ As mentioned in Key Debates, **LRA 2002** represents a considerable shift towards the mirror principle, and as part of this, the overriding interests in **s 70(1), LRA 1925** have been greatly modified and reduced; they are now 'interests which override' in **Schedule 3** to the **2002 Act**. Various changes and modifications have been pointed out in the answer to part (a) of this question, and part (b) is a general overall view of the changes.

DIAGRAM ANSWER PLAN

(a) Discuss the following:
- the 'mirror' principle of the register;
- overriding interests, which represent a serious flaw in this, but the justification for them is that they are the interests of persons unable to protect them, or even unaware of them;
- the relevant date for overriding interests to exist to be binding on a purchaser.
- s 70(1)(g), LRA 1925 and its replacement by Schedule 3, para 2, LRA 2002.
- case law on the nature of 'actual occupation' for the purposes of the section, indicating any changes under the LRA 2002.

▼

(b) Discuss the following:
- interests overriding on a first registration of title and on a registered disposition (Schedules 1 and 3, LRA 2002);
- s 70(1)(a), LRA 1925 and provision for legal easements under the LRA 2002;
- equitable easements under the LRA 1925 and changes under the LRA 2002;
- s 70(1)(f), LRA 1925, which makes overriding rights acquired (or being acquired) under the Limitation Acts, but these are not applicable to registered land under the LRA 2002;
- s 70(1)(g), LRA 1925 and judicial interpretations of it in the cases. The new Schedule 3, para 2, LRA 2002 is narrower and would reverse some of these decisions;
- how legal leases are dealt with under the LRA 2002.

A **SUGGESTED ANSWER**

[1] Start by establishing the basics.

The fundamental principle[1] of registered conveyancing is that the purchaser is bound by everything on the register, which provides a mirror of the title and all the interests affecting the land. As part of the 1925 legislation, the **LRA 1925** was concerned to simplify conveyancing and provide certainty for the purchaser. The **LRA 1925** was repealed and replaced by **LRA 2002**.

[2] Now show what happened before 2002.

Under the system of registration before **LRA 2002**,[2] legal freeholds and leases of more than twenty-one years were registrable substantively with their own title number and land certificate (so were legal rentcharges, but these are now virtually extinct as the **Rentcharges Act 1977** provided for them to cease after sixty years and a procedure for their redemption before then in certain cases). Certain interests are now registrable dispositions (such as the express grant or reservation of a legal easement within **s 1(2), LPA 1925** and the grant of a legal charge), which must be completed by registration in order to be legal and binding. Other interests can be protected as minor interests by means of a notice or restriction under the **LRA 2002**. Thus, many interests affecting the land are to be found on the register of title.

But 'the register of title is not a perfect mirror of the title to a registered property. It is not possible to rely on entries on the register as the complete record of everything that affects the title'[3] (*per* Peter Gibson LJ, *Overseas Investments Ltd v Simcobuild Construction Ltd* (1995) 70 P & CR 322 at 327). This limitation to the mirror principle is primarily to be found in the category of overriding interests. These are interests which, although not registered or protected on the register, bind a registered proprietor regardless of his state of knowledge as to their existence (**LRA 2002, Schedule 3**).

[4] Having set the stage, now deal with overriding interests—the heart of the problem.

The list of overriding interests[4] is contained in **Schedule 3, LRA 2002**. It includes a range of interests such as certain rights of way, rights under local land charges, property rights of a person in actual occupation, and legal leases for seven years or less.

[5] You may not agree with this opening gambit. The point is to be analytical, not just descriptive.

Overriding interests are a blemish upon the mirror of the title to which the system of registration ultimately aspires.[5] The **LRA 2002** has therefore modified and reduced these interests in various ways.

[6] Include for complete coverage (and gaining extra points).

Interests which override on a first registration of title are contained in **Schedule 1, LRA 2002**, whilst interests which override on a registered disposition are contained in **Schedule 3**.[6] They are largely the same, except for the rights of a squatter, but **Schedule 1** is slightly wider in scope. For example, the 'occupation' paragraph in **Schedule 1** is not quite so specific and restricted as **para 3** of **Schedule 3**, presumably to allow for the doctrine of notice which applies in unregistered conveyancing. Also, there is no restriction on the types of legal easement which will be overriding as there is in **Schedule 3**. **Section 11(4)(c), LRA 2002** provides that a first registered proprietor takes subject to interests acquired under the **Limitation Act 1980** of which he has notice, whereas the rights of a squatter are no longer overriding under the new Act and there is no equivalent of

[7] Use the Law Commission reports.

s 70(1)(f), LRA 1925 in **Schedule 3**. The Law Commission[7] did not see rights of adverse possession as consistent with a system of registered title. Various other old rights, such as customary rights, public rights, and franchises, are to be found in both Schedules, as are local land charges.

[8] Now go on to work your way through the list.

Section 70(1)(a), LRA 1925[8] made overriding certain specific rights in the nature of easements, profits à prendre, and other easements not being equitable easements. By a liberal interpretation of r 258 of the **Land Registration Rules**, in *Celsteel Ltd v Alton House Holdings Ltd* [1985] 2 All ER 562 (and confirmed in *Thatcher v Douglas* (1996) 146 *NLJ* 282) an equitable easement which was openly exercised and enjoyed was held also to be an overriding interest. Under **LRA 2002**, an express easement cannot become a legal easement until it is registered against the title of the servient tenement; merely meeting the formality of a deed is not enough. This recognises that most easements are created on the transfer of part of a plot of land. Provision is made in **Schedule 3, para 3** for legal easements or profits created by implied grant and by prescription, of which the purchaser knows, or which could have been discovered on a reasonably careful inspection of the land, or which have been exercised within one year of the purchase. The paragraph does not include equitable easements (thereby reversing the decision in *Celsteel*), which become minor interests binding on a purchaser only if they are protected by a notice on the register.

The Act makes a profound change to the law of adverse possession. Rights acquired or being acquired under the **Limitation Acts** were overriding interests under **s 70(1)(f), LRA 1925**. Rights under the **Limitation Acts** are viewed as incompatible with the concept of registration of title, however, and **Part 9** and **Schedule 6** of the Act provide that the **Limitation Acts** do not apply to a registered title. There is provision for a person who has adversely possessed land for ten years to apply to the Registry for registration as proprietor, but the Registry must then serve notice on the present registered proprietor. If the registered proprietor serves a counter-notice objecting within the prescribed period (some three months), the adverse possessor will only obtain registration if he can show that one of three grounds set out in **para 5** of **Schedule 6** applies. If he is unable to do so, then the registered proprietor has two years in which to recover possession of the land. If the registered proprietor takes no action, then the adverse possessor may apply again for registration after the two years have expired. These changes should assist local authorities and other large landowners and prevent cases such as *Ellis v Lambeth LBC* **(1999)** *The Times*, **28 September 1999**, which caused much public indignation.

Section 70(1)(g), LRA 1925, the overriding interest which has caused most litigation, is to be found in a very much more specific and restricted form in **para 2, Schedule 3** to the **2002 Act. Paragraph 2** seems to indicate that the time of the disposition is the relevant time for actual occupation, thus endorsing the decision in *Abbey National v Cann* and followed in *Cook v The Mortgage Business plc* [2012] EWCA Civ 17; but the point had previously been left open in *Thompson v Foy* [2009] EWHC 1076 (Ch). When electronic conveyancing has been introduced there will be no 'registration gap' at all, as the disposition and registration of it will be simultaneous.

The interest is only overriding as regards land of which a person is in actual occupation (so reversing the decision in *Ferrishust Ltd v Wallcite Ltd* [1999] 1 All ER 977).

As before, enquiry and non-disclosure of an interest will mean that a purchaser takes free of it, but only when 'such person' with the right could reasonably have been expected to disclose it. This recognises the criticism of *Hypo-Mortgage Services Ltd v Robinson* [1997] **2 FLR 71** (see P H Kenny, 'Children are Spare Ribs' [1997] *Conv* 84), but would also include persons in occupation who are senile or of unsound mind.

Paragraph 2(c)(i) would appear to be capable of a wide interpretation, which might exclude interests which have been held to be overriding under **s 70(1)(g)**. It exempts a purchaser from the rights of an occupier whose occupation would not have been obvious on 'a reasonably careful inspection of the land' and of which occupation the purchaser does not have actual knowledge. It remains to be seen how the courts will apply it. **Paragraph 2(d)** excludes a reversionary lease which is not to take effect for more than three months after its grant. This, no doubt, is to encourage a person with a lease who is not in occupation to register it substantively, or to protect it by an entry on the register if it is not capable of being registered substantively. The previous alternative to actual occupation in **s 70(1)(g), LRA 1925**, that a person is in receipt of the rents and profits of the land, has disappeared altogether.

There is no further definition in the section of 'actual occupation' so that the case law on **s 70(1)(g)** will still apply. The legislature has obviously heeded Lord Oliver's warning in *Abbey National v Cann* that 'it is, perhaps, dangerous to suggest any test for what is essentially a question of fact, for occupation is a concept which may have different connotations according to the nature and purpose of the property which is claimed to be occupied'. **Schedule 3, para 2** refers to an 'interest' rather than a 'right' and this would seem to emphasise that it must be an interest of a proprietary nature, as for **s 70(1)(g)**. The paragraph can be seen as an attempt to 'plug the hole' made by some of the decisions which have given a liberal interpretation to **s 70(1)(g)**.

The final significant change to overriding interests is the way in which the **LRA 2002** deals with legal leases. Whereas under **LRA 1925** legal leases not exceeding twenty-one years were overriding interests under **s 70(1)(k)** and legal leases of over twenty-one years were registrable substantively with their own title, **LRA 2002** extends the substantive registration of legal leases to those exceeding seven years (with the expressed ultimate aim of further reducing this period to leases exceeding three years). **Schedule 3, para 1** therefore makes overriding legal leases not exceeding seven years. There are three exceptions to this (a reversionary lease to take effect in possession more than three months after it is granted and certain leases arising under the **Housing Act 1985**).

[9] And wind up.

It is apparent[9] that the intention of **LRA 2002** is greatly to reduce the categories of overriding interests that formerly applied under **s 70(1), LRA 1925**. It achieves this by making some of these interests registrable (leases of over seven years and express easements), and by restrictions on the 'actual occupation' provision. Rights of adverse possession under the **Limitation Acts** have disappeared altogether as overriding interests, and an entirely new regime has been introduced for adverse possession.

+ LOOKING FOR EXTRA MARKS?

- Cover all the technical detail (eg distinction between **Schedules 1** and **3**).
- Take an analytical and critical approach to the question—is the mirror principle a diabolical breach of registration principles or a wise and sensible approach to protecting interests?

Q QUESTION 3

Until last year, Walter, an elderly retired farmer, was the registered proprietor of Sheepdale Farm. He lived in Bluebell Cottage on part of the farm. His daughter Delia and son-in-law Steve ran the farm and lived with their two children, Bill aged seventeen and Ben aged six, in the farmhouse.

Last year, Steve exercised undue influence over Walter to persuade him to transfer Sheepdale Farm to Tick and Tock to hold upon trust for himself (Steve) and Delia for life, with remainder to Bill and Ben absolutely. As a result of a foot-and-mouth epidemic, the farm stock was destroyed, and Steve and Delia decided to take the opportunity to make a prolonged visit to Australia for three months to investigate the possibilities for sheep farming there. Steve's brother and his wife Joan went to live in the farmhouse while they were away to look after Bill and Ben and to ensure that Walter was properly cared for.

Jasper, a neighbouring farmer, has been in adverse possession of Pony Field on the farm for over ten years.

Delia and Steve returned recently to discover that Tick and Tock, who were the registered proprietors of the farm, had charged it to the Abbey Bank plc for £60,000 and absconded with the mortgage monies.

(a) **Advise Walter, Delia, and Steve whether they could obtain alteration of the register against Tick and Tock and the Abbey Bank plc, and if so, advise whether any indemnity might be payable to anyone.**

(b) **Advise Jasper if he is likely to obtain alteration of the register to reflect his adverse possession, and whether this could give rise to a claim for indemnity in any circumstances.**

! CAUTION!

■ There have been comparatively few orders for rectification of the register and it is not an area of law which has given rise to much litigation so don't be concerned that you can't find much authority.

■ Draw attention to the point that the law relating to indemnity was amended by **LRA 1997** and is largely unaffected by **LRA 2002**, although there does seem to be an omission in **Schedule 8** to the **2002 Act**.

◯ DIAGRAM ANSWER PLAN

Identify the issues	■ The legal issue is the remedy of rectification of the register.
Relevant law	■ This is **LRA 2002, s 65** and **Schedule 4**.

Apply the law	(a) Alteration of the register to restore Walter as registered proprietor:
	■ Walter's right to avoid transfer for undue influence takes effect as an equitable interest capable of binding successors in title:
	  ● Tick and Tock take subject to that right to avoid, as transfer to them was not for valuable consideration.
	  ● So, Walter should be able to have the register altered to restore his name as registered proprietor.
	  ● Alteration of register would not be 'rectification' (since it is not a mistake and does not prejudice the title of Tick and Tock—they took subject to Walter's equity)—so no indemnity would be payable to the trust.
	■ Undue influence binds the bank because, although the bank's registered charge was for valuable consideration, Walter was in actual occupation and so his equity to avoid gained protection as an overriding interest:
	  ● So, Walter should be able to have the register altered to remove the bank's charge.
	  ● The alteration would not be a 'rectification' because the bank's charge was subject to Walter's overriding interest.
	  ● So, no indemnity would be payable to the bank.
	■ If in either case no alteration is ordered, Walter cannot obtain an indemnity, so he can have only a personal action against Steve, Tick, and Tock.
	(b) Jasper may have an overriding interest as a person in actual occupation under **Schedule 3, para 2**.
	■ He may apply for registration after ten years, but the application will usually be unsuccessful. Furthermore, the registered proprietor must be given notice of the application and (assuming it is unsuccessful) has a further two years to bring an action for possession before the squatter can re-apply.

Conclude	(a) Advise Walter, Delia, and Steve. (b) Advise Jasper.

SUGGESTED ANSWER

[1] Set out the issues—there are two, so say so. This is the I in IRAC.	(a) There are two issues in this part of the question.[1] The first[2] is whether the register of title of Sheepdale Farm will be altered to restore Walter as the registered proprietor and, if so, whether any indemnity is payable to the trust (and so will benefit the beneficiaries).
[2] Issue number 1.	
[3] Issue number 2.	The second)[3] is whether the register will be altered to remove the registered charge, and, if so, whether any indemnity is payable to the bank.
[4] Set out the law (IRAC fashion).	The grounds[4] for obtaining alteration of the register are set out in **LRA 2002, s 65** and **Schedule 4**. These provisions replace those contained in **LRA 1925, s 82(1)(a)–(h)**. Any change made to the register is now called an 'alteration', and the term 'rectification' is reserved for alterations that involve correction of a mistake and that prejudicially affect the title of a registered proprietor: **LRA 2002, Schedule 4, para 1**.
[5] This is a key point of fact, which is critical to the application of the law to the problem, so state this carefully.	As the transfer by Walter to Tick and Tock was a result of the undue influence[5] exercised by Steve, the transfer is voidable in equity. Such right to avoid is a mere equity which has effect from the time the equity arises as an interest capable of binding successors in title: **LRA 2002, s 116**. Walter's equity therefore has priority over the transfer to Tick and Tock as, although the disposition to them was completed by registration, it does not appear to have been for valuable consideration: **LRA 2002, s 28**. Walter should therefore be able to obtain an alteration of the register to restore his name as the registered proprietor.
[6] You are quoting from the statute so put it in quotes and then follow up with a precise reference to the statutory source.	As Tick and Tock took the transfer subject to Walter's equity, an alteration to the register to restore Walter as the registered proprietor would be giving effect to a 'right or interest'[6] excepted from the effect of registration: **LRA 2002, Schedule 4, paras 2(1)(c) (court), 5(c) (registrar)**.[7] It seems, however, that the alteration would not rank as a 'rectification', both because the registration was not a mistake and because the title of the registered proprietors would not be prejudicially affected by the alteration. The registration would not be a 'mistake' because a mistake seems to refer to a mistake in the process of obtaining registration from the Land Registry. An analogy may be drawn with an earlier provision:[8] under **LRA 1925, s 82(1)(d)** rectification was allowed where any entry on the register had been obtained by fraud; but in ***Norwich and Peterborough Building Society v Steed* [1993] Ch 116**, the Court of Appeal construed that provision narrowly to mean fraud in obtaining registration, rather than to a fraudulent transaction subsequently registered correctly. The fraud had to be practised on the Land Registry: ***Norwich and Peterborough Building Society***, p 134. In contrast, there had been a 'mistake' in ***Baxter v Mannion* [2010] EWHC 573 (Ch)**,[9] where the
[7] You can make these precise references if you have looked at your statute book when studying the topic. It becomes familiar to you that way.	
[8] Nice point, worth extra marks.	
[9] Setting out the contrasting case works really well and earns extra marks.	

register was rectified against a registered proprietor because he had obtained registration by swearing in a statutory declaration that he had been in adverse possession for ten years when he had not: the mistake was his supply of inaccurate information to the Land Registry. The registration of Tick and Tock, however, is not a mistake. The significance of the alteration not being a rectification is that no indemnity would be payable to the trust as a result of the alteration.

[10] Now go on to the next point.

The next issue[10] is whether the register may be altered to remove the Abbey Bank plc's registered charge. As the registered charge was made for valuable consideration, Abbey will take free of Walter's equity to avoid the transfer for undue influence unless it was protected either as a notice on the charges register or as an overriding interest through actual occupation: **LRA 2002, s 30**. Walter clearly did not protect such right by notice, but as he appears to have been living in Bluebell Cottage throughout, he was probably in actual occupation of Sheepdale Farm when Tick and Tock charged the farm to Abbey: **LRA 2002, Schedule 3, para 2**. As Abbey did not evidently ask Walter if he had any rights, it will have taken its registered charge subject to his overriding interest. The registrar may alter, or the court may order the registrar to alter, the register to give effect 'to any estate, right or interest excepted from the effect of registration': **LRA 2002, Schedule 4, paras 5(c)** (registrar), **2(1)(c)** (court). Walter should therefore be able to obtain an alteration of the register to remove Abbey's charge.

[11] Combining overriding interest with rectification.

As an overriding interest is excepted from the effect of registration,[11] neither of the alterations (namely the removal of the bank's charge from the title of the farm, and the closure of the bank's registered charge) ranks as a rectification because the alterations merely give effect to the overriding interest to which Abbey's registration was subject. Under the former law, it was the case that whilst an indemnity is payable when a 'rectification' is ordered against a registered proprietor (unless he contributed to the registration through his own fraud or lack of proper care), no indemnity is paid where the register is altered to give effect to an overriding interest. The rationale was that the registered proprietor suffers no 'loss' when the register is altered in this way, as the alteration merely gives effect on the face of the register to an interest to which the registered proprietor was already subject (*Re Chowood's Registered Land* [1933] Ch 574, 582 and *Malory Enterprises Ltd v Cheshire Homes (UK) Ltd* [2002] Ch 216 (CA)). However, in *Swift 1st Ltd v Chief Land Registrar* (2015) EWCA Civ 330, which did not follow Malory, it was held that the effect of **para 1(2)(b)** of **Schedule 8** ('the deeming provision')—which states: 'The proprietor of a registered estate or charge claiming in good faith under a forged disposition is, where the register is rectified, to be regarded as having suffered loss by reason of such rectification as if the disposition had not been forged'—was that provided the registered proprietor had acted in good faith and had suffered loss by its security having disappeared, it was accordingly entitled to an indemnity to reflect the value of the charge as though it had never been forged.

If the court or the registrar were to refuse to alter the register to restore Walter as the registered proprietor or to remove the bank's registered charge (or both), Walter would obtain no indemnity as, unlike the earlier provision in **LRA 1925, s 83(2)**, nothing in the **LRA 2002, Schedule 8** enables an indemnity to be paid where loss is suffered when the register is not altered. In the event of Walter's failing to obtain alteration of the register, he would be left to pursue his personal remedies for compensation against Steve, Tick, and Tock.

[12]Set out the adverse possession point at the beginning.

(b) Rights acquired or being acquired under the **Limitation Act**,[12] which were overriding rights under **s 70(1)(f), LRA 1925**, are no longer overriding under **Schedule 3, LRA 2002**. Furthermore, a squatter is not regarded as being in possession of land so as to satisfy the requirements of **s 131(1), LRA 2002 (s 133(3))**. A squatter does, however, have an overriding interest if he is in actual occupation within **LRA 2002, Schedule 3, para 2**. Jasper will not be regarded as in adverse possession while the estate is subject to a trust, unless the interest of each of the beneficiaries is an estate in possession: **LRA 2002, Schedule 7, para 12**. This is clearly not the case in relation to the trust for Steve, Delia, and their two sons. Furthermore, under the **2002 Act**, a squatter cannot acquire the title of the registered proprietor unless the squatter first applies for registration after having been in adverse possession for ten years, and (unless he then satisfies specified conditions) he then remains in adverse possession for a further two years and applies for registration a second time. As the registrar will notify the registered proprietor when the first application for registration is made, the registered proprietor is likely to take action to evict Jasper before he has time to make a second application. However, if Jasper were able to satisfy all these requirements, then on his second application for registration, the register would be altered to substitute his name as registered proprietor. The former registered proprietor would have no claim for an indemnity as his registered estate would have been subject to Jasper's overriding interest in any event.

✚ LOOKING FOR EXTRA MARKS?

- Using analogous cases is a very lawyerly approach and worth extra marks.

- This is not a tricky topic and does not have much case law, so you need to present a very thorough examination of the statutory authority for extra marks.

- The one exception to the previous point is the decision in *Swift 1st Ltd v Chief Land Registrar*. For extra marks, you could argue that this case is problematic, as it leaves unanswered the question of what the application of the 'deeming provision' is, where the transaction is not achieved by forgery—say where *non est factum* applies. Be careful about its application though if your question does not cover a forgery. In that case, your examiner will be looking for an argument about its application. Your lectures are likely to have guided you on that point.

➚ TAKING THINGS FURTHER

- Dixon, M, 'HM Adjudicator to the Land Registry and Questions of Rectification' [2010] 74 *Conv* 207.
  Discusses the remedy of rectification.

- Law Commission, Updating the Land Registration Act 2002 (2018) Law Com Report No 380. This Report contains fifty-three recommendations for reform and includes a draft Bill— the Land Registration (Amendment) Bill—to give effect to these recommendations. For a discussion of this report, see the editorial by Nick Hopkins and Joshua Griffin, 'Updating the Land Registration Act 2002' (2018) 3 *Conv*, 207–12.

- Law Commission, Third Report on Land Registration, Law Com No 158 (1989) (HC 269) and Land Registration for the Twenty-first Century, Law Com No 254 (1998).
  These two Law Commission Reports *provide some useful background analysis of the issues relating to overriding interests and the mirror principle.*

 Online Resources   www.oup.com/uk/qanda/

For extra essay and problem questions on this topic, as well as advice on revision and exam technique, please visit the online resources.

Successive Interests and Trusts of Land

6

ARE YOU READY?

In order to attempt the questions in this chapter, you will need to have covered the following topics:

- Trusts of Land and Appointment of Trustees Act 1996 (TLATA 1996);
- trusts of land.

KEY DEBATES

Debate: how should applications for the sale of land held under a trust for sale be treated?

TLATA 1996 has achieved a simplified and more coherent form of a trust of land. The large body of case law on **s 30, Law of Property Act (LPA) 1925** (applications for sale of land held under a trust for sale) has been reflected in **s 15(1), TLATA 1996**, but there are conflicting decisions at first instance as to how **s 15(1)** should be interpreted: contrast, on the one hand, *Judd v Brown* [1998] 2 FLR 360, *Mortgage Corporation v Shaire* [2000] 1 FLR 973, and *Edwards v Lloyds TSB Bank* [2005] 1 FCR 139; and, on the other *TSB Bank plc v Marshall* [1998] 3 EGLR 100 and *Bank of Ireland Home Mortgages v Bell* [2001] 2 FLR 809.

QUESTION 1

What rights have the beneficiaries under a trust of land?

! CAUTION!

- A trust of land may be expressly created by deed or by will or may arise from a situation, such as co-ownership, where statute imposes a trust of land. The definition of a trust of land in **s 1, TLATA 1996** also includes a bare trust and implied, resulting, and constructive trusts, which arise by operation of law or under equitable principles. So, take care to note that the question considers the rights of beneficiaries under a trust of land, however the trust arises.

- This is a very straightforward question and it is tricky to avoid just listing everything. Try to get the argument in around the judicial interpretation of applications for sale (as explained in the Key Debate).

◯ DIAGRAM ANSWER PLAN

Beneficiaries under a trust of land:

> have an interest in the land itself; if beneficially entitled to an interest in possession;

▼

> may have a right to occupy in certain circumstances: **s 12, TLATA 1996;**

▼

> may have management power delegated to them: **s. 9;**

▼

> if at least eighteen and absolutely entitled, may require the trustees to partition the land amongst them: **s 7;**

▼

> have a right, if at least eighteen, to be consulted by trustees about the exercise of their powers: **s 11;**

▼

> if at least eighteen, may be able to withhold consent to an exercise by the trustees of certain powers, if the trust instrument expressly requires their consent: **s 10;**

▼

> may apply to the court under **s 14** for an order concerning a wide range of matters, including sale of the land. The court must have regard to the matters set out in **s 15. Section 335A, Insolvency Act 1986** applies to an insolvency rather than **s 15.**

SUGGESTED ANSWER

[1] See the Caution! feature.

[2] Explain the exception.

The rights of the beneficiaries under **TLATA** are the same however the trust arises,[1] but[2] the Act makes a distinction between beneficiaries who are of full age and beneficially entitled in possession, and those who have a future interest. There are some rights given to the beneficiaries under **TLATA**, however, which apply to a pre-1997 trust for sale converted into a trust of land only if they are expressly adopted by deed. If the trust arises from a will or disposition, then the beneficiaries may be given additional powers to those under **TLATA**, or certain **TLATA** powers may be restricted.

[3] A key point to make, which was introduced by **TLATA**.

[4] Explain this point (and get it out of the way early on in your answer).

Although the legal estate in land held on trust is vested in the trustees, who are given all the powers of an absolute owner (**s 6(1)**), the beneficiaries under the trust have an interest in land.[3] The equitable doctrine of conversion[4] applied to trusts for sale created before 1 January 1997 so that the beneficiaries had an interest in the proceeds of sale of the land, which was sometimes regarded by the courts as personalty. The doctrine was abolished by **s 3, TLATA**, however, and the beneficiaries' interests are now in land and are therefore realty. (There is an exception made for testators who died before 1 January 1997 leaving 'realty' to one person and 'personalty' to another, but this is of limited practical importance, not merely because of the number of years that have passed since that date, but because testators rarely did this.) In *Bull v Bull* **[1955] 1 QB 234**, Lord Denning MR decided that all co-owners of property have a right of possession[5] and so cannot be excluded from occupation by any other co-owner.

[5] Make sure you understand a right of possession.

[6] Good to mention *Bull v Bull* *(and Lord Denning)* and then follow up with the current statutory position, which is quite nuanced.

Section 12, TLATA[6] provides that a beneficiary of full age with an interest in possession has a right of occupation of the land provided that this is contemplated by the trust, or the trustees so decide, having regard to the intentions of the settlor, the purposes for which the land is held, and the circumstances and wishes of any other beneficiaries who also have a right of occupation. The right does not apply if the land is unavailable or unsuitable for occupation by the beneficiary. In addition to co-owners of full age, any persons entitled to a life interest under a trust under which there are successive interests in land will also be persons with an interest in possession and have a right to occupy the land under **s 12**. Under a trust for sale, because co-owners all had rights of possession, one co-owner could not charge another one rent unless the conduct of the occupying co-owner was such as to make it impossible for them to live together (*Dennis v McDonald* **[1982] Fam 63**, where the occupying co-owner was violent towards the other one). **Section 13, TLATA** gives guidance to the trustees about which beneficiary they should allow to occupy the premises (if more than one is entitled) and restrictions that they should impose.

A prudent trustee will probably want to give the beneficiary a written document, similar in terms to a lease, specifying the care of the premises. **Section 13(6)**[7] provides that, where a beneficiary is excluded by reason of the occupation of another entitled beneficiary, then the one in occupation should 'make payments by way of compensation' or forego other benefits under the trust in favour of the one excluded.

Section 9 allows trustees to delegate their functions (other than giving a good receipt for capital money) to a beneficiary or beneficiaries entitled in possession, and if more than one, the delegation may be to them either jointly or severally. **Section 9A** requires trustees to exercise the general duty of care applicable to all trustees under **s 1, Trustee Act 2000** as regards both the decision to delegate and overseeing and if necessary withdrawing the delegation.

The trustees must consult the beneficiaries of full age entitled in possession as to the exercise of their very wide powers (**s 11**) unless there is a trust instrument dispensing with the requirement or the trust was created by a will made before 1 January 1997. The duty to consult does not apply to an express trust created before that date unless it is adopted by deed after that date. The exception to the requirement for consultation is where all the beneficiaries under the trust are of full age and capacity, in which case the trustees may decide to convey the land to them (**s 6(2)**). Such beneficiaries may themselves decide to terminate the trust and require the trustees to convey the land to them, under the rule in *Saunders v Vautier* (1841) 4 Beav 115.

One way of terminating co-ownership of land is (and always has been) for the co-owners of full age and capacity to agree to partition the land physically between them. If co-owners under a trust are all of full age and absolutely entitled to the trust property, then the trustees may agree with them to partition the land, dividing it physically between them (**s 7**). This would, of course, be one way of applying the rule in *Saunders v Vautier* if the beneficiaries wanted the land instead of a share of the proceeds of sale.

In an expressly created trust, **s 8** allows the settlor to restrict the powers of the trustees under **ss 6** and **7** by requiring the consent of certain persons before such powers are exercised. As **s 6** gives the trustees all the powers of an absolute owner, this will include the power of sale. Any such restriction should be entered on the register of a registered title in order to warn a purchaser of its existence. The effect of **s 26, Land Registration Act 2002 (LRA 2002)** is that a disponee of a registered title takes it free from any limitations that are not entered on the register, but this does not affect the lawfulness of the disposition. This appears to put the beneficiaries in the same position as beneficiaries under a trust for sale, who could not impeach the sale but who could still sue the trustees for equitable compensation (damages) for a breach of trust if they failed to fulfil any requirements, such as obtaining a consent, before selling. A purchaser of unregistered land will take free from it unless he has actual notice of the restriction by virtue of **s 16, TLATA**.

The beneficiaries can require a trustee to retire from the trusteeship (**s 19**) or can designate any new trustee whom they would like to be appointed, unless the trust instrument prevents this. The new trustee cannot be appointed by the beneficiaries (who do not have the legal estate and so cannot vest it in him) and will be appointed by the existing trustees or the person (if any) to whom the trust instrument gives the power. Like the requirement for consultation in **s 11**, these rights do not apply to a pre-1997 trust unless adopted by deed made by the settlor or settlors.

Under **s 14, TLATA**, a trustee or any person with an interest in the land may apply to the court for an order relating to any functions of the trustees, and the court may make such order as it thinks fit. Like the parallel **s 30, LPA**, relating to trusts for sale, this is a very widely drawn section and clearly includes a beneficiary. In addition, obviously to a sale of the land, the section also specifically mentions the requirements of consultation (under **s 11**)[8] and to obtain any necessary consents (under **s 8**). The Act then specifies, in **s 15**, the matters that the court is to have regard to in determining what order to make. **Subsections (2) and (3)** reiterate the considerations that the trustees must have regard to in **s 13** in allowing a beneficiary entitled in possession to occupy the land, and the requirement to consider the views of the majority in value of the beneficiaries' interests in the event of a dispute. **Section 15(1)** appears to be a codification of the old case law on **s 30, LPA** and will be primarily applicable in considering whether or not to make an order for the sale of the property. However,[9] in *Mortgage Corporation v Shaire* **[2001] Ch 743**, Neuberger J had to consider the application for sale by a secured creditor, and took the view that the legislature had intended to widen the previous case law under which it was determined that an order for sale should be made on an application by a creditor, unless there were exceptional circumstances. Neuberger J's wider interpretation was not adopted by the Court of Appeal in *Bank of Ireland Home Mortgages v Bell* **[2001] 2 FLR 809** (although on facts that would have caused considerably more hardship to a chargee than in *Shaire*) and has been criticised (see Susan Pascoe, 'Section 15 of the Trusts of Land and Appointment of Trustees Act 1996—A Change in the Law?' [2000] *Conv* 315). Nevertheless, in *Edwards v Lloyds TSB Bank plc* **[2005] 1 FCR 139**, Park J took account of the fact that there was likely to be enough equity in the house for the bank to be repaid in full, with interest for a few years, and ordered that a sale be postponed for five years until the youngest child attained the age of eighteen. An amendment was made by **TLATA** to the **Insolvency Act 1986** by the addition of **s 335A**, and **s 15(4)** excludes the provisions of **s 15** if **s 335A** applies. **Section 335A** provides that, on a bankruptcy, the court may have regard to all the circumstances set out therein in

[8] Good to reference the previous provision.

[9] Here starts the consideration of the case law which has moved the position on.

deciding whether or not to order a sale, but that, after one year, the interests of the unsecured creditors should be paramount and an order for sale should be made unless there are exceptional circumstances. It is perhaps curious that Neuberger J's approach would be less favourable to a secured creditor as against a beneficiary than **s 335A** is to an unsecured creditor! *Dicta* in ***Barca v Mears* [2005] 2 FLR 1** raise the possibility that the extent to which **s 335A** leans in favour of a creditor might contravene **Article 8** of the **European Convention on Human Rights** (respect for a home and family life), but in ***Nicholls v Lan* [2006] EWHC 1255 (Ch)**, the court held that the criteria in **s 335A** were not inconsistent with the rights in **Article 8**.

[10] A short concluding point.

It is clear that,[10] although the trustees of a trust of land are given very wide powers under **TLATA**, the beneficiaries are also given rights that enable them to control considerably the way in which the trustees exercise those powers. The abolition of the trust for sale under the **LPA** and substitution of a trust of land were necessary because the application of the doctrine of conversion, whereby the beneficiaries' interests were regarded as interests in the proceeds of sale and not in land, had led to some extraordinary and inconsistent decisions. There is still not much litigation involving the new Act—but this may perhaps be a testimony to its adequacy.

✚ LOOKING FOR EXTRA MARKS?

- As with all transitional pieces of legislation, it will be a while before the old traces are gone so be ready to know and understand the workings of **s 30, LPA 1925**.
- Analyse the cases (don't just describe them).

QUESTION 2

James, who died earlier this year, appointed Tick and Tack as executors and trustees of his will and left all his property in trust for his wife Emma for life, and then to his two children John and Jane absolutely (who are thirty-nine and thirty-five, respectively). His property included the Owl House, a listed building, and his will directed that this should not be sold without the consent of John and Jane.

Polly, who has always liked the house, made a good offer for it to the trustees, which was in excess of its likely market value. Polly knew that Jane did not want to sell the house, but did not know that the sale needed the consent of John and Jane. Tick and Tack consulted Emma, who was keen to sell, but overlooked the fact that they should have obtained John and Jane's consent to a sale. The trustees have now conveyed the house to Polly.

Advise John and Jane on the basis that the title to Owl House is:

(a) **unregistered**; and

(b) **registered**.

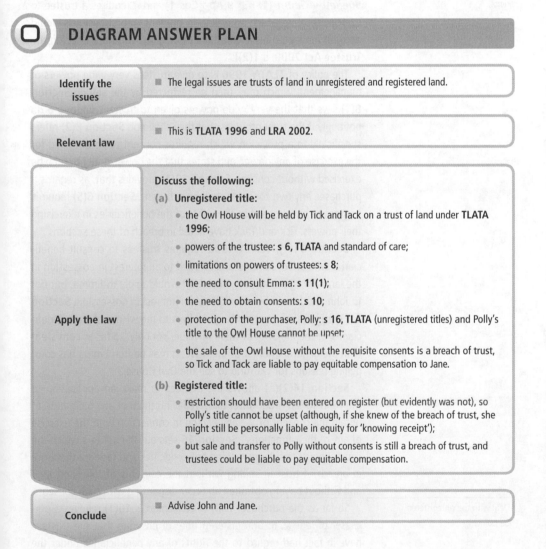

! **CAUTION!**

- The question requires you to have a knowledge of the different sections of **TLATA 1996** relating to the powers of trustees and the effect of a limitation on those powers. Because the sections impose a general fiduciary duty on the trustees, you also need to be aware of the general standard of care which applies to trustees.

- The question also requires a consideration of the effect on a purchaser of a breach of the limitation period. As regards unregistered land, **s 16, TLATA** specifically provides for this, but there was some argument as to the position of a purchaser in registered title. **LRA 2002** resolves this.

O **DIAGRAM ANSWER PLAN**

Identify the issues	■ The legal issues are trusts of land in unregistered and registered land.

Relevant law	■ This is **TLATA 1996** and **LRA 2002**.

Apply the law	**Discuss the following:** **(a) Unregistered title:** • the Owl House will be held by Tick and Tack on a trust of land under **TLATA 1996**; • powers of the trustee: **s 6, TLATA** and standard of care; • limitations on powers of trustees: **s 8**; • the need to consult Emma: **s 11(1)**; • the need to obtain consents: **s 10**; • protection of the purchaser, Polly: **s 16, TLATA** (unregistered titles) and Polly's title to the Owl House cannot be upset; • the sale of the Owl House without the requisite consents is a breach of trust, so Tick and Tack are liable to pay equitable compensation to Jane. **(b) Registered title:** • restriction should have been entered on register (but evidently was not), so Polly's title cannot be upset (although, if she knew of the breach of trust, she might still be personally liable in equity for 'knowing receipt'); • but sale and transfer to Polly without consents is still a breach of trust, and trustees could be liable to pay equitable compensation.

Conclude	■ Advise John and Jane.

SUGGESTED ANSWER

[1] Set out the basics to start.

[2] Set out the precise statutory provisions.

[3] Use case law to illustrate the points.

(a) The disposition in James's will creates a trust of land under the **TLATA 1996**, which, by its definition in **s 1(1)**,[1] is a trust of any property which 'includes' land, even though it also includes personalty. The trustees, Tick and Tack, have all the powers of an absolute owner for the purpose of exercising their functions 'as trustees' (**s 6(1)**), but must have regard to 'any rule of law or equity' (**s 6(6)**).[2] These provisions suggest that trustees are subject to the usual fiduciary duties, and that the general standard of care applicable to all trustees applies to them. This is the standard of care established in the case of *Speight v Gaunt* **(1883) 9 App Cas 1**[3] and it requires a trustee to exercise the care which an ordinarily prudent man of business would apply in managing his own affairs (now given statutory effect in the **Trustee Act 2000, s 1(2)**).

The policy of **TLATA 1996** is to give trustees very wide powers of management, which may then be restricted by the settler. **Section 8(1)** says that the very wide powers given to trustees under **s 6** do not apply if the trust provides that they shall not. **Section 8(2)** refers specifically to a provision which requires consent to be obtained for the exercise of any power, and states that the power shall not then be exercised without consent. **Section 10(1)** provides that, as regards a purchaser, any two consents shall be sufficient. **Section 6(5)** requires trustees to have regard to the rights of the beneficiaries in exercising their powers. Tick and Tack have acted in breach of these sections.

Section 11(1), TLATA 1996 requires trustees to consult beneficiaries who are of full age and entitled to an interest in possession in the land. This general duty to consult would apply to Emma, but not to John and Jane, who do not have an interest in possession. **Section 11(1)(b)** requires trustees to give effect to the wishes of such beneficiaries, or the majority of them in value, but only 'so far as consistent with the general interest of the trust'. It may be that Emma has compelling reasons for wanting to sell the Owl House.

Section 14(2)(a) allows the trustees to make an application to the court for an order (*inter alia*) 'relieving them of any obligation to obtain the consent of . . . any person in connection with the exercise of any of their functions'. **Section 15** sets out the matters which the court should consider in making any order. Tick and Tack are therefore in breach of trust in selling without the consents of John and Jane and without having obtained an order dispensing with such consents.

[4] Deal with the unregistered title point.

So far as the purchaser Polly is concerned, **s 16(1)** relieves a purchaser of land with unregistered title[4] of ensuring that the trustees have in fact had regard to the rights of any beneficiaries under the trust, as they are required to do by **s 6(8)**. **Section 16(2)** provides that a contravention of **s 6(8)** shall not invalidate the conveyance, if the purchaser does not have actual notice of it. Polly knew that Jane did not want to sell the Owl House and has made a very good offer for it, suggesting that she might have had constructive notice (ie the notice she would have had if she had made enquiries) of the need for consent, or that as regards Jane she might not have acted entirely in good faith. **Section 16** refers specifically to *actual* notice, however, which Polly did not have, and the conveyance to her is therefore valid. Even though her title to the Owl House is secure, if Polly knowingly received the trust property in breach of trust, she might be personally liable to pay equitable compensation to the beneficiaries if they have suffered any loss.

[5] Deal here with the actual notice point.

The fact that Polly will obtain a good title if she does not have actual notice[5] of the limitation does not relieve Tick and Tack from a breach of trust in that they have sold without first obtaining a requisite consent or an order dispensing with it. They are also in breach of **s 16(3)(a)** (applicable only to unregistered land), which requires them to take all reasonable steps to bring any limitation on their powers to the notice of a purchaser. To have overlooked the requirement for consents to a sale of the Owl House is probably also a breach of the standard of care imposed upon trustees by **s 1(2)**, **Trustee Act 2000**, and Jane would be able to claim equitable compensation from them for breach of trust.

[6] Give precise statutory provision.

[7] A key point regarding restrictions.

(b) **Section 16(7)** excludes the application of **s 16** to registered titles.[6] **Sections 40(2)** and **40(3)(b)**, **LRA 2002** allow for a restriction to be entered on the proprietorship register. A restriction should have been entered requiring the consent of John and Jane to any transfer.[7] It is the duty of the trustees to apply for the registration of such a restriction (**Land Registration Rules, 2003, r 94(4), Schedule 4**), but an application for entry of a restriction may also be made by any person with an interest in the registered estate (clearly John and Jane) (**Land Registration Rules, 2003, Schedule 4, r 93(c)**). If such restriction had been entered, the registrar would have declined to register Polly as the registered proprietor of the Owl House. The fact that she has been registered indicates that no such restrictions had been entered.

There having been no restriction on the register, Polly has obtained legal title and takes free from the trustees' obligation to obtain consents (**s 26(1)**, **LRA 2002**). **Section 26(3)** makes it clear, however, that the purpose of the section is to give the purchaser a good title, notwithstanding that the disposition is in contravention of a limitation on the powers of the trustees, and 'it does not affect the lawfulness of a disposition'. So, although Polly obtains title to the Owl House without the requisite consents, the disposition to her is still a breach of trust by the trustees, who will be liable to pay equitable compensation to John and Jane.

LOOKING FOR EXTRA MARKS?

■ You should not only know but should reference the precise statutory provision—not too much of a hardship when you most likely will have your statute book in the exam with you.

TAKING THINGS FURTHER

■ Dixon, M, 'Resulting and Constructive Trusts of Land: The Mist Descends and Rises' [2005] *Conv* 79.
Considers the issues around successive interests in property.

■ Smith, R, *Plural Ownership* (OUP 2005).
Explains how the important trusts of land legislation operate and provides a full analysis of the fundamental and problematic area of concurrent interests.

Online Resources

www.oup.com/uk/qanda/

For extra essay and problem questions on this topic, as well as advice on revision and exam technique, please visit the online resources.

Co-ownership and Trusts of Land

7

ARE YOU READY?

In order to attempt the questions in this chapter, you will need to have covered the following topics:

- **Trusts of Land and Appointment of Trustees Act 1996 (TLATA 1996);**
- joint tenancies and tenancies in common;
- co-ownership under constructive and resulting trusts.

KEY DEBATES

Debate: what should be taken into account in order to determine the beneficial interests of the parties in a domestic context?

Stack v Dowden **[2007] 2 AC 432** and *Jones v Kernott* **[2011] UKSC 53** have started a new phase in the determination of this question. It is likely that this topic of trusts in the family home will feature extensively in your course, as it is an area of much modern concern, prompting Law Commission reports.

Q QUESTION | 1

A testator who died recently devised his freehold four-bedroomed house Dunroamin to trustees upon trust for his three children, Susan, Tom, and Ursula, in equal shares. The will provides that should any of the three children wish to do so, they may live in the house.

Advise the trustees under the following sets of circumstances:

(a) **Tom, who is married with five children, would like to live in the house, but Susan and Ursula would prefer it to be sold and the proceeds of sale divided amongst them.**

⊙

(◄)

(b) If Tom and his family do go to live in the house, advise whether Susan and Ursula would be entitled to any rent for his occupation.

(c) Tom is single, aged seventeen, and without children, and wishes to occupy the house with his aunt and guardian, with whom he is now living.

How would your answer differ if there had been no provision in the will for any of the three children to live in the house if they so wished?

CAUTION!

■ This is a question on the powers of the trustees and the rights of the beneficiaries under a trust of land. It requires knowledge of **TLATA 1996**, case law on which is developing very slowly.

DIAGRAM ANSWER PLAN

Identify the issues	■ The legal issue is co-ownership.
Relevant law	This is (a) ss 11, 12, 13, 14, 15, TLATA 1996; (b) s 13, TLATA 1996; (c) ss 11 and 15, TLATA 1996.
Apply the law	**(a)** ■ The right to occupy: **s 12(1)**, TLATA 1996; ■ consultation with beneficiaries: **s 11**; ■ possible application to court (**s 14**) and relevant matters (**s 15**). **(b)** ■ Condition of occupation could be payment of compensation: **s 13(5)**; ■ possible payment of rent by Tom (consider former case law). **(c)** ■ Welfare of minor relevant factor for court to consider, but consideration of suitability of house: **s 15**; ■ duty to consult and importance of majority view: **s 11(1)**; ■ rights of occupation of other beneficiaries.
Conclude	■ Advise the trustees.

A

[1] Establish the basics.

(a) This disposition will take effect as a trust of land[1] under **TLATA 1996**, which came into force on 1 January 1997. It is recognised that the interests of the beneficiaries under trusts of land are interests in land, as opposed to interests in the proceeds of sale of land (as they were under the trust for sale under the **Law of Property Act 1925 (LPA 1925)**, which the trust of land replaced).[2]

[2] Extra marks—shows knowledge of legal development.

[3] Give precise statutory reference.

Section 12(1), TLATA 1996[3] gives a beneficiary who is beneficially entitled to an interest in possession the right to occupy the land if the trust makes it clear (as it does here) that the property is to be available for occupation, or the trustees hold land that is so available, and the land is not for any reason unsuitable. In *I R C v Eversden* (2002) STC 1109, it was held that the 'purpose' of a trust[4] is primarily to be found in the trust instrument, and even if the purpose is found outside the trust, it must be consistent with it. A four-bedroomed house might be regarded as reasonably suitable for a family with five children.

[4] This is the big issue here, so be ready with case law.

[5] Paraphrase the section—don't quote it.

Section 11 requires the trustees[5] to consult the beneficiaries who are at least eighteen and entitled to a beneficial interest in possession in the land, and, so far as is consistent with the general interests of the trust, to give effect to their wishes, or of the majority of them in value. The duty to consult may be excluded by the settlor, but does not appear to have been excluded here.[6]

[6] Applying the facts of the question.

[7] Bracket precise reference to show authority for your point.

The trustees may not unreasonably exclude any beneficiary's entitlement to occupy land (s 13(2)),[7] but may impose reasonable conditions with regard to his occupation (s 13(3)), including obligations with regard to the use of the land and payment of outgoings (s 13(5)). In *Rodway v Landy* [2001] Ch 703, it was held that **s 13** allows trustees to divide a building between the beneficiaries, so that each is entitled to occupy a defined part but has his or her entitlement to occupy the rest either excluded or restricted. Commentators have pointed out that these provisions will almost certainly require the trustees to give to a beneficiary a written licence to occupy the property, setting out the terms of occupation. **Section 9** also allows trustees to delegate any of their functions (other than the receipt of capital money) to a beneficiary who is at least eighteen and who is beneficially entitled in possession, and if Tom is to occupy the house, the trustees may wish to consider this. Any delegation must be made by a power of attorney to the beneficiary for a fixed or indefinite period.

Section 6 of the Act, which gives the trustees all the powers of an absolute owner of the land, also requires them to have regard to the rights of the beneficiaries in exercising those powers (s 6(5)). They must not exercise their powers contrary to 'any rule of law or equity'. However, there is no presumption in favour of a right of sale under the Act.

As the testator has specifically mentioned occupation by the beneficiaries as a possible purpose of the trust, it seems probable that the trustees could properly decide to allow Tom and his family to occupy Dunroamin. If Ursula and Susan were aggrieved by this decision, they could apply to the court under **s 14**, whereby the court may make any order, including one not to sell. The matters to which the court must have regard in deciding what order to make are set out in **s 15** and include the intention of the settlor, the purpose for which the property is held, and the welfare of any minor (*Bagum v Hafiz* **[2015] EWCA Civ 80**). It is therefore important to know whether any of Tom's children are minors. As occupation by a beneficiary is stated as a purpose of the trust, this might tilt the decision in Tom's favour.[8]

[8] You can't be categorical in your answer, as it depends on the facts.

(b) One of the conditions which the trustees may impose for occupation of the property under **s 13(5)** is the payment of compensation to any beneficiary who is excluded from occupation, or that the beneficiary who occupies the property should forego other benefits under the trust. Under the old case law[9] on co-ownership, it was recognised that if one co-owner was effectively excluded from occupation, he could be awarded rent from the occupying co-owner (*Dennis v McDonald* **[1981] 1 WLR 810**; *Bernard v Josephs* **[1982] Ch 391**). Although Lady Hale cautioned in *Stack v Dowden* **[2007] 2 AC 432**, at **465 (para 94)**,[10] that the criteria in **TLATA 1996** should be applied rather than the cases decided under the old law, she conceded that the results may often be the same. Susan and Ursula could therefore probably require Tom to pay a rent, presumably of two-thirds of the rack-rent value of the house.

[9] This is a nice point to make—see Lady Hale's comment which follows.

[10] You are unlikely to remember the exact paragraph—this is included here to assist your studies.

(c) If Tom were a minor and the aunt's house were unsuitable for him to live in for any reason, the trustees should consider very seriously allowing Tom and the aunt to occupy Dunroamin, bearing in mind that the welfare of any minor is specifically mentioned in **s 15(1)** as a factor which the court should consider in making any order. However, in *Chan v Leung* **[2003] 1 FLR 23**, the statutory right of occupation was not available where the house was disproportionate to the needs of the beneficiary. So, Susan and Ursula may be able to argue that a four-bedroomed house is unsuitable for only two people and that consideration of Tom's minority would be for only a further twelve months (although there are provisions in the Act for protecting a beneficiary who has taken up occupation from being disturbed: **s 13(7)**). As Tom, at seventeen, is close to achieving majority, less weight will be given to consideration of his welfare than if he had been a younger child (*Bank of Ireland Home Mortgages Ltd v Bell* **[2001] 2 FLR 809**, *per* Peter Gibson LJ at 816).

Had there been no specific provision in the will allowing any of the three children to live in the house if they so wished, the duty to consult and to have regard to the wishes of the majority in value under **s 11(1)** applies, and the trustees might have to do what Susan and

Ursula wish, and exercise their power of sale. The trustees, or Tom's guardian on his behalf, could apply to the court under **s 14**, but **s 15(2)** specifically requires the court to have regard to the wishes of other beneficiaries who would (but for the exercise of the trustees' powers) be entitled to occupy (Susan and Ursula), as well as to the welfare of any minor who 'might reasonably be expected to occupy [the property] as his home' (**s 15(1)(c)**). Should an application to the court be necessary, the Court of Appeal decision in *Bagum v Hafiz* **[2015] EWCA Civ 801** indicates that the objects of **ss 14 and 15** are to confer upon the court a substantially wider discretion than otherwise given to trustees when acting without the consent of the beneficiaries or an order of a court. Where the wishes of the beneficiaries are in conflict, then the court will be able to make an order which provides a solution to the conundrum. Given that Tom is a minor for only another year, and that a four-bedroomed house may not be entirely suitable, it is possible that the wishes of Susan and Ursula might prevail.[11]

[11] Again, you can't be categorical—you just need to discuss the point.

LOOKING FOR EXTRA MARKS?

- Precision in citing the correct statutory source is a mark of the lawyer.
- Discussion of the cases to show the importance of distinction of facts and the flexibility of the statute shows a mature understanding.

QUESTION | 2

In 2004, Angus, Belinda, Connie, and David, who were medical students, decided to buy a large house in which to live while they were studying. They contributed to the purchase price equally. Connie was only seventeen at the time, but the other three were all eighteen.

At the end of his first year at University, Angus unfortunately failed his examinations and, having decided that medicine did not suit him, went to Spain to train as a toreador. He wrote enthusiastically in 2005 to Belinda and Connie (who was by then eighteen) about his life in Spain, but not to David. He said that as he did not feel he would have much use for the house in future, he would like them to buy his share or to have the house sold.

In 2006, Belinda mortgaged her interest in the house to buy a horse. Later that year, Belinda was killed in a riding accident. She had made a will in 2004, leaving all her realty to her sister Iris and all her personalty to her brother James.

David married in 2015, and while Angus was staying with them to attend the wedding, David took the opportunity to have dinner with Angus and Connie to discuss the future of the house. The occasion was a convivial one, and all three agreed that their shares in the property should be separate and distinct in future, although nothing was put into writing to this effect.

○◀

Sadly, Angus perished in 2016 on the horns of a bull. He had made a will earlier that year, leaving all his realty to Ronnie and his personalty to Penny.

David would like the house to be sold; but Connie, who is working at a hospital nearby, would like to keep it.

(a) If the house is sold, how should the proceeds of sale be divided?

(b) If the house is sold, who will be able to give a good title to it?

(c) Advise Connie whether she might successfully oppose a sale.

! CAUTION!

- This is a fairly typical examination-type question on co-ownership. Before you can say who will be entitled to the proceeds of any sale and who will be able to convey the legal estate to a purchaser, you will have to trace logically the devolution of both the legal estate and the equitable interests. You should do this in the answer to the question, of course, but you may find it easier to set it out first in diagrammatic form in rough, as set out in the following table. Joint tenants are indicated in square brackets.

- In case your transcription to essay form is erroneous, it might be preferable to put only two or three lines through your rough working but still leave it legible! A kind-hearted examiner might be prepared to give some credit for a correct rough working erroneously transcribed.

- Such questions will often involve (as this one does) facts where it is uncertain whether the equitable joint tenancy has been severed or not. If so, be prepared to answer the question in the alternative, ie showing how the equitable interests devolve if there has been a severance, and if there has not been one. After all, you can hardly be expected to predict what the judge would decide in any particular circumstance!

- Complete your diagram of the devolution of titles before you begin writing your prose answer and keep referring to it as a guide as you write. It could be a lifeline!

LEGAL TITLE	TRUST OF LAND	EQUITABLE INTERESTS
2004		
[ABD]		[ABCD]
2005 Angus's letter no change: not an effective severance	Ditto	Ditto

LEGAL TITLE	TRUST OF LAND	EQUITABLE INTERESTS
2005 Connie eighteen and can hold legal estate, but no change	Ditto	Ditto
2006 Belinda's mortgage		
[ABD]	Ditto	[ACD] (¾); B (¼)
2006: Belinda's death		
[AD]	Ditto [ACD] (¾); I (¼)	
[AD]	Ditto	Ditto
2015 Agreement		
If no severance:		
Ditto	Ditto	Ditto
If severance:		
Ditto	Ditto	ACDI (¼ each)
If no severance:		
Ditto	Ditto	[DC] (¾); I(¼)
2016: death of A		
If severance in 2015:		
D	Ditto	DCIR (¼ each)
If no severance in 2015:		
D	Ditto	[DC] (¾); I(¼)

◉ DIAGRAM ANSWER PLAN

Identify the issues	■ The legal issues are the distinction between joint tenancies and tenancies in common and the split between legal and equitable interests.
Relevant law	This is the **Trusts of Land and Appointment of Trustees Act 1996 (TLATA 1996)**.
Apply the law	**(a)** ■ Legal title vests only in A, B, and D as joint tenants; not in C, as she is a minor.
	■ A's letter was not sent to all joint tenants, so there is not notice of severance in equity within **s 36(2), Law of Property Act (LPA) 1925**.
	■ B's mortgage effects a severance as an act operating on her own equitable share, but cannot sever her legal joint tenancy. On B's death, her share of the legal estate accrues by survivorship to A and D. Since B died after 1996, her three-quarters severed equitable share passes as realty to I.
	■ It is uncertain whether informal agreement between all three of the remaining equitable joint tenants is valid: **s 2(1), Law of Property (Miscellaneous Provisions) Act 1989**. But there might be severance by a course of dealing: *Burgess v Rawnsley* [1975].
	■ On A's death, his share of the legal estate passes to D by survivorship. If there had been a severance in 2006, A's equitable interest passes to R as realty. If there had been no severance, it accrues by survivorship to the two remaining joint tenants, C and D.
	(b) ■ As there is still co-ownership in equity, D must appoint a second trustee so that the purchaser can overreach the beneficial interests under the trust (**s 2(1), LPA 1925**).
	(c) ■ Consider applications to court (**s 14, TLATA 1996**) and powers of court (**s 15**).
	■ This is pre-**TLATA 1996** trust, so there is no duty to consult beneficiaries unless expressly adopted by deed (**s 11(3)**).
	■ Discuss the criteria for deciding whether to order a sale: **s 15, TLATA 1996, paras (a)** and **(b)** and the conflicting decisions on the impact of **s 15** on previous law; also, the effect of **s 12(2)** on suitability of the property for a beneficiary to occupy.
Conclude	■ Advise, if the house is sold, how the proceeds of sale will be divided; who can give good title; and advise Connie whether she might successfully oppose a sale.

[1] There's a lot to get through in this answer, so go straight into the application.

[2] Discuss the options and support with case law.

[3] You can never, ever sever a legal joint tenancy!

(a) As Connie was only seventeen when the house was purchased,[1] she could not hold a legal estate in land, and the legal estate will therefore be vested in Angus, Belinda, and David as joint tenants at law. So, Angus, Belinda, and David held the house as legal joint tenants upon trust for themselves and Connie in equity. Assuming that there are no words of severance in the conveyance (such as 'in equal shares') then they would have been joint tenants in equity also, as they contributed equally to the purchase price. The presumption of equity of a tenancy in common only applies where contributions to the purchase price are unequal.

It might be argued that the content of Angus's letter in 2005 to Belinda and Connie was sufficient to constitute a notice of severance for the purposes of **LPA 1925, s 36(2)**. The section, however, requires any such notice to be given to 'the other joint tenants', therefore notice to only two of them would not be sufficient, so the joint tenancy would continue in equity.

It is possible[2] also that the letter might qualify as an act of severance, being 'an act of any one of the persons interested operating on his own share' (*per* Page-Wood V-C in *Williams v Hensman* (1861) **1 John & H 546**). A declaration of intention to sever by one party was accepted by Havers J in *Hawkesley v May* [1956] **1 QB 304** as a sufficient act of severance, and this was approved by Plowman J in *Re Draper's Conveyance* [1969] **ChD 486**, where he found that a summons and affidavit in support filed by a wife asking for the sale of the matrimonial home and division of the proceeds was sufficient to sever the joint tenancy held by her and her husband. The problem remains, however, that the letter to only two of the joint tenants cannot effect a severance with one-third to whom there has been no 'declaration', as it would still lack the necessary element of mutuality for severance. There was, therefore, no severance.

Connie's attaining her majority in 2005 did not automatically make her a co-trustee and owner of the legal estate, which therefore continued to be vested only in Angus, Belinda, and David. For Connie to become a trustee and joint tenant at law, there would have to be a deed of appointment by the existing trustees vesting the legal estate in her and them as joint tenants (completed by registration at the Land Registry).

Belinda's mortgage of her share in 2006 would have been an act operating on her own share within the *dictum* of Page-Wood V-C (mentioned above). It therefore severed her equitable joint tenancy. The legal joint tenancy can never be severed,[3] however, so Belinda remained as a joint tenant of the legal estate with Angus and David. She became a tenant in common in equity, although the joint tenancy continued as regards the other joint tenants. So, the position was that Angus, Belinda, and David held the legal estate as joint tenants on trust for sale for Angus, Connie, and David as joint tenants in equity as to three-quarters, together with Belinda, who was a tenant in common as to a one-quarter share.

The position in 2006 was that Angus and David held the legal estate as joint tenants (Belinda's share having accrued to them by the right of survivorship), and they held as trustees of a trust of land for themselves and Connie as joint tenants in equity as to three-quarters, together with Iris as a tenant in common as to a one-quarter share.

Although the legal joint tenancy cannot be severed (because a tenancy in common cannot exist at law after 1925), the equitable joint tenancy may be severed either by notice (**LPA 1925, s 36(2)**), or by any of the three ways described by Page-Wood V-C in *Williams v Hensman* (discussed above).[4] The first, an act of any one of the persons interested operating on his own share, has already been considered in relation to the letter from Angus and Belinda's mortgage. The other two ways of severance (which should be considered in relation to the dinner party) are severance by mutual agreement, or a course of dealing sufficient to intimate to all the joint tenants that their interests were mutually to be regarded as being held under a tenancy in common in future.

Although all three joint tenants appear to have agreed upon a severance of the equitable joint tenancy, it is a purely oral agreement. In *Burgess v Rawnsley* [1975] Ch 249, Lord Denning MR expressed the opinion that severance of the equitable joint tenancy could be oral as it was not a contract for the sale or other disposition of land, and so did not have to comply with **LPA 1925, s 40** (now repealed), or be a specifically enforceable contract. This was probably justified only by regarding the interests of the joint tenants as personalty because of the operation of the doctrine of conversion to a trust for sale. From 1 January 1997, the joint tenants have an interest under a trust of land, so severance by agreement probably has to comply with **s 2, Law of Property (Miscellaneous Provisions) Act 1989** [5] as being 'a contract for the sale or other disposition of an interest in *land*'. Any such agreement will then have to be in writing and signed by all parties, so that the oral agreement over dinner would not have sufficed.

Even if the oral agreement was not a severance by mutual agreement,[6] it might still have operated as a severance if it could be regarded as a sufficient course of dealing to sever: this is essentially a matter of evidence.

[4] Don't repeat yourself—cross-reference.

[5] This is a neat point—no case law authority though. Definitely worth extra marks.

[6] Discuss the options.

Assuming that there had been no effective severance of the equitable joint tenancy, when Angus died the right of survivorship would operate to vest his legal share in the surviving joint tenant, David. Angus's equitable interest would pass—again, by the right of survivorship—to Connie and David as joint tenants. If there had been a severance of the equitable joint tenancy, when Angus died the right of survivorship would still operate to vest his legal share in David, but Angus's equitable interest would pass under his will. Since the abolition of a trust for sale and conversion, a beneficiary's share under a trust of land is regarded as realty, and Angus's share as tenant in common would therefore have passed to Ronnie.

The division of the proceeds of sale therefore depends upon whether the informal agreement at the dinner party could be regarded as a course of dealing sufficient to sever the equitable joint tenancy. If it could not,[7] Angus's interest under the equitable joint tenancy accrued to Connie and David by the right of survivorship. Connie and David would then have been entitled to three-quarters as joint tenants, and Iris to one-quarter. If the informal agreement was sufficient to sever, Ronnie will have taken Angus's one-quarter share as tenant in common under Angus's will, whilst David, Connie, and Iris would each also have a one-quarter share as tenants in common.

(b) Although David is the sole remaining trustee and owner of the legal estate, there is still co-ownership in equity. In order to overreach the equitable interests,[8] therefore, a purchaser should require the appointment of a second trustee (who may be Connie or someone else) to give a good receipt for the purchase moneys (**s 2(1) LPA, 1925**).

(c) One of the main purposes of the **TLATA 1996** was to abolish the presumption in favour of a sale which applied to a trust for sale under **LPA 1925**. **Section 11(1), TLATA 1996** requires trustees to consult the beneficiaries[9] as to the exercise of their extensive powers and to have regard to the wishes of the majority in value. If there had been an effective severance, and David, Ronnie, and Iris, together holding three-quarters of the equitable interest, all wanted the property sold, this would suggest that the property should be sold.

If there was no severance, so that David and Connie together have three-quarters of the equitable interest as joint tenants, Iris's wishes could be decisive. **Section 14 of the 1996 Act** allows a trustee or a person with an interest in property to apply to the court for an order. As a **s 14** application can be for any order, Connie could apply for an order resisting sale.[10]

Section 15, TLATA 1996 sets out statutory criteria which the court should consider when making an order under **s 14**, and the two relevant ones here would appear to be 'the interests of the persons who created the trust' (**s 15(1)(a)**), and 'the purposes for which

[7] Again—discuss the options.

[8] Don't forget the doctrine of overreaching.

[9] Not all exam questions add on this extra point.

[10] **Section 14** is wide enough to allow this and it is a nice point to add.

[11] Still worth stating, even though **s 30** is now long gone.

the property subject to the trust is held' (**s 15(1)(b)**). This latter sub-section reflects the case law on **s 30** of the **1925 Act**.[11] There are two conflicting decisions at first instance on this: that of Wroath J in **TSB Bank v Marshall** [1998] 2 FLR 769, who said that the previous case law under **s 30, LPA** should apply, and that of Neuberger J in **Mortgage Corporation v Shaire** [2000] 1 FLR 973, who found eight reasons for concluding that the legislature had not necessarily intended the courts to be bound by the previous case law. **Mortgage Corporation v Shaire** was cited with approval by the Court of Appeal in **Bank of Ireland Home Mortgages Ltd v Bell** [2001] 2 FLR 809, although the court took a relatively limited view of the discretion available under **s 14**. More relevant to the circumstances here might be the Court of Appeal decision in **Chan Pui Chun v Leung Kam Ho** [2002] EWCA Civ 1075, which considered the effect of **s 12(2)**, **TLATA** on the suitability of a particular property for a particular beneficiary to occupy. A house bought for four students to occupy might well not be suitable for Connie alone to live in.

LOOKING FOR EXTRA MARKS?

■ There are a lot of points to make here and the diagram will help you capture them all (and then not forget them as you write them down). Getting all the points will be rewarded with extra marks.

QUESTION | 3

Consider the significance of the decision of the House of Lords in *Stack v Dowden* [2007] AC 432.

CAUTION!

■ This question gives you scope to discuss the case, both in the context of the previous law and also in the light of subsequent decisions.

■ In an essay question on a particular case, it can be useful to set out the facts, the reasoning of the court, and the decision itself, and then to go on to consider the scope of the decision and to comment on it. But academic examiners nowadays nearly always expect you to engage in a critical commentary around a case, especially one as controversial as this one, so they will be awarding marks for that. The suggested answer builds its critique on an interesting lecture given by Lord Neuberger, who gave the only dissenting opinion in *Stack v Dowden*. The suggested answer is framed by an introduction, which sets out the basic legal issue in the case, and a conclusion, which draws the discussion together.

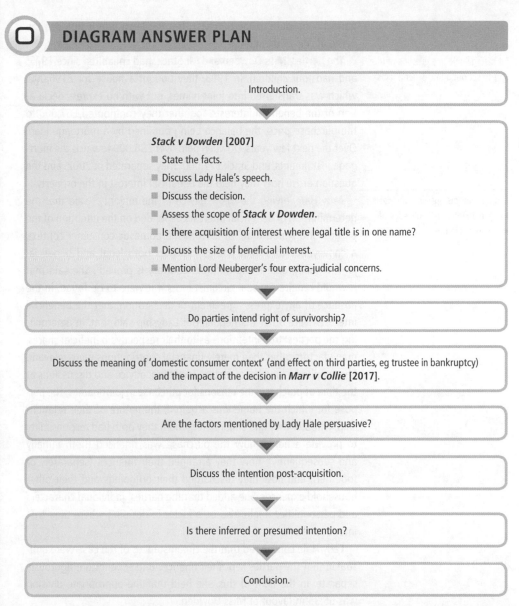

DIAGRAM ANSWER PLAN

Introduction.

▼

Stack v Dowden [2007]
- State the facts.
- Discuss Lady Hale's speech.
- Discuss the decision.
- Assess the scope of **Stack v Dowden**.
- Is there acquisition of interest where legal title is in one name?
- Discuss the size of beneficial interest.
- Mention Lord Neuberger's four extra-judicial concerns.

▼

Do parties intend right of survivorship?

▼

Discuss the meaning of 'domestic consumer context' (and effect on third parties, eg trustee in bankruptcy) and the impact of the decision in **Marr v Collie [2017]**.

▼

Are the factors mentioned by Lady Hale persuasive?

▼

Discuss the intention post-acquisition.

▼

Is there inferred or presumed intention?

▼

Conclusion.

A SUGGESTED ANSWER

[1] Give the narrow point, then explain the broader significance.

The decision of the House of Lords in **Stack v Dowden** was narrowly concerned[1] with the determination of the beneficial shares of cohabitees who had purchased in joint names a family home but without expressly declaring how they held their shares in equity. The decision is of broader significance, however, because it is clear that the House of Lords intended their decision to be applicable to cases where both parties contribute to the purchase, but the legal title is put into the name of one of them only.

[2] It is forgivable in a question of this sort to set out a few (salient) facts.

The parties, Miss Dowden and Mr Stack, had cohabited since 1975[2] and had four children. In 1993, they bought a house for £190,000, which was transferred into joint names, but with no express declaration of the beneficial interests. Together they contributed £67,000 to the purchase price, the balance being obtained by a mortgage loan. Over the next few years, Dowden paid over £38,000 towards the mortgage instalments, and Stack £27,000. They separated in 2002, and the question arose how they held the beneficial interest in the property.

[3] To answer this question, you need to have an intimate knowledge of the opinions in the court.

Lady Hale, giving the main speech of the majority,[3] said that the determination of beneficial interests depended on the intention of the parties. She stated that, 'at least in the domestic consumer context, a conveyance into joint names indicates both legal and beneficial joint tenancy, unless and until the contrary is proved'. She said that it would require unusual circumstances if it were to be found, in the absence of any express agreement or declaration, that the beneficial interests were other than equal. Her Ladyship said that, in determining the parties' true intentions as to their respective beneficial shares, many factors other than merely financial contributions were relevant. She supplied a long list of factors, including: advice and discussions at the time of purchase; the reasons for purchase in joint names; the purpose for which the home was acquired; the nature of their relationship; whether they had children for whom they both had responsibility to provide a home; how the purchase was financed (both initially and subsequently); how they arranged their finances (separately or together); and how they discharged their outgoings and their other household expenses. She added that the parties' individual characters and personalities might also be a factor in deciding where their true intentions lie.

Lady Hale considered that the circumstances of the case were unusual in that the parties kept their finances and expenditure rigorously separate. In the light of this, she held that the appropriate division was 65:35 in favour of Miss Dowden.

[4] Important new presumption.

As a result of the case, there is now a strong presumption[4] that a transfer of property into joint names in the context her Ladyship described creates a joint tenancy in equity. This is the new starting point, even if one of the parties makes no contribution to the purchase price. The previous starting point in cases of transfer into joint names, namely that of resulting trust according to financial contributions, has been abandoned in the context her Ladyship described, and therefore has no role to play. If the presumption were rebutted by evidence of the parties' contrary intentions, the parties would then hold on a constructive trust for themselves in unequal shares.

The *ratio* of **Stack v Dowden** is narrow, because the House of Lords was dealing with a case where the property had been transferred into joint names.[5] Where the property is transferred into the name of one of the parties only (A), the starting point is different, as then the party whose name is not on the legal title (B) must first establish that he or she has acquired a share in equity in the first place. Nothing in **Stack v Dowden** affects the need for B to establish that he or she has acquired an equitable interest.[6] Before **Stack v Dowden**, B could have no equitable interest unless he or she could show the acquisition of such an interest.[7] Lord Walker, however, thought[8] that now the courts, in seeking to ascertain the parties' intentions, could take account of the parties' whole course of conduct, and that a common intention constructive trust might be inferred from other than the direct contributions to which Lord Bridge in *Lloyd's Bank v Rosset* [1991] AC 107 had referred. Lady Hale approved this statement in *Abbott v Abbott* [2008] 1 FLR 1451.[9] If this is what Lord Walker and Lady Hale intended, then their remarks are inconsistent with the earlier decisions of the House of Lords in *Pettitt v Pettitt* [1970] AC 777 and *Gissing v Gissing* [1971] AC 886. However, in *Thomson v Humphrey* [2009] EWHC 3576 (Ch), Warren J was unable to infer an agreement that the beneficial interest should be shared merely from the non-legal owner's taking care of the housekeeping; so, it seems that the principle of **Burns v Burns** survives **Stack v Dowden**.

There is no doubt, however, that Lady Hale's observations are relevant to the cases of purchase in a sole name at the second stage: namely in ascertaining, in the absence of any express agreement between the parties, the size of B's share. Lady Hale emphasised[10] that the search was for the parties' intentions, not what the court considered fair. She indicated that, whilst the starting point was different where the legal title was in the name of A alone from where it had been vested in A and B jointly, the same factors that she mentioned as relevant in determining the parties' true intentions should be applicable to both. Thus, in *Abbott v Abbott* [2008] 1 FLR 1451 (PC), where land had been transferred into the husband's sole name, the wife, who had contributed only 8.3 per cent through building a house on it, was nevertheless held entitled to half the beneficial interest. It was significant that the parties had contributed to the property jointly, had a joint bank account, and had joint legal liability for the mortgage repayments and insurance. The fact that **Stack v Dowden** excludes the application of the doctrine of resulting trusts was of concern to Lord Neuberger,[11] who delivered the sole dissenting speech in the House of Lords in that case. His dissent was not on the result, but on the majority's reasoning.[12] He said that the determination of the beneficial interests should depend initially on an application of the principles of the resulting

[5] Many students miss this crucial point—**Stack v Dowden** is a 'joint names' case.

[6] An obvious point, but state it—it shows understanding.

[7] For example by declaration of trust **(LPA 1925, s 53(1)(b))**, or by evidence of an actual informal agreement, or, by showing a direct contribution to the purchase price or to the mortgage instalments (plus inference of a common intention, **Rosset**).

[8] In other words, he thought that the law had moved on since Lord Bridge in **Rosset**.

[9] If these observations (which were strictly *obiter*) are interpreted widely, the decision in **Burns v Burns** [1984] Ch 317, where a woman acquired no beneficial interest through seventeen years of housework and child care, might now be different; see M Dixon, 'The Neverending Story—Co-ownership after Stack v Dowden' [2007] *Conv* 456.

[10] Lady Hale was critical of Chadwick LJ's comment in *Oxley v Hiscock* [2004] 3 All ER 703 (para 69) that the parties were each entitled to 'that share which the court considers fair having regard to the whole course of dealing between them in relation to the property'.

[11] Now deal with the dissent.

[12] Watch out for this point.

[13] One that takes into account not merely the initial contributions to the purchase price, but also the payment of mortgage instalments.

[14] If you missed this speech, you will need to rely solely on his speech in the case.

trust, which might then be supplanted by the doctrine of constructive trust arising from an express or inferred agreement supported by detriment. It should also be noted that the size of the shares that the House of Lords determined in *Stack v Dowden*, applying the factors that Lady Hale set out, were about the same as the parties' overall financial contributions: in other words, the decision itself would have been the same even on a broader resulting trust approach.[13]

Speaking extrajudicially, Lord Neuberger has since expressed four concerns about the decision in *Stack v Dowden*: see Lord Neuberger, 'The Conspirators, the Tax Man, the Bill of Rights and a Bit about the Lovers', Chancery Bar Association Annual Lecture, 28 March 2008.[14]

First, his Lordship doubted whether most couples can be taken to have intended a joint tenancy in equity, with the consequent right of survivorship. Second, Lord Neuberger was concerned about what Lady Hale meant by suggesting that the principle she was laying down applied 'at least in the domestic consumer context', although the Privy Council in *Marr v Collie* [2017] has now determined that *Stack* also applies where a cohabiting couple purchased investment properties, thus extending the principle from the domestic context to a commercial one. The presumption has been applied where the joint legal owners have had a long-term sexual relationship: *Fowler v Barron* [2008] EWCA Civ 377 and *Edwards v Edwards* [2008] All ER (D) 79 (Mar) (Ch); but was held not to apply where a mother and daughter had bought property for letting: *Laskar v Laskar* [2008] 2 P & CR 245; and see also *Close Invoice Finance Ltd v Abaowa* [2010] EWHC 1920 (QB).

[15] In such circumstances, the trustee in bankruptcy ought to be able to take any larger share arising from the presumption in *Stack v Dowden*, as such additional share would have been acquired under a voluntary disposition made by the bankrupt: cf *Densham v Densham* [1975] 1 WLR 1519 and *Segal v Pasram* [2007] BPIR 881 (ChD).

It is also difficult to see why the presumption in *Stack v Dowden* should be binding on a trustee in bankruptcy of one of the parties.[15]

Third, Lord Neuberger was not persuaded by some of the factors that Lady Hale had mentioned as pointing away from a beneficial joint tenancy. If unequal contributions rebutted the presumption of equal beneficial shares, then the presumption was of no value, since the issue would arise only where the contributions were not equal. He also doubted whether the fact that the parties keep their finances separate was at all unusual.

Fourth, he was concerned that the reference to the court's need to determine the parties' true intentions, and the list of factors that Lady Hale mentioned as relevant, tend towards uncertainty and will therefore lead to more, not less, litigation. This is a powerful criticism: the list of factors is long, and some of them—such as the parties' characters and personalities—are entirely subjective. The difficulties of determining the size of the shares are illustrated in *Barnes v Phillips* [2015] EWCA Civ 1056; *Adekunle v Ritchie* [2007] EW Misc 5 (EWCC); and *Hapeshi v Allnatt* [2010] EWHC 392 (Ch).

If the parties hold the property as beneficial joint tenants at the time of acquisition, to what extent, following *Stack v Dowden*, can those beneficial interests be subsequently varied? In *Jones v Kernott* **[2011] UKSC 53**, the Supreme Court said that the *Stack v Dowden* presumption can be varied by the parties' subsequent common intention. Unfortunately, *Jones v Kernott* did little to clarify *Stack v Dowden*.[16] The point of contention concerned the determination of the size of the parties' respective beneficial interests in circumstances where no common intention can be inferred from the evidence. In a joint judgment, Lady Hale and Lord Walker[17] were content to accept the first-instance judge's finding that the parties' intentions had changed. They nevertheless thought that,[18] whilst there might be a conceptual distinction between inferring and imputing an intention, in practice it was a distinction without a difference (*Barnes v Phillips*).

Although it is now a few years since the controversial decision[19] in *Stack v Dowden*, many issues remain unclear: first, what circumstances will be regarded as exceptional to rebut the strong presumption that it laid down; second, the extent to which the decision applies where the legal title is in one name only; and, third, how the size of beneficial interests is calculated using the 'holistic' approach favoured by Lady Hale. Subsequently, the decision in *Jones v Kernott* has revealed disagreement amongst the members of the Supreme Court over whether a common intention relating to the size of the beneficial interests is a matter of inference or imputation. To date, therefore, whilst the decision in *Stack v Dowden* has shifted the nature of the legal arguments over beneficial interests in the family home, it has not produced clear legal principles that enable parties to settle their disputes without recourse to the courts. Indeed, the volume of litigation since the House of Lords' decision seems rather, as Lord Neuberger feared, to have increased.

[16] In *Jones v Kernott*, where the beneficial interests were joint, after the break-up, Ms Jones paid all the mortgage interest and insurance premiums out of her own funds, as well as all the costs of bringing up their two children. The Supreme Court awarded Ms Jones a 90 per cent share based on a finding that the parties' intentions had changed after they had split up.

[17] However, whilst Lord Collins was broadly supportive of this view, Lord Kerr and Lord Wilson were not.

[18] Lords Kerr and Wilson thought it more realistic to recognise that what the court was doing was simply imputing to the parties an intention to share in such proportions as the court considered fair.

[19] Was it controversial, do you think? You can express your own view.

LOOKING FOR EXTRA MARKS?

■ When a question focuses on a single key case, then an intimate knowledge of the different judgments in the case is critical. An overview will earn poor marks.

■ Reference to extrajudicial statements was made here. Just like citing relevant academic articles, this will earn extra marks.

■ Further argument could be made for extra marks on the issue of the status of *Lloyds Bank plc v Rosset* [1991] 1 AC 107 (see 'Taking Things Further' for recommended reading on this point).

Q

QUESTION | **4**

In 2009, Nancy bought a house which was transferred into her name as the sole registered proprietor. Her father, who had been recently widowed, moved in with her. He had paid to her £10,000 for the deposit on the house, and he spent £5,000 of his life insurance money on adapting part of the ground floor so that he had a bedroom with en suite bathroom for his own use. In 2012, Nancy met and fell in love with Bill, who moved in with her. Bill, who was unemployed, spent a good deal of time on improving and renovating the house. He also did all the housework and cooking. He spent most of his £5,000 redundancy money on the renovations and also contributed to the housekeeping bills. Last year, Nancy mortgaged the house with the Fagin Finance Emporium to secure a loan of £125,000. Tiring of Bill's obsessive housekeeping, she bought a round-the-world air ticket and left. The Fagin Finance Emporium is now seeking possession of the house as a preliminary to sale.

(a) **Advise Bill and Nancy's father.**

How would your answer differ if:

(b) **Nancy and Bill had been married?**

(c) **Nancy had been declared bankrupt?**

! **CAUTION!**

- Although *Stack v Dowden* [2007] AC 432 concerned the acquisition of beneficial interests where the title to domestic property was in joint names, it appears that the House of Lords intended the same principles to apply to cases where the legal title is in one of the parties' names only. How *Stack v Dowden* applies to the latter situation has not yet been completely clarified, however, and the suggested answer draws attention to this. As *Stack v Dowden* established that, where the legal title is in joint names, there is a strong presumption that the beneficial interests are also held jointly, so it would seem to follow that, where the legal title is in one name, there is a strong presumption that the equitable interest is with the legal owner. If this is so, it seems to place a heavier burden on the non-legal owner to show that he or she has a beneficial interest than was the position before *Stack v Dowden*.

- This is a problem question, so take advantage of it, and use the points in it as hooks on which to hang your argument.

○ **DIAGRAM ANSWER PLAN**

Identify the issues	▪ The legal issues are constructive and resulting trusts.
Relevant law	▪ This is *Stack v Dowden* [2007] and related case law; **Matrimonial Proceedings and Property Act 1970, s 37**; **Matrimonial Causes Act 1973**; **Insolvency Act 1986, s 335A**; and **Article 8 ECHR**.

Apply the law	**Discuss the following:**
	(a) Nancy's father:
	  ▪ Is the deposit as gift, loan, or acquisition of beneficial interest?
	    ● acquisition of constructive trust under *Stack v Dowden*.
	  ▪ Adapting a ground-floor bedroom:
	    ● Is this a factor in determining the size of share under acquisition of the constructive trust?
	    ● If not, the nature of the work depends on whether one can infer common intention for post-acquisition constructive trust.
	
	Bill:
	  ▪ Housekeeping—there is no beneficial interest absent express agreement.
	  ▪ Renovation—there is possible interest under post-acquisition constructive trust, depending on the nature of the work.
	
	(b)
	  ▪ Improvements—**Matrimonial Proceedings and Property Act 1970, s 37**.
	  ▪ Property adjustments on divorce—**Matrimonial Causes Act 1973**.
	
	(c)
	  ▪ **Insolvency Act 1986, s 335A**.
	  ▪ Are there exceptional circumstances?
	  ▪ **Article 8 ECHR**.

Conclude	▪ Advise Bill and Nancy's father.

A

SUGGESTED ANSWER

The Fagin Finance Emporium (the Emporium) may be seeking possession because the mortgage instalments are in arrears. Whether it will be able to obtain possession of the house depends, however, on whether Nancy's father and Bill (or either of them) has a beneficial interest in the house[1] that is binding on the Emporium.

The legal title to the house is in Nancy's sole name,[2] but her father may try to establish a beneficial interest on the basis that he provided £10,000 for the deposit and spent £5,000 in adapting the ground floor. It is first necessary to determine the basis on which the £10,000 for the deposit was provided. If the evidence shows that it was intended to be a gift, the father will have no beneficial interest in the house. In the absence of evidence, the presumption of advancement [3] will have applied to the transfer of the money, as it was a transfer from father to child. Although that presumption is to be abolished by the **Equality Act 2010, s 199**, that section is not yet in force and will in any event not be retrospective, and so the presumption will apply here. The presumption is easily rebutted,[4] however, by evidence of surrounding circumstances; and in *McGrath v Wallis* **[1995] 2 FLR 114**, it was rebutted by the fact that the person who had contributed to the purchase of a house was to share occupation with the legal owner. Another possibility is that the £10,000 was intended to be a loan; but, absent evidence to support this construction, it is unlikely.

As the legal title is in Nancy's sole name, there is a strong presumption[5] that she has the entire beneficial interest: cf *Stack v Dowden* **[2007] AC 207**. Nancy's father might be able to rebut this presumption by showing that he acquired a beneficial interest in the house by virtue of paying the £10,000 deposit. Before *Stack v Dowden*, this direct contribution to the purchase price would, in the absence of any agreement between them, have given him a proportionate share of the beneficial interest in the house; so that if, for example, it had been bought for £200,000, he would thereby have obtained a 5 per cent share. In many instances, however, once it was established that the non-legal owner had a beneficial interest under a resulting trust, the court could infer that the parties had agreed that they were to share the beneficial interest, and could, where the non-legal owner had acted to his or her detriment in reliance on the common intention, award such person a larger share under a constructive trust: *Midland Bank v Cooke* **[1995] 4 All ER 562**. In practice, therefore, the resulting trust would usually be superseded in these sorts of cases by a constructive trust. In the House of Lords in *Stack v Dowden*, however, it was established that, in the domestic consumer context, both

---

[1] The issue.

[2] Always state where the legal title is at the outset.

[3] Explain this presumption.

[4] An example of a rebuttable presumption.

[5] Another presumption—from *Stack v Dowden*.

the acquisition of a beneficial interest and the size of any interest obtained are to be determined, not according to principles of resulting trust, but in accordance with the parties' intentions, whether express or (more likely) inferred. In *Stack v Dowden*, the legal title was in the parties' joint names; but it is clear that the House of Lords intended the principles they laid down to apply also to cases where the legal title is (as in the question) in one person's name only. Even though there is no sexual relationship involved, the facts in this part of the problem indicate a domestic context within *Stack v Dowden*. On this basis, Nancy's father's payment of the £10,000 deposit would be treated both as evidence that he and Nancy had a common intention that he should have an interest in the property, and also that he had changed his position to his detriment in reliance on such agreement; these are the ingredients of a common-intention constructive trust, which would be outside the statutory formalities of **LPA 1925, s 53(1)(b)** by virtue of **s 53(2)**. In determining the size of the share, Lady Hale, with whose speech in *Stack v Dowden* the majority agreed, favoured a 'holistic' approach, and she listed the many factors that are to be taken into account, including the parties' individual characters and

[6] This is one interpretation of the case.

personalities. This being so, it is impossible to predict[6] what the court might determine the size of Nancy's father's share to be. However, one factor which might be taken into account to enlarge his share under such a constructive trust might be his later expenditure of £5,000 in adapting the ground floor for his bedroom.

If, however, the initial deposit was intended as a gift or a loan, the moneys spent on the bedroom later on might not give the father a beneficial interest. Although in *Lloyds Bank plc v Rosset* **[1991] 1 AC 107, 131–2**, Lord Bridge suggested that, in the absence of an express agreement, only direct contributions, such as by the payment of mortgage instalments, suffice to justify the inference of a constructive trust, such narrow approach was not favoured in *Stack v Dowden* **[2007] 2 AC 432, 445 (para 26)** (Lord Walker). Much therefore depends on whether the work amounts to an improvement that enhances the house's value. If it does, it may be evidence from which the court could infer that he and Nancy had agreed that he was to have an interest.

[7] Now get ready for an in-depth exposition of the relevant case law on this point.

In respect of Bill,[7] the situation is different since he did not make a contribution at the outset. It would seem extremely unlikely that a constructive trust would arise either from Bill's contribution of £5,000 to the renovation of the house (which is unlikely to increase its value) or from his payment of the housekeeping costs, as these are not direct contributions to the purchase price, nor would they amount to the equivalent of purchase money (*Burns v Burns* **[1984] Ch 317** and *Pettitt v Pettitt* **[1970] AC 777**). An indirect contribution could only act as a detriment where there was an express agreement or where the payment of the household expenses enabled Nancy to pay the mortgage: *Grant v Edwards* [1986] Ch 638. In the absence of an express agreement, a common-intention constructive trust can arise if there is detrimental reliance on an implied bargain. Bill could argue that the use of his redundancy money is clear evidence of detrimental conduct. His labour alone is unlikely to be sufficient to establish detrimental conduct. In *Eves v Eves* [1975] 1 WLR 1338, the woman's arduous work of renovation was held to have been carried out in reliance on a common intention that she should share the beneficial ownership. The conduct of the man in inducing her to agree that the property should be put in his name alone because she was under twenty-one was clear evidence of an express common intention and her work would not have been carried out without such an agreement. However, in the present case, Bill's work may not fall into the same category. On its own, without any express agreement as to beneficial ownership, it might be viewed as solely an anxiety on his part to improve his living conditions. In *Lloyds Bank plc v Rosset*, the woman's work in assisting in the renovation of the house was simply attributed to her anxiety to move the family in quickly. It was not sufficient evidence to point to an agreement to share beneficial ownership. It seems that Bill's payment of the housekeeping expenses cannot establish beneficial ownership in the absence of an express agreement (*Rosset*). In *Gissing v Gissing*, it was held that the wife's contribution to the household expenditure and her labour in caring for the family was insufficient evidence of detrimental conduct in reliance on a common intention to share beneficially in the ownership. It seems unlikely that Bill will be able to establish a constructive trust. Lord Walker, in *Stack v Dowden* [2007] 2 AC 432,[8] considered that the law had moved on since Lord Bridge in *Rosset*, and said that a common-intention constructive trust might now be inferred from other than direct contributions. This view was approved by the Privy Council in *Abbott v Abbott* [2008] 1 FLR 1451. These observations, however, were made in cases involving a transfer into joint names, and it seems unlikely that they were intended to be inconsistent with *Pettitt v Pettitt* [1970] AC 777 and *Gissing v Gissing* [1971] AC 886, both of which rejected the possibility of imputing an agreement that the parties never made. The better view is that the observations are applicable only to determining the size of a beneficial interest the existence of which, but not the quantum, has already been established. They do not affect the earlier case law that establishes whether the claimant has acquired a beneficial interest in the first place. *O'Kelly v Davies* [2014] EWCA Civ 1606 and *Geary v Rankine* [2012] EWCA Civ 555 both accept the broader principles of

[8] A close knowledge of this case will pay dividends.

the application of *Stack* to single-person acquisitions—at least at the second stage of the determination of the size of the beneficial share.

The court will not therefore infer an agreement between Nancy and Bill that the latter should have a beneficial interest merely from his housework and cooking: *Thomson v Humphrey* [2009] EWHC 3576 (Ch).

If either Nancy's father or Bill has an equitable interest in the house, then, as they are both in actual occupation, this may constitute an overriding interest under the **Land Registration Act 2002, Schedule 3, para 2**, provided they do not fall within the exceptions in **paras 2(b)** and **(c)**. As the capital money is paid to only one trustee (Nancy) by the Fagin Finance Emporium, the doctrine of overreaching will not operate (*Williams & Glyn's Bank Ltd v Boland* [1979] **Ch 312**). The Fagin Finance Emporium will, therefore, take subject to the rights of any beneficiaries.

The Fagin Finance Emporium will need to apply to the court for an order for sale under **s 14, TLATA 1996**.[9] The court must have regard to the matters set out in **s 15**, which include the intentions of the person who created the trust, the purposes for which the property is held, the welfare of minors occupying the trust property as a home, and the interests of secured creditors (*Bagum v Hafiz* [2015] EWCA Civ 80).

There is no indication in **s 15** of the relative weights to be given to the competing interests of the creditors and other parties with an interest. Each case must depend on its facts, and it is for the court to make a value judgement (*Re Domenico Citro* [1991] **Ch 142**; *Abbey National v Moss* [1994] **1 FLR 307**; and *Bagum v Hafiz* [2015] EWCA Civ 80). In *Bank of Baroda v Dhillon* [1998] **1 FLR 524**, the priority to be given to the interests of the creditors in preference to those of a spouse with an overriding interest was recognised where an application for an order for sale was made under the statutory predecessor of **s 14, TLATA 1996**. If the family relationship has broken up, the purpose will be regarded as spent (*Re A; A v A* [2002] EWHC 611 (Admin/Fam); *First National Bank plc v Achampong* [2003] EWCA Civ 487).

In *Bank of Ireland Home Mortgages Ltd v Bell*, it was held that a powerful factor was whether a creditor was being recompensed for being kept out of his money.

If the Emporium obtained possession and sold the house, the issue would then be how much of the proceeds of sale they would have to pay to Nancy's father or to Bill. This depends on the extent to which their beneficial interests bind the Emporium. Lady Hale emphasised that the principle in *Stack v Dowden* applies in the domestic consumer context. It is not clear, however, whether an action

[9] This gives you full coverage of all the points.

by a mortgagee against a beneficial owner has a domestic or a commercial context. If the context is domestic, the Emporium will first have to apply the sale proceeds in paying Nancy's father the share to which he is entitled under the constructive trust. If the context is commercial, the Emporium will have to pay him only the interest he will have acquired under the principles that apply outside *Stack v Dowden*: namely, his interest under a resulting trust (which might be smaller). In *Densham v Densham* **[1975] 1 WLR 1519**, a wife had contributed the original deposit on a house, this being one-ninth of the purchase price. The house was conveyed into the sole name of her husband, who later became bankrupt. It was held that the one-ninth share that she had under a resulting trust was binding on the trustee in bankruptcy, as it was obtained for valuable consideration before the bankruptcy. The larger share that she claimed under a constructive trust, however, was held voidable by the trustee in bankruptcy, as it involved an element of voluntary disposition. It may therefore be that Nancy's father would be able to claim from the Emporium only the share obtained under a resulting trust by his £10,000 payment of the deposit.

➕ LOOKING FOR EXTRA MARKS?

■ There are a lot of points to be found in this question, so a good plan at the outset will help you find them all. Picking up all the points is key to earning full marks.

TAKING THINGS FURTHER

■ Law Commission, *'Sharing Homes': A Discussion Paper* (Law Com No 728, 2002).

Discusses, as its title suggests, the shared homes problem.

There are a number of commentaries on *Stack v Dowden* to be found, so these are listed below. Any of them make excellent reading, but Lord Neuberger's speech is one of the best:

■ Cooke, E, 'In the Wake of *Stack v Dowden*: The Tale of TR1' [2011] *Fam Law* 1142.

■ Dixon, M, 'Casenotes: Editor's Casenotes (Jul/Aug)' [2007] *Conv* 352 (case comment).

■ Dixon, M, 'The Never-Ending Story' [2007] *Conv* 456.

■ Moran, A, 'Anything to Declare?' [2007] *Conv* 364.

■ Lord Neuberger, 'The Conspirators, the Tax Man, the Bill of Rights and a Bit about the Lovers', Chancery Bar Association Annual Lecture, 28 March 2008, http://www.chba.org.uk/for-members/library/annual-lectures/the-conspirators-the-taxman-the-bill-of-rights.pdf.

■ Pawlowski, M, 'Beneficial Entitlement No Longer Doing Justice?' [2007] *Conv* 354.

- Piska, N, 'Intention, Fairness and the Presumption of Resulting Trust after *Stack v Dowden*' (2008) 71 *MLR* 120.
- Sparkes, P, 'Non Declarations of Beneficial Co-ownership' [2012] *Conv* 207.
- Swadling, W, 'The Common Intention Trust in the House of Lords: An Opportunity Missed' (2007) 123 *LQR* 511.

Likewise, there are many commentaries on ***Jones v Kernott***, and here is a selection:

- Dixon, M, 'The Still Not Ended, Never-Ending Story [2012] *Conv* 82.
- Gardner, S and Davidson, K, 'The Supreme Court on Family Homes' (2012) 128 *LQR* 177.
- Mee, J, '*Jones v Kernott*: Inferring and Imputing in Essex' [2012] *Conv* 167.
- Mills, M, 'Single Name Family Home Constructive Trusts: Is Lloyds Bank v Rosset Still Good Law?' [2018] 4 *Conv*, 350–66.

Discusses the current status of **Lloyds Bank v Rosset**:

- Sloan, B, 'Keeping Up with the Jones Case: Establishing Constructive Trusts in "Sole Legal Owner" Scenarios' [2018] 35 *Legal Studies* 226.

A reflection on both **Stack v Dowden** *and* **Jones v Kernott**.

For a case commentary on the impact of **ss 14** and **15 Trusts of Land and Appointment of Trustees Act 1996**, see:

- Goldsworth J G, 'Bagum v Hafiz—A Cautionary Tale' (2017) 4 *Conv* 296–302.

Online Resources

www.oup.com/uk/qanda/

For extra essay and problem questions on this topic, as well as advice on revision and exam technique, please visit the online resources.

8 Proprietary Estoppel

ARE YOU READY?

In order to attempt the questions in this chapter, you will need to have covered the following topics:

- the doctrine of proprietary estoppel;
- remedies satisfying a proprietary estoppel;
- licences and constructive trusts.

KEY DEBATES

Debate: the question of the role of unconscionability in the doctrine of proprietary estoppel remains topical (*Guest v Guest* [2020]; *Yeoman's Row Management v Cobbe* [2008]; and *Thorner v Major* [2009]).

As Professor Nicholas Hopkins argues in his article, 'Understanding Unconscionability in Proprietary Estoppel' (2004) 20(3) *J Contract L* 210–32, the courts have reasserted unconscionability as the basis of proprietary estoppel, moving away from the structured form of discretion envisaged in the classic *Taylors Fashions* [1982] formula. Proprietary estoppel now provides a vehicle for examining the increasing emphasis on the role of unconscionability in judicial decision making. The issue of proportionality between the detriment and remedy is also now a key concern of the courts when using proprietary estoppel as a remedial device. *Guest v Guest* [2020] EWCA Civ 387 and *Moore v Moore* [2018] EWCA Civ 2669, long-running cases concerning the family farm, are both Court of Appeal decisions on the difficult question of how to satisfy the equity. But there is a plethora of estoppel cases hitting the courts, so keep an eye on the reports. For a short editorial on the topic, see M Dixon, 'Proprietary Estoppel: The Law of Farms and Families' (2019) 2 *Conv* 89–92.

The overwhelming weight of authority shows that detriment is required. But the authorities also show that it is not a narrow or technical concept. The detriment need not consist of the expenditure of money or other quantifiable financial detriment, so long as it is something substantial. The requirement must be approached as part of a broad enquiry as to whether repudiation of an assurance is or is not unconscionable in all the circumstances.

(*per* Robert Walker LJ in *Gillett v Holt* [2001] Ch 210)

In the light of this statement, consider the extent to which the strict requirements set out in *Willmott v Barber* (1880) for establishing the equitable doctrine of proprietary estoppel have been modified by subsequent cases.

CAUTION!

- This essay question requires a knowledge of the classic exposition of the equitable doctrine of proprietary estoppel and its subsequent development through judicial precedent. There has been an increasing number of cases which have rested on the application of this doctrine and *Gillett v Holt*, a quotation from which is part of the question, provided an opportunity in the Court of Appeal for a review of the doctrine.

- There is a difficulty in seeking to establish separate categories for proprietary estoppels, and it can often overlap with issues relating to licences and constructive trusts. You do need to have read thoroughly the two leading cases in the House of Lords: *Yeoman's Row Management Ltd v Cobbe* [2008] UKHL 55 and *Thorner v Major* [2009] UKHL 18.

- When a question contains (as it does here) a quotation, it has been put there for a purpose. In the present question, your answer must be framed 'in the light' of Walker LJ's statement, so take care to reference it in your answer.

DIAGRAM ANSWER PLAN

The modern approach is taken in *Taylors Fashions Ltd v Liverpool Victoria Trustee Co Ltd* [1982].

⬇

The strict fivefold criteria is displayed in *Willmott v Barber* (1880).

⬇

Discuss *Gillett v Holt* [2001].

⬇

Analyse the modern approach:
- the promise;
- detrimental reliance;
- unconscionability.

[1] Start straight off from the beginning by referencing the quotation.

The extract from the judgment[1] in *Gillett v Holt* demonstrates that the equitable doctrine of proprietary estoppel has moved from a rigid requirement for proof of strict elements to a broader approach, depending ultimately on the unconscionability of the action.

[2] The basic explanation of the doctrine.

Proprietary estoppel[2] is an equitable doctrine whereby an owner of real property is prevented from insisting on his strict legal rights in relation to that property, when it would be inequitable for him to do so, having regard to the dealings which have taken place between the parties (*Hughes v Metropolitan Railway Co* (1877) 2 App Cas 439).

[3] Start to demonstrate the breadth of the case law—ancient to modern.

Modern case law[3] appears to show that there has to be some assurance of an individual's rights and some detrimental reliance on those rights. This approach was confirmed in *Taylors Fashions Ltd v Liverpool Victoria Trustees Co Ltd* [1982] QB 133, where Oliver J said (*obiter*) that it is necessary to ascertain whether, in the particular circumstances, 'it would be unconscionable for a party to be permitted to deny that which, knowingly, or unknowingly, he has allowed or encouraged another to assume to his detriment'. This was to be preferred to an attempt to fit every conceivable case within the strictures of some preconceived formula.

[4] Another reference to the quotation.

The formula to which Oliver J was referring[4] is to be found in *Willmott v Barber* (1880) 15 ChD 96, which followed the views of Lord Kingsdown (in a dissenting opinion) in *Ramsden v Dyson* (1866) LR 1 HL 129. These criteria were necessary, according to Fry J, in order to establish that it would be tantamount to fraud for individuals to assert their strict legal rights. This fraudulent conduct comprised the legal owner remaining silent in the face of someone else's mistaken belief. In this case, it was considered that the mistake must be unilateral; ie only that of the person who believes he has a right.

[5] This question really requires you to set out the criteria so you can show how they have (or have not) changed.

The strict criteria are fivefold:[5]

(a) the claimant must have made a mistake as to his legal rights;

(b) the claimant must have spent money or done some act on the faith of his mistaken belief;

(c) the defendant, as holder of the legal right, must know of the existence of his own right which is inconsistent with the right claimed by the claimant;

(d) the defendant must know of the claimant's mistaken belief; and

(e) the defendant must have encouraged the claimant in his expenditure of money or the other acts performed, either directly or by abstaining from asserting his legal right.

[6] Showing how they changed.

Originally,[6] these criteria were followed diligently and there have been some cases which have continued to follow this approach, such as *Matharu v Matharu* (1994) 68 P & CR 93, although these have been criticised. In general, the approach adopted in *Taylors Fashions Ltd v Liverpool Victoria Trustees Co Ltd* [1982] QB 133 is considered to be the preferred approach, and this is borne out by the decision in *Gillett v Holt*, which cites with approval the earlier decisions in *Re Basham* [1986] 1 WLR 1498, *Jones v Watkins* [1987] CAT 1200, and *Wayling v Jones* [1993] EGCS 153. Further, the House of Lords' decision in *Yeoman's Row Management Ltd v Cobbe* [2008] UKHL 55 confirms that a claim to a proprietary interest by virtue of the application of the doctrine of proprietary estoppel requires 'clarity as to what it is that the object of the estoppel is to be estopped from denying, or asserting, and clarity as to the interest in the property in question that the denial, or assertion, would otherwise defeat' (Lord Scott at 28).[7] If there is no mistake by the claimant as to their legal rights, then no claim in proprietary estoppel can be made out.

[7] Included here to assist you, but unlikely (and it is not expected) that you would remember the precise paragraph.

In *Gillett v Holt*,[8] a close relationship developed between a prosperous gentleman farmer, the defendant, and a schoolboy, the claimant, which lasted over forty years and extended to include the family of the claimant once he grew up and married. The relationship which developed was both on a social and a business basis, the boy going to work for the farmer and also becoming a surrogate son to him. Over the years, many unambiguous and public assurances were given that the claimant would become the owner of the estate. The claimant relied on these assurances, investing all his life in the business of his employer and friend until the relationship eventually broke down when the defendant came to rely instead on someone else.

[8] Important here to set out some facts to support the argument.

The Court of Appeal held that the claim had been made out. In reaching this decision, they considered that the assurances that were made were tantamount to a promise, even though they amounted to a promise to make a testamentary disposition in itself a revocable act. On this point, they criticised the earlier case of *Taylor v Dickens* [1998] 1 FLR 806 (which has since been compromised on appeal), where it had been held that since the promise was revocable, the estoppel claim could not be made out. The criticism was made on the point that the very nature of every such promise is that it is revocable; it is the subsequent detrimental reliance which makes it irrevocable.

[9] Part of your conclusion.

Thus,[9] the first requirement under the modern broad approach to a successful claim is the establishment of an unambiguous promise by the defendant to the claimant that he would acquire some interest or benefit over his real property. This is described in the earlier cases as 'encouragement or acquiescence' (*Ramsden v Dyson* (1866) LR 1 HL 129) and was one of the elements that was missing in *Yeoman's Row Management Ltd v Cobbe* [2008] UKHL 55. The promise does not have to be the exclusive reason why the claimant acted to his detriment in reliance on it (*Amalgamated Property Co v Texas Commerce International Bank* [1982] QB 84).

The promise could take the form of a written assurance (*Dillwyn v Llewelyn* (1862) 4 De GF & J 517; *Ely v Robson* [2016] EWCA Civ 774) or an oral one (*Pascoe v Turner* [1979] 1 WLR 431; *Guest v Guest* [2020] EWCA Civ 387; *Gillett v Holt; Jennings v Rice and others* [2003] 1 P & CR 100; *Liden v Burton* [2016] EWCA Civ 275). It could include a request to act in a particular manner (*Plimmer v Mayor of Wellington* (1884) 9 App Cas 699) or passive encouragement (*Ward v Kirkland* [1967] Ch 194), where the defendant knows that the claimant mistakenly believes he will obtain an interest. However, if the promise is not clearly made, then it will be insufficient to support the claim. So, where, in *James v Evans* (2000) EGCS 95; (2000) 42 EG 173, negotiations for the grant of a ten-year tenancy had been undertaken 'subject to contract', there was no basis for an estoppel claim. A similar result was reached in *Attorney-General of Hong Kong v Humphreys Estate (Queen's Gardens) Ltd* [1987] AC 114. In *Yeoman's Row Management Ltd v Cobbe*, the claimant, a commercial property developer, entered into an oral agreement with the defendant that he would purchase a block of flats for £12 million, would develop it, and then split the profits with the defendant. Relying on this agreement, the claimant then spent eighteen months drawing up plans, engaging architects and other professional consultants, and applying for planning permission. When planning permission was eventually granted, the defendant refused to honour the oral agreement. The House of Lords made it clear that, as a commercial person, the claimant knew that there was no legally enforceable contract and therefore knew that he 'was free to discontinue the negotiations without legal liability that is liability in equity as well as at law' (Lord Walker at 91).

[10] This lengthy discussion of the case law is absolutely required in this question.

Shortly after *Cobbe*,[10] the House of Lords heard another estoppel case, *Thorner v Major* [2009] UKHL 18, the facts of which were similar to those of *Gillett v Holt*. In the case, Peter, a taciturn farmer, by conduct and laconic statements over many years, led a younger relative, David, to believe that he would inherit the farm on his death; in reliance on this, David worked for fifteen years on the farm without pay. The House of Lords held that the minimum equity to satisfy the estoppel was to declare David entitled to the farm. Lord Neuberger's speech clearly distinguished *Cobbe*, most importantly on the ground that the parties were not businesspeople, and had never even contemplated entering into a contract for the disposition of the farm on Peter's death. Peter simply made an assurance over a period of years and David had acted on it to his detriment over a long period.

11 Linking back to your criteria.

The second essential ingredient[11] of the doctrine is that the claimant must show that he relied to his detriment on the promise. There must be a link between this promise and the detrimental reliance (*Eves v Eves* [1975] 1 WLR 1338; *Wayling v Jones* [1993] EGCS 153; *Davies v Davies* [2016] EWCA Civ 463). This link can be demonstrated by the bare link between the owner encouraging the claimant to incur expenditure on his land as in *Inwards v Baker* [1965] 2 QB 29, where a father allowed his son to build a bungalow on his land.

But the requirement for detrimental reliance is not narrow. It must simply consist of something substantial. In *Mollo v Mollo* [1999] EGCS 117, it consisted of both the time (valued at £11,900) and the money (£31,900) that the claimant had spent renovating property held in his wife's name. Similarly, in *Yaxley v Gotts* [2000] All ER 711, the claimant undertook the refurbishment and conversion of a property into three flats in reliance on a promise that he would have the ground floor flat.

The detriment relied on must, however, be more than minimal expenses and must be something substantial and long-lasting (*Guest v Guest* [2020] EWCA Civ 387; *Dr Kong Bok Gan v Wood & Choudhury* (1998) EGCS 77, CA). The reliance can be inferred from the conduct of the claimant, as where a former servant looked after a family without pay, relying on the promise that she could stay in the house for life (*Greasley v Cooke* [1980] 3 All ER 710; [1980] 1 WLR 1306; *Davies v Davies*). In *Jennings v Rice*, it consisted of years of unpaid work comprising gardening, shopping, maintenance, and nursing care. There must be sufficient conduct on the part of the claimant for the inducement to detrimental reliance to be inferred. Once this hurdle has been cleared, then the burden of disproving it shifts to the defendant.

Ultimately, the test as to whether the detriment is sufficiently substantial to be relied on is determined on the basis of whether it would be unjust or inequitable to allow the owner to renege on the assurance given in the particular circumstances of the case—the test of unconscionability.

In *Gillett v Holt*, the claimant relied on: his continued employment with the defendant and refusal of offers elsewhere; his contributions beyond that of an ordinary employee; his failure to take any other steps to secure his future wealth, such as through a pension; and, his expenditure and labour on the defendant's farmhouse, which he occupied. It was argued that the claimant was simply acting as an employee and that, had he moved on, he might have done no better than staying under the protection of his employer and benefactor. However, the court considered that it was sufficient that the family deprived themselves of the opportunity of trying to better themselves. This clearly draws the test for detrimental reliance very wide.

The fact that the claimant also derives benefit from the acts of reliance does not preclude there being a detriment; in assessing whether there is sufficient overall detriment, any advantages are weighed against the disadvantages: *Jennings v Rice*, approved in *Henry v Henry* **[2010] UKPC 3, 51**.

[12] Linking back again to the criteria.

The third requirement[12] of the doctrine is that of unconscionability. This is a broad requirement which underpins the other elements and generally informs the doctrine of proprietary estoppel. It must be shown that it would be unconscionable for the owner of the land to deny the claimant the benefit he has promised him and on which he has relied to his detriment. This element might be traced back to the earliest exposition of the doctrine in *Ramsden v Dyson* **(1866) LR 1 HL 129**, where Lord Kingsdown opined that the doctrine of estoppel could arise where there was a fostering of an expectation in the minds of the parties which, once acted upon, it would be unconscionable to deny later.

In *Gillett v Holt*, this element was considered to have been made out by the very fact that the claimant had devoted himself for more than forty years, both at an employment level and a social one, to the betterment of the defendant's life. There must be a broad enquiry as to the circumstances which it is alleged give rise to the unconscionability, although this does not permit the judge to exercise a 'completely unfettered discretion' according to his notion 'of what is fair in any particular case' (*Jennings v Rice* **[2003] 1 P & CR 8**, *per* Robert Walker LJ). Nor does it permit a claimant to rely on a promise that he clearly knows (perhaps because of his commercial expertise) not to be legally binding (*Yeoman's Row Management Ltd v Cobbe*). Thus, the particular circumstances of each case will be the pertinent factors to decide whether the tests for unconscionability have been made out and whether there has been an assurance given and sufficient detrimental reliance resulting from it for that promise to become irrevocable. The fact that the property has since passed into the hands of a purchaser might be a factor affecting unconscionability: *Henry v Henry* **[2010] UKPC 3**.

LOOKING FOR EXTRA MARKS?

■ You really need an excellent knowledge of the cases to get full marks here. This includes understanding how the law has developed.

Q

QUESTION | 2

Cyril was the registered proprietor of Acacia Lodge. Five years ago, he told his Aunt Agatha that she could live there rent-free for as long as she wanted, provided she did any necessary repairs. Agatha gave up her council flat and moved in. Agatha was very nervous about intruders, so she spent £2,000 on security locks and a burglar alarm. Cyril found out about this only when he visited her one day and accidentally set off the alarm.

Last year, Cyril sold Acacia Lodge to Derek at half the market value for a vacant property of that type. Cyril told Derek about the arrangement with Aunt Agatha and Derek assured him that he was looking at the property as a long-term investment.

Earlier this year, Aunt Agatha decided to replace the windows, as the house was very cold. She had double-glazed units installed at a cost of £5,000, which absorbed practically all of her life savings. When Derek came to visit Acacia Lodge, he told her he was absolutely delighted about the windows. He said, 'As long as you carry on paying for all the outgoings and repairs you can do what you want with the place as we agreed.'

Derek was killed in a road accident last week. The devisee of Acacia Lodge now wishes to sell it with vacant possession.

Advise Aunt Agatha.

!

CAUTION!

■ It can be difficult to decide whether the circumstances presented give rise to a constructive trust, to a contractual licence, or to the doctrine of proprietary estoppel. If in doubt, go in with all guns firing. Separate out the arguments for each type of equitable remedy or you might shoot yourself in the foot. There are overlaps, but it is easier to handle the issues if you keep the points separate.

■ This is a question that requires the inclusion of a lot of case law to illustrate the points. Know your case law.

■ As the answer involves a discussion of several distinct legal issues, it can be helpful to use subheadings in your answer to make it clear when you move from one issue to another.

DIAGRAM ANSWER PLAN

Identify the issues	▪ The legal issues are contractual licences, constructive trusts, and proprietary estoppel.
Relevant law	▪ This is *Bannister v Bannister* [1948]; *Binions v Evans* [1972]; *Taylors Fashions Ltd v Liverpool Victoria Trustees Co. Ltd* [1982]; *Wayling v Jones* [1993]; *Campbell v Griffin* [2001]; *Gillett v Holt* [2001]; *Jennings v Rice* [2002]; *Stack v Dowden* [2007]; *Yeoman's Row Management Ltd v Cobbe* [2008]; *Davies v Davies* [2016]; and associated case law.

Apply the law	**Discuss the following:**
	▪ Contractual licence:
	  ● *Binions v Evans*, *per* Lord Denning MR; not an interest in land.
	▪ Constructive trust:
	  ● If agreement gave rise to a trust of land, Derek took subject to Agatha's rights through her actual occupation; as Derek took expressly subject to Agatha's right to occupy and paid a reduced price; by virtue of Agatha's expenditure on property?
	  ● Is there common-intention constructive trust?
	  ● (Or mere restitutionary claim for reimbursement of expenditure?)
	▪ Proprietary estoppel:
	  ● Discuss unconscionability and proportionality between acts of reliance and remedy.

Conclude	▪ Advise Agatha.

A | **SUGGESTED ANSWER**

[1] A concise opening, then go straight into the issues.

There are several potential causes of action based upon a contractual licence, a constructive trust, and the doctrine of proprietary estoppel.[1]

[2] Using subheadings helps not only you to keep the issues separate, but also your examiner.

Contractual Licence[2]

Agatha was told by Cyril that she could live in the property rent-free provided she undertook repairs. Such an agreement is capable of forming the subject matter of a licence. However, the property was subsequently transferred to Derek, so the issue is whether this licence is enforceable against Derek's devisee as a successor in title who was

[3] You don't know for sure, so put it this way.

not a party to the licence agreement. The facts suggest[3] that when Acacia Lodge was sold to Derek, it might have been sold subject to her rights, as reflected by the low price. In *Binions v Evans* [1972]

Ch 359, it was agreed between the trustees of the Tredegar Estate that Mrs Evans should occupy a cottage on the estate for the rest of her life. The trustees sold the cottage to purchasers who bought at less than the market price because they took expressly subject to Mrs Evans' rights of occupation. All three judges agreed that the purchaser could not evict Mrs Evans, but the legal reasoning of Lord Denning MR was different from that of the majority. He considered that the agreement between Mrs Evans and the trustees gave her a right to reside in the cottage for the rest of her life, and that this conferred on her an equitable interest that was binding on the purchasers as they took with notice. In Lord Denning's judgment, therefore, the contractual licence was an interest in land. Lord Denning MR's view is inconsistent with the earlier House of Lords' authority of *King v David Allen & Sons (Billposting) Ltd* [1916] 2 AC 54, and the *dicta* in *Ashburn Anstalt v Arnold* [1989] Ch 1, that a licence cannot be an interest in land, although it is in line with *Errington v Errington* [1952] 1 KB 290. The view that contractual licences do not bind land has been confirmed in further cases, such as *Camden LBC v Shortlife Community Housing* (1992) 90 LGR 358, *Canadian Imperial Bank of Commerce v Bello* (1992) 64 P & CR 48, *Nationwide Building Society v Ahmed* (1995) 70 P & CR 381, and *Lloyd v Dugdale* [2002] 2 P & CR 167. In the light of these authorities, it cannot now be contended that the contractual licence is itself an interest in land; thus, Agatha's contractual licence cannot per se bind the purchasers.[4] However,[5] it will now be considered whether her licence might become binding by reason of a constructive trust.

[4] Include your conclusions on each point as you go along.

[5] Lead into the next point.

[6] Next issue—a subheading also means you don't need an explanatory opening sentence.

Constructive Trust[6]

In *Bannister v Bannister* [1948] 2 All ER 133, the defendant agreed to sell two cottages to the plaintiff on the basis that she was to be able to live in one of them rent-free for the rest of her life. The sale, which was at a considerably lower price than market value, was completed, and then the plaintiff tried to turn her out. The Court of Appeal held that, as the defendant had obtained the title to the cottages only because he had agreed that the defendant should be able to live there rent-free, it would be fraud on him to rely on the absolute nature of the conveyance. As the agreement intended to confer a beneficial interest on her, it held that the defendant held the cottage in which she was living on a constructive trust for her for her life, determinable on her ceasing to live there. The effect was that she became a tenant for life under the **Settled Land Act 1925** (**SLA 1925**).

In *Binions v Evans*, the majority of the Court of Appeal applied *Bannister v Bannister* and held that the agreement between

Mrs Evans and the Tredegar Estate gave her a beneficial interest, which meant that she became a tenant for life under the **SLA 1925**. If the agreement between Agatha and Cyril is construed in a similar way, it would give her a beneficial interest under a trust for land under the **Trusts of Land and Appointment of Trustees Act 1996 (TLATA 1996)**. This beneficial interest would bind Derek because, although not protected by a restriction in the charges register, Agatha was in actual occupation when Acacia Lodge was transferred to Derek: **Land Registration Act (LRA) 2002, Schedule 3, para 2**. Derek's estate would continue to be bound by this interest after Derek's death, as it could be in no better position than Derek.

Lord Denning MR in *Binions v Evans* took a different view from the majority. As an alternative to his holding that the contractual licence created an equitable interest (a view which now seems untenable), he argued that, as the purchaser took the cottage expressly subject to Mrs Binions' licence to occupy, and at a reduced price, it would be fraud on the purchasers to attempt to turn her out. He quoted with approval the statement of Cardozo J in *Beatty v Guggenheim Exploration Co* (1919) 225 NY 380, 386: '[a] constructive trust is the formula by which the conscience of equity finds expression'. Lord Denning would have held that in the circumstances the purchasers would have taken the conveyance subject to a constructive trust under which Mrs Evans had a right to remain in the cottage for the rest of her life. Lord Denning's constructive trust analysis was later applied in *Lyus v Prowsa Developments Ltd* [1982] 2 All ER 953. As Derek paid half price for Acacia Lodge, it might be inferred that this was because he had agreed to take it subject to Agatha's occupation rent-free for life. He might therefore have taken the transfer of Acacia Lodge subject to a constructive trust under which Agatha would be a beneficiary under a trust of land with a right to reside there for life, and such trust would continue to bind his estate after his death.

There is another way in which Agatha might possibly be able to argue that she has an interest under a constructive trust, and so can resist eviction: this is if she can establish that she has acquired a beneficial interest in Acacia Lodge through having spent £2,000 on the security lock and burglar alarm, and £5,000 on double-glazing. In order to establish this, Agatha would have to show that there was an agreement, either express or inferred, with either Cyril or Derek (or both), that she was to have a beneficial interest in the property, and that she acted to her detriment by spending her life savings in reliance on such agreement. As there appears to be no express agreement, she would have to argue that the court could infer an agreement merely from her expenditure on the cottage. The court cannot impute an agreement that the parties never made merely because it thinks it

[7] The common-intention constructive trust.

fair, and the onus is on Agatha to establish a common intention[7] that can lead to the imposition of a common-intention constructive trust: *Stack v Dowden* **[2007] UKHL 17**. As there is a strong presumption that the beneficial ownership follows the legal title, it may be difficult, on the facts of the problem, for Agatha to establish a common intention that secures for her a post-acquisition beneficial interest. If the works have increased the value of the property, the most that Agatha might therefore hope for is that Derek's estate would be unjustly enriched[8] were it to take the benefit of her expenditure, and that she might therefore be awarded compensation on a restitutionary basis for her expenditure on Acacia Lodge.

[8] A little reference to restitution here.

[9] Next subheading.

Proprietary Estoppel[9]

To rely on the doctrine of proprietary estoppel, Aunt Agatha must show that it would be unconscionable for her to be evicted from the property when she has been encouraged or allowed to assume to her detriment that she will be permitted to remain there for as long as she wished (*Taylors Fashions Ltd v Liverpool Victoria Trustees Co Ltd* **[1982] QB 133**). Her mistaken belief appears to fall into the category of domestic cases envisaged in *Yeoman's Row Management Ltd v Cobbe* **[2008] UKHL 55**. She could rely on the promise made by Cyril and the assurance given her by Derek. Her actions in giving up her council flat and spending money on Acacia Lodge could amount to the detrimental conduct in reliance on the representations, which is necessary for her to establish to succeed under this head (*Crabb v Arun District Council* **[1976] Ch 179**; *Davies v Davies* **[2016] EWCA Civ 463**).

It is not necessary to show a written agreement, as the requirements contained in **s 2** of the **Law of Property (Miscellaneous Provisions) Act 1989** need not be satisfied when the elements of proprietary estoppel are made out (*Yaxley v Gotts* **[2000] All ER 711**). Aunt Agatha is an example of 'the typical domestic claimant' personified by Lord Walker, at 68 in *Yeoman's Row Management Ltd v Cobbe*, who does not know that some further legal formality is necessary to complete title.

The court will take account of the proportionality between the remedy and the detriment it is designed to avoid. In *Bawden v Bawden* **[1997] EWCA Civ 2664 (CA) (7 November 1997)**, it was accepted that the court needed to adopt a flexible approach; that is, the minimum required to do justice in the case. It would therefore be appropriate to consider the balance in Aunt Agatha's case between her interest and that of the devisee of Derek's estate.

Once Aunt Agatha has established the doctrine, an equity arises and the court would seek a way to satisfy her claim on the basis of proportionality and justice. In *Dodsworth v Dodsworth* **(1973) 228 EG 1115**, the defendants spent £700 on improvements to a bungalow in the expectation that they would be able to remain there for as long as they wished. The Court of Appeal held that the defendants would be allowed to remain in occupation until their expenditure was reimbursed. A more extreme example can be found in *Pascoe v Turner* **[1979] 1 WLR 431**, where the Court of Appeal ordered that the fee simple should be conveyed to the defendant who had spent £1,000 on the property in reliance on the promise that the property was hers. However, it is also possible for the court to award compensation (*Wayling v Jones* **[1993] EGCS 153**; *Campbell v Griffin* **[2001] EWCA Civ 990**; *Gillett v Holt*; *Jennings v Rice* **[2003] 1 P & CR 100**). In contrast to these cases, is *Sledmore v Dalby* **(1996) 72 P & CR 196**, where, although an equity had been raised, the Court of Appeal considered that it had been already satisfied. In both *Moore v Moore* **[2018] EWCA Civ 2669** and *Guest v Guest* **[2020] EWCA Civ 387**, the Court of Appeal considered that the process for deciding how to satisfy the equity rested on a discretionary basis subject to broad principles of equity.

Before **LRA 2002**, it was uncertain in registered titles whether the inchoate equity created an equitable proprietary right which could constitute an overriding interest, or whether that would only arise once the right had been crystallised by the court (*Birmingham Midshires Mortgage Services Ltd v Sabherwal* **(2000) 80 P & CR 256, CA**). **Section 116** of the **LRA 2002**[10] resolves this point, as it confirms the proprietary status of an equity arising by estoppel in relation to registered land. It can therefore be protected by entry of notice on the register or (if the claimant is in actual occupation) it will be protected without the need for registration, provided it falls under **LRA 2002, Schedule 3, para 2**.

Thus, Aunt Agatha may seek to rely on the doctrine of proprietary estoppel. Any such estoppel will bind Derek's devisee, who is not a purchaser for valuable consideration: **LRA 2002, s 29**. As the devisee intends to sell Acacia Lodge, however, Agatha should be warned that, although her estoppel interest will bind any purchaser (**LRA 2002, s 116**) provided she remains in actual occupation (**Schedule 3, para 2**), the test for unconscionability might need to be considered afresh if the property has since passed into the hands of a third-party purchaser. In *Henry v Henry* **[2010] UKPC 3**, the Privy Council did not rule this out, but did not comment further as the point had not been pleaded: **paras 46–68, 56**.

[10] A good point to capture here.

LOOKING FOR EXTRA MARKS?

- Knowledge of the case law is going to get you the marks here.
- Showing the ability to distinguish the different heads of claim is crucial for a high mark.

TAKING THINGS FURTHER

- Dixon, M, 'Proprietary Estoppel: The Law of Farms and Families' (2019) 2 *Conv* 89–92.
  A short editorial, worth a read to get the flavour of the current flow of case law on this topic.
  The case law has prompted quite a few articles on proprietary estoppel—here are some examples:
- Etherton, T, 'Constructive Trusts and Proprietary Estoppel' [2009] 2 *Conv* 104.
- Low, K, 'Nonfeasance in Equity' (2012) 128 *LQR* 63.
- McFarlane, B and Robertson, A, 'Apocalypse Averted: Proprietary Estoppel in the House of Lords' (2009) 125 *LQR* 535.
- Owen, G and Rees, O, 'Section 2(5) of the Law of Property (Miscellaneous Provisions) Act 1989: A Misconceived Approach?' [2011] 6 *Conv* 495.
  An older article, but still useful, on licences and how they affect third parties:
- Wade, H W R, 'Licences and Third Parties' (1952) 68 *LQR* 337.

Online Resources
www.oup.com/uk/qanda/

For extra essay and problem questions on this topic, as well as advice on revision and exam technique, please visit the online resources.

9 Leases and Licences

In order to attempt the questions in this chapter, you will need to have covered the following topics:

● leasehold agreements;
● licences;
● leasehold covenants.

KEY DEBATES

Debate: what is the fundamental distinction between a lease and a licence?

This debate remains important (despite changes on the statutory protection of leases) in determining whether rights granted to an occupier bind a third party. Until the early 1980s, owners of residential properties might prefer occupiers to be licensees rather than tenants, as the latter usually enjoyed both security of tenure and rent control (latterly under the **Rent Act 1977**). For this reason, what were, in substance, leases were sometimes dressed up to resemble licences: the parties to the written agreement entered into might have been called 'licensor' and 'licensee', the regular sums payable might have been termed a 'licence fee', and there might have been terms designed to prevent the occupier from obtaining exclusive possession (such as the occupiers being required to vacate the premises for a minimum number of hours each day). In **Street v Mountford** [1985] AC 809, however, the House of Lords held that whether a lease or a licence was created did not depend on what the parties labelled the arrangement, but on its substance, and for this purpose sham terms were to be ignored. If the arrangement conferred exclusive possession at a rent, it would give rise to a lease. Moreover, a person who occupies the premises for the purpose of a business will have the security of tenure provided by the **Landlord and Tenant Act 1954, Part II** (unless it is expressly excluded) only if the occupation is under a lease. Even in a residential context, the distinction can still be important: both the tenancy deposit scheme (under which landlords are required to protect any deposit they receive from a residential tenant), and the statutory obligations (under the **Landlord and Tenant Act 1985, s 11**) to keep the premise in repair and the services in working order apply only to leases.

Q

The year before last, George inherited a large Victorian house, title to which is registered. He decided to convert it into three flats, from which he might derive an income. He therefore made the following arrangements three months ago:

(a) He completed the conversion of the two-bedroomed ground-floor flat, and signed a document, which described itself as a 'licence', giving Annie the right to occupy the flat with any other person whom George should select for three years for a fee of £400 per month. A week later, George signed an identical document, similarly called a 'licence', giving Bob the right to occupy the flat with Annie or any other person whom George should select for three years for a fee of £400 per month.

(b) He completed the conversion of the small, one-bedroomed attic flat, and gave each of Joe and his fiancée, Linda, a document headed 'licence'. Each document gave the 'licensee' a right to occupy the attic flat for three years at a fee of £400 per month. Joe was named as licensee in one document, and Linda was named as licensee in the other; apart from this, the documents were identical. Joe and Linda signed their respective 'licences', and returned them to George, who also signed each document and dated each the same date. Each 'licence' reserved to George the right either to nominate another occupier of the attic flat or to occupy the flat himself. Last week, Linda vacated the attic flat.

(c) The conversion of the basement flat is not yet completed, but George's niece, Marie, who recently left her husband and had nowhere to live, moved into it last month and is paying George £80 per week under a 'licence' agreement for three years, terminable earlier by the 'licensee' on two months' notice. George has kept a key to the premises in order to supervise the workmen and has entered the premises a few times for this purpose.

George has now received a very attractive offer for the freehold of the house from Horace.

Advise Horace whether he will be able to obtain vacant possession of the flats if he buys the house and has the legal title transferred to him.

!   CAUTION!

■ This question is on an area of law which has been the source of much litigation. Security of tenure and any significant rent control for residential tenants under leases created since the early 1980s meant that there was generally less reason for landlords to try to create licences rather than leases. Under an 'assured shorthold tenancy', a landlord has a right to possession at the end of the term, and the tenant can be charged a market rent.

■ When a question, such as this one, is in several parts, your answer should deal with each part in turn and indicate clearly which part you are dealing with. It can be helpful to leave a line between your answer to each part.

DIAGRAM ANSWER PLAN

Identify the issues	■ The legal issue is the distinction between leases (interest in land) and licences (personal right).
Relevant law	■ This is *Street v Mountford* [1985].
Apply the law	■ Distinguish 'exclusive possession' (necessary for a lease) from 'exclusive occupation' (that might be enjoyed under a licence). ■ Explain the significance of the owner's retention of a key. ■ Discuss the circumstances that might indicate no intention of creating legal relations.
Conclude	■ Advise Horace.

A SUGGESTED ANSWER

[1] Set out the first issue.

It is first necessary to determine whether the occupiers of each flat have leases or licences,[1] as only leases are capable of binding Horace if he takes a transfer of the legal title to the house.

(a) As Annie and Joe share occupation of the ground-floor flat, they will each be licensees until it can be established that, together, they have exclusive possession of the flat, and so are joint tenants under a single lease. The fact that each agreement is called a licence is inconclusive: ***Addiscombe Garden Estates v Crabbe* [1958] 1 QB 513**. In ***Street v Mountford* [1985] AC 809**, Lord Templeman said that wherever exclusive possession of premises is granted for a term at a rent, *prima facie* a lease will be created. He warned that judges must be wary of 'sham' agreements, where a lease is disguised as something else, such as a licence or a service occupancy.

[2] Explain the meaning of this term.

Exclusive possession[2] means, however, that the tenant may exclude everyone else, including the landlord, from the premises. Where premises are shared, therefore, it is necessary to consider the nature of the sharing arrangements to decide whether the occupiers all have equal rights and interest in the whole of the property, in which case they may together have exclusive possession (and so are legal joint tenants), or whether their obligation to share the premises with others means that all are merely licensees. It is the reality of the arrangement that is determinative.

[3] Deal with the associated cases.

In the conjoined appeal[3] in *A G Securities v Vaughan* **[1990] 1 AC 417**, four occupiers who signed different licence agreements on different dates and for different terms and for different individual payments were held to be licensees of a four-bedroomed flat, as the necessary four unities were not present to make them joint tenants. Although they each had an exclusive right to occupy the flat with the other three, they did not collectively have exclusive possession.

Although Annie and Bob between them occupy the flat, the different agreements entered into on different dates and for different payments, the absence of any apparent pre-existing relationship between them, and the fact that there are two bedrooms all suggest that, as in *A G Securities v Vaughan*, they are merely licensees.

[4] The second part—note the importance of the joint tenancy point.

(b) The factors here are suggestive of a joint tenancy.[4] In *Antoniades v Villiers* **[1990] 3 WLR 139**, the two occupiers of a small, one-bedroomed flat, who were an unmarried couple, each entered into a 'licence' agreement with the owner of the flat, under which each agreed to share occupation with the 'licensor' or with such other persons as he might permit to use the premises, and to pay a specified sum each month. Each agreement was entered into on the same day. It was held that, looking at the circumstances, including the fact that it was a one-bedroomed flat and that the 'licensees' were a couple, the landlord's purported right to share occupation or to put another person into occupation was a sham. In reality, the arrangements conferred exclusive possession on the couple jointly, so they had a lease. In the problem, various factors point strongly to a joint tenancy: the attic flat having only one bedroom, the pre-existing relationship between Joe and Linda, the entering of the agreements on the same date, and the similarity of the monthly payments. The two agreements would therefore be treated as creating a single lease under which Joe and Linda are joint tenants at law and pay a rent of £400 per month. Under a joint tenancy, each joint tenant is liable for the entire rent. George can therefore demand that Joe pay £400 a month.

[5] Go straight into explaining the issue.

(c) The issue here[5] is whether George's entering of the flat occupied by Marie in order to supervise the completion of the conversion precludes her from having the exclusive possession necessary for a lease. An arrangement under which the owner is entitled to enter for certain purposes is not necessarily a licence, since even in a lease a landlord may reserve a 'right of entry' (usually upon notice) for specified purposes. Indeed, if the agreement under which Marie occupies expressly reserves George a 'right of entry' to enable the conversion to be completed, this might, paradoxically, point to a lease. This was the position in *Street v Mountford*, where, although the agreement purported to be a licence, it was held to be a lease, as the landlord had expressly reserved the right to enter the room to inspect and maintain it and to read the meters. It was held that the reality was that a lease had been created whereby the tenant had exclusive possession for a term at a rent.

[6] Nice word to explain a doubtful point.

The fact that George retains a key to the basement flat is equivocal.[6] On the one hand, it might suggest that Marie does not have exclusive possession, but only exclusive occupation. In *Luganda v Service Hotels Ltd* [1969] 2 Ch 209, where the landlord retained a key to enter a room and carry out certain minimal services such as cleaning, the occupier was held to have exclusive occupation, which enabled him to exclude everyone except the landlord, but he did not have exclusive possession as against the landlord, and did not therefore have a tenancy. In *Abbeyfield (Harpenden) Society Ltd v Woods* [1968] 1 WLR 374, although the occupier had exclusive occupation of a room in a retirement home, the various services provided made the agreement as a whole a licence. On the other hand, retention of the key might merely be pursuant to a landlord's limited rights of entry under a lease. In *Family Housing Association v Jones* [1990] 1 WLR 779, the retention of a key for purposes not related to shared occupation, but in order to discuss re-housing and inspect the state of repair of the premises, was not sufficient to negate exclusive possession. Therefore, it may well be that George's retention of a key for purposes not relating to his agreement with Marie does not detract from her having exclusive possession under a lease.

[7] It is important to show good knowledge of this leading case.

Although Lord Templeman said in *Street v Mountford*[7] that exclusive possession of premises for a term at a rent would *prima facie* create a lease, he did recognise that some arrangements were not intended to create legal relations. These could well be the types of agreement referred to by Lord Denning MR in *Facchini v Bryson* [1952] 1 TLR 1386, being those affected by 'circumstances such as of family arrangement, and an act of friendship or generosity or such like'. As Marie is George's niece and her payments are evidently substantially below the market rent, the arrangement may fall within this category. However, a small rent paid to a relative is not necessarily conclusive of a licence rather than a tenancy: *Ward v Warnke* [1990] 22 HLR 496 (CA). If the arrangements made by George have merely created licences then, as a licence is not an interest in land (*Ashburn Anstalt v WJ Arnold* [1989] Ch 1), the licensees will not have any rights binding upon Horace if he takes a transfer of the title, and he would be able to evict them. As each of the flats is a 'dwelling', however, the **Protection from Eviction Act 1977, s 5** requires Horace to give twenty-eight days' notice to vacate the premises; and if the licensees are residing at the premises, he may re-enter only by court order. The only course of action open to an evicted licensee would be to sue George for damages for breach of contract.

8 Easy to miss this point.

Although the arrangements are not by deed, they can create legal leases[8] if they are for terms not exceeding three years at the best rent reasonably obtainable: **Law of Property Act 1925 (LPA 1925), s 54(2)**. A lease 'granted' for a term not exceeding seven years is an overriding interest, and so binding on Horace: **LRA 2002, Schedule 3, para 1**. If Marie's lease was not at the best rent reasonably obtainable, and so was not a legal lease for lack of a deed, it would not have been 'granted'. She would nevertheless have an equitable lease, which, as a proprietary interest, would be binding on Horace if she is in actual occupation: **Land Registration Act 2002 (LRA 2002), Schedule 3, para 2**.

If Horace takes a transfer of the legal estate and the leases are binding on him, Horace will not be able to obtain vacant possession of a flat until its three-year term is completed, unless he is able to forfeit for breach of covenant (assuming there is a proviso for re-entry), or if a tenant surrenders his or her lease, or, in the case of Marie, if the lease is determined early by her serving a notice to break.

LOOKING FOR EXTRA MARKS?

- Knowledge of the case law (including any recent cases) is critical here. Getting the point about legal leases is also going to earn extra marks.

QUESTION | 2

Consider the validity and effect of the following dispositions:

(a) A grants to B a lease of a flat for one day.

(b) A grants a lease to B 'for the life of B' at a rent of £10,000 per annum.

(c) A grants a lease of Bleak House to B 'until A shall marry'.

(d) A grants B a lease for seven years with an option to renew 'on exactly the same terms as the present lease'.

(e) A grants a lease in writing of Red House to B for two years at a market rent of £10,000 per annum to take effect in possession.

(f) A grants B a yearly tenancy of White House, 'not to be terminated by A unless B becomes unemployed'.

! **CAUTION!**

■ This is a straightforward question on leases if you know your general basic law on the subject well. The different parts of the question require a knowledge of the operation of case law and statutory provisions on certain grants. It is the type of question to which you will either know the answer or not!

■ Unless your exam paper specifically states that all parts of the question merit equal marks, some parts may be worth more than others. Part (c) of this question, for instance, is a very short point on the wording of the **Law of Property Act (LPA) 1925, s 149(6)**, whereas part (f) involves a fundamental point of law on the nature of leases, reaffirmed by the House of Lords in 1992, upsetting the decision in *Re Midland Railway Co's Agreement* **[1971] Ch 725**, which had stood since 1971. Part (f) gives a student the opportunity to show an understanding of the decision and its effect, and to pick up more marks than may be possible on part (c). It would be a strange examiner who did not regard an explanation of this as deserving of more marks than the short point in part (c)!

O **DIAGRAM ANSWER PLAN**

Identify the issues	■ The legal issues are leases: certainty of term; determinable leases; creation of legal leases; and options to renew.
Relevant law	■ This is **LPA 1925, ss 54(2), 149(6)**, and **LPA 1922**.
Apply the law	**Discuss the following:** (a) certainty of term and rent; (b) leases terminable on death or marriage: **LPA 1925, s 149(6)**; (c) options to renew and perpetually renewable leases: **LPA 1922**; (d) leases not required to be granted by deed: **LPA 1925, s 54(2)**; (e) certainty of term applied to periodic tenancies.
Conclude	■ Advise on the validity and effect of each disposition.

[1] Explain that this is an essential requirement.

(a) One of the essential requirements[1] of a lease is that it must be for a certain term. Although the technical name for a lease is 'a term of years', **LPA 1925, s 205(1)(xxvii)** specifically includes in the definition 'a term for less than a year'. It is therefore possible to have a lease for just one day. The same definition section also includes a term of years 'whether or not at a rent', so that it could still be a lease if no rent were reserved, although this is a factor which might suggest that it is instead a licence.

[2] Legal lease point.

As the lease is for a term that does not exceed three years,[2] it may also be a legal lease provided that it fulfils the other requirements of **LPA 1925, s 54(2)**, ie it is at the best rent obtainable (a market rent) and takes effect in possession.

[3] The key point.

(b) A lease determinable upon death is for an uncertain duration[3] and is therefore *prima facie* void. **LPA 1925, s 149(6)**, states that a lease at a rent 'for life or lives' becomes a term of ninety years terminable by one month's written notice on the death. The grant to B for life is therefore converted into a term of ninety years, which may be determined by the grantor or B's personal representatives by one month's written notice on B's death.

As the lease is for a period exceeding seven years, it will not operate at law until it is registered substantively with its own title number (**LRA 2002, s 27(1)** and **s 27(2)(b)(i)**).

[4] Don't hunt for anything more complex than this answer.

(c) This grant is also for an uncertain duration.[4] Although **LPA 1925, s 149(6)** saves a lease for an uncertain term terminable on the *tenant's* marriage and by converting it into a term of ninety years determinable on such marriage, it does not apply to render valid a lease for an uncertain term terminable on the marriage of anyone else. As the term is expressed to last until the marriage of A, not B, the purported grant is void.

(d) The grant of a lease containing an option to renew on exactly the same terms confers on B the right to require another lease with the same option to renew, so making the lease perpetually renewable.[5]

[5] This is the key point to make.

LPA 1922, s 145 converts such leases into terms of 2,000 years, with the tenants having a right to terminate, on ten days' written notice, on a date when the lease would have expired but for its conversion into a 2,000-year term. The tenant must give notice of any assignment to the landlord. A tenant who has assigned the lease is no longer liable for breaches of covenant committed after assignment: **LPA 1922, Schedule 15, para 11**. This is an express statutory exception to the principle of a tenant's continuing contractual liability after assignment (which principle still applies to leases created before 1996).

In construing a renewal option in a lease, however, the courts will lean against interpreting it as giving a right to perpetual renewal. In *Marjorie Burnett Ltd v Barclay* **[1981] 1 EGLR 41**, the lease was construed as giving only one further right to renew after the first renewal, and the provision for rent review every seven years was said to be inimical to the creation of a 2,000-year term.

If conversion applies, the lease for a term of 2,000 years, since it exceeds seven, must be registered substantively in order to operate at law. If, however, the option is construed so as to enable the lease to be renewed for one period only, the lease, being granted for a term of only seven years, will not be registrable substantively; it will, however, be an overriding interest under **Schedule 3, para 1**.

(e) A lease for a term not exceeding three years at 'the best rent which can reasonably be obtainable without taking a fine' and which takes effect in possession is a legal lease within **LPA 1925, s 54(2)**. Although the subsection refers to leases 'by parol' (ie by word of mouth), it has been held to include leases in writing: *Wright v Macadam* **[1949] 2 KB 744 (CA)**. The written lease for two years is therefore a legal lease, provided that the £5,000 per annum specified is indeed the market rent.

(f) A periodic tenancy satisfies the requirement that a lease must be for a fixed and definite duration,[6] as it is regarded as being a lease for one period at a time, the lease being automatically renewed and running from one period to the next unless notice is given by either party. In *Breams Property Investment Co Ltd v Stroulger* **[1948] 2 KB 1**, a restriction prohibiting the landlord from giving notice to quit during the first three years was accepted as valid. In effect, it created a lease for a fixed term of three years determinable by the tenant, and then a periodic tenancy: *Berrisford v Mexfield Housing Co-operative Ltd* **[2011] UKSC 52**, at **para 55** (Lord Neuberger).

In *Re Midland Railway Co's Agreement* **[1971] Ch 725**, the Court of Appeal held valid a periodic tenancy in which the landlord was precluded from giving notice to quit unless it required the demised premises for the purposes of its undertaking. In *Prudential Assurance Co v London Residuary Body* **[1992] 2 AC 386**, however, the House of Lords affirmed the rule in *Lace v Chantler* **[1944] KB 368** that the duration of a lease must be certain. They expressed the opinion that the *Midland Railway* case had been wrongly decided, as the restriction on one party's giving notice to quit was governed by events which were uncertain, thus rendering the duration of the term uncertain. In *Prudential*, a local authority had granted

[6] Students often don't make this point about periodic tenancies.

a lease of land until it was 'required by the Council for the purposes of the widening of Walworth Road and the street paving rendered necessary thereby'. It was held that, as the term was of uncertain duration, the grant was void. Instead, the tenant had a yearly tenancy, which arose by reason of his occupation and payment of rent on a yearly basis. In *Berrisford v Mexfield Housing Co-operative Ltd*, the Supreme Court, whilst considering that the requirement of a maximum fixed term lacks any practical justification, nevertheless affirmed the decision in the *Prudential* case.

A's grant of the yearly tenancy not to be terminated by A unless B becomes unemployed is therefore void for uncertainty of term. However, if B occupies White House and pays rent annually, he acquires an implied yearly periodic tenancy.

+ LOOKING FOR EXTRA MARKS?

■ This is a mix of statute and case law—include all the cases, and you will be getting very high marks.

Q QUESTION | 3

Frieland Ltd is the freehold owner of a shop with a separate flat above it.

In 2015, Frieland Ltd granted a seven-year lease of the shop to Curlywig, a firm of hairdressers. The lease includes covenants not to assign, sublet, or part with the possession of the whole or any part of the property without the consent in writing of the landlord, to pay the rent of £20,000 per annum, and not to use the premises for any purpose other than that of a hairdressing business.

In 2016, Frieland Ltd granted a yearly tenancy of the flat above the shop to Susie.

Last year, Curlywig applied in writing to Frieland Ltd for consent to assign the lease of the shop to Kingpin, a hairdresser, but some four months later had received no reply, in spite of repeatedly reminding Frieland Ltd of its application. Kingpin refused to wait any longer, so Curlywig assigned the lease to him, and Kingpin has paid the rent ever since to Frieland's agents.

Nine months ago, Kingpin started to have financial problems and so allowed Minnie to use part of the shop premises in the evenings as a massage parlour in return for a money payment. Kingpin is now three months in arrears with the rent.

Susie has been disturbed by unpleasant clients of the massage parlour ringing her bell and leaving the shop premises as late as 2.00 am.

The staircase to Susie's flat is in a bad state of repair and the metal window frames are badly rusted through condensation.

▶

Advise:

(a) **Frieland Ltd;**

(b) **Susie**

as to what possible remedies they may have.

! **CAUTION!**

■ This question requires you to consider the effect of certain covenants commonly found in leases. It requires a consideration of the different forfeiture procedures for non-payment of rent and for breach of any other covenant in a lease. You also require some knowledge of landlord's covenants which are implied into a lease, including the statutory obligations relating to dwelling-houses. Although most land law courses will include these, this is one of the more peripheral areas of the subject and it is possible that some courses may omit it. You will have to be guided on this by your lecture notes and tutorials.

■ Although there is an assignment, it is not an immensely complicated question with a series of dispositions, so a diagram is probably unnecessary. Questions that deal with assignments and subleases may sound complicated, but often become clearer when reduced to diagrammatic form. You should therefore sketch out a rough diagram (as in Figure 9.1) before embarking upon your answer.

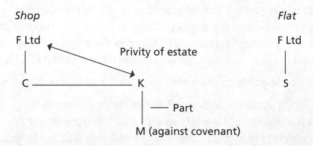

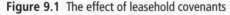

Figure 9.1 The effect of leasehold covenants

Once you have achieved this, you may be surprised at how comparatively simple the whole question becomes. The diagrammatic form (used in some textbooks also) is to indicate a lease or a sublease by a vertical line and an assignment by a horizontal one. L leases to T. T assigns to T1. T1 assigns to T2. T2 sublets to S. S assigns to S1. L assigns the reversion to L1. (It may, of course, also be important to note the order in which the dispositions occur.) The significance of this diagram is that wherever two parties are joined by a vertical line, there will be privity of contract between them; wherever it is possible to join two parties by a single diagonal line, there will be privity of estate on the lease or sublease assigned. If it is necessary to draw two diagonal lines, however, there will be no privity of estate or of contract.

DIAGRAM ANSWER PLAN

Identify the issues	▪ The legal issue is leasehold covenants.

Relevant law	(a) **LTA 1927; LTA 1988; LPA 1925, s 146; Common Law Procedure Act 1852.** (b) **LTA 1985, s 11** and ***Liverpool City Council v Irwin*** **[1977].**

Apply the law	(a) **Frieland Ltd**
	 ▪ Discuss the nature of covenant against assignment, etc—qualified—consent must not be unreasonably refused. The landlord must give reasons in writing for a refusal within a reasonable time.
	 ▪ Discuss the effect of assignment in breach of covenant—privity of estate.
	 ▪ Consider forfeiture proceedings for any covenant other than payment of rent—notice:
	   • enforceability of restrictive covenants in leases;
	   • forfeiture proceedings for non-payment of rent;
	   • right of recovery of rent from original tenant Curlywig under the **Landlord and Tenant (Covenants) Act (LT(C)A) 1995** and procedure.
	 (b) **Susie**
	 ▪ Discuss implied covenant by the landlord to repair.
	 ▪ Discuss the tenant's remedies for breach of a repairing covenant.
	 ▪ Consider the landlord's implied covenant for quiet enjoyment and its limitations.

Conclude	▪ Advise: (a) Frieland Ltd; (b) Susie.

SUGGESTED ANSWER

[1] Concise introduction to issue.

(a) A covenant not to assign or sublet without the consent of the landlord is a qualified` form of such a covenant and is therefore subject to the **Landlord and Tenant Act (LTA) 1927, s 19(1),**[1] which implies that such consent shall not be unreasonably withheld. The **LTA 1988** provides that where a tenant applies in writing for such consent, the landlord must give his decision in writing to the tenant within a reasonable time, stating any reasons for refusing consent.

The burden of proof to show that he has complied with **LTA 1988** is on the landlord, and Curlywig could have had a claim for damages for breach of the statutory duty imposed by the Act if Frieland Ltd has delayed unreasonably in replying. Recent cases indicate that what constitutes a reasonable time will vary according to the complexity of the circumstances that the landlord has to consider (*NCR Ltd v Riverland Portfolio No 1 Ltd* [2004] 16 EG 110 (CS)) but that, in a fairly straightforward matter, it should be no more than a few weeks, so that four months would seem to be an unreasonable delay for which Frieland Ltd could have been liable in damages.

However, Curlywig has gone ahead and assigned the lease, so that he may not have suffered any actual loss giving rise to a claim for damages. As Frieland Ltd's agents have accepted rent from Kingpin, Frieland Ltd will be deemed to have waived any breach of covenant. The assignment, in any event, is effective to dispose of the lease, and the landlord must proceed against the assignee Kingpin for any breach of covenant, and not against Curlywig (*Old Grovebury Manor Farm v W Seymour Plant Sales & Hire Ltd (No 2)* [1979] 1 WLR 1397).

In allowing Minnie to use part of the premises,[2] Kingpin may be in breach of the covenant not to part with the possession of the whole or any part of the premises without the landlord's consent. In *Akici v L R Butlin Ltd* [2005] EWCA Civ 1296, however, Neuberger LJ held[3] that sharing possession of premises was a different breach of covenant from parting with the possession of part of premises. If this is correct and Kingpin is using the premises during the daytime, then it may be that Kingpin is not in breach of the covenant at all. If there is a breach, however, this is a landlord and tenant covenant, the burden of which would pass to Kingpin, and Frieland Ltd would therefore be able to sue Kingpin for forfeiture or damages or both.

If Frieland decides to sue for forfeiture, then, once the contractual right to re-entry has arisen (*Toms v Ruberry* [2019] EWCA Civ 128), it must first serve a notice under **LPA 1925, s 146**, informing Kingpin of the breach complained of, requiring it to be remedied, and requiring compensation for it. The notice need not require the breach to be remedied if it is irremediable. In *Scala House & District Property Co Ltd v Forbes* [1974] QB 575, the Court of Appeal held that a breach of covenant against assignment was irremediable, although in *Akici* Neuberger LJ, whilst accepting that he was bound by *Scala House*, expressed doubts about this. The notice need not require compensation if the landlord does not want this (*Governors of Rugby School v Tannahill* [1935] 1 KB 87). An immoral user of the premises may well be irremediable (*Rugby School v Tannahill*). Kingpin may apply for relief against forfeiture under **LPA 1925, s 146(2)**, although he would be unlikely to obtain it. Breach of a covenant against assignment without consent is an irremediable breach.

[2] The section here deals with possible breach of covenant not to part with possession.

[3] Shows knowledge of the case.

The covenant not to use the premises for any purpose other than

that of a hairdresser's business is a restrictive covenant.[4] It is therefore binding upon anyone who occupies the premises, including a squatter, other than a *bona fide* purchaser for value of the lease without notice of it (*Re Nisbet and Potts' Contract* [1905] 1 Ch 391). Frieland Ltd may therefore seek an injunction against Minnie to restrain the

[5] Good point for extra marks. breach of the covenant. Under the **Senior Courts Act 1981**, the court may award Frieland Ltd equitable damages against Minnie either in lieu of, or in addition to, an injunction.[5]

Frieland Ltd may also forfeit the lease for non-payment of the rent, but the procedure here is entirely different from that for forfeiture for breach of any other covenant. It is not necessary to first serve a **s 146** notice, as it is for breach of any other covenant.

Forfeiture for non-payment of rent is governed by the **Common Law Procedure Act 1852**. Unless the lease provides otherwise (as most leases do), the landlord must first make a formal demand for rent. Such demand is, however, unnecessary if at least half a year's rent is in arrears, and there are insufficient goods on the premises available for distress to satisfy the amount due (**Common Law Procedure Act 1852, s 210** (High Court); **County Courts Act 1984, s 139** (county court)).

If Frieland Ltd brings its action in the High Court, and at least half a year's rent is in arrears, Kingpin has an automatic right to relief if, before the trial, he pays off all the arrears and costs. Failing this, if Frieland Ltd re-enters under an order of the court, Kingpin has six months after re-entry in which to pay off the arrears and costs and to apply for relief. The court has a discretion to grant relief, and it would not be granted if this will prejudice the position of a *bona fide* purchaser of the lease without notice of Kingpin's right to seek relief. After six months, any application for relief is barred (**Common Law Procedure Act 1852, s 210**).

If Frieland Ltd brings its action in a county court, the procedure, though differing in detail, is broadly similar in effect. If Kingpin fails to pay off the arrears and costs within the period specified by the court, he may apply for discretionary relief for six months after Frieland Ltd's re-entry (**County Courts Act 1984, s 138(9A)**). If Kingpin does not apply within this time, he is barred from all relief both in the county court and in the High Court (*Di Palma v Victoria Square Property Co Ltd* [1986] Ch 150).

If Frieland Ltd peaceably re-enters without a court order, the High Court has an inherent equitable jurisdiction to grant relief (*Howard v Fanshawe* [1895] 2 Ch 581). Although there is no statutory time limit, in practice the court will not be prepared to grant relief unless the application is made within six months (or a few days exceeding six months) of the re-entry (*Thatcher v C H Pearce & Sons (Contractors) Ltd* [1968] 1 WLR 748).

Under a lease made before 1996,[6] Frieland Ltd would also have been able to sue the original tenant Curlywig for any arrears of rent and for damages for breach of the user covenant, as the privity of covenant between them made an original tenant liable to a landlord on covenants in the lease throughout the term. The main purpose of the **LT(C)A 1995** was to limit an original tenant's liability once he had assigned the lease. Provided the assignment is a lawful assignment with the landlord's consent, then the original tenant will be released from his liability on covenants in the lease under privity of contract. However, the landlord may be able to require the assigning tenant to give an authorised guarantee agreement guaranteeing the performance of the covenants by his immediate assignee.

If, however, the assignment is unauthorised or occurs by operation of law (eg on the death of the tenant), then the assigning tenant's liability will continue until there is an authorised assignment. In the circumstances of this question, Frieland Ltd would appear to have been in breach of their obligation under **LTA 1988** to consent to a proposed assignment or to give reasons for their refusal to consent within a reasonable time, in spite of repeated requests from Curlywig. So, the assignment may be treated as authorised and Frieland Ltd would no longer have any right of action against Curlywig.

Frieland Ltd could only recover rent arrears from Curlywig if it had first served a notice under **s 17, LT(C)A 1995** within six months of Kingpin's default. A tenant against whom a landlord proceeds to recover rent on the default of an assignee (whether the lease was made before or after the Act came into force) has a right under **s 19** to require the landlord to grant him an overriding lease, effectively making him the immediate (intervening) landlord of the defaulting assignee.

(b) Susie's lease, being a yearly tenancy, is within the **Landlord and Tenant Act 1985, s 11(1)**, which applies to residential leases of less than seven years.[7] The section requires a landlord to maintain the structure and exterior of a dwelling-house, and installations for water, gas, electricity, sanitation, and space and water heating. The section was extended by the **Housing Act 1988, s 116** to include the common parts of a building of which the dwelling-house forms only part, and any installations used by all the tenants, such as a central heating boiler. The staircase would now be within this section, and Frieland Ltd would be liable to repair this.

Frieland Ltd would also be liable under the principle of *Liverpool City Council v Irwin* [1977] AC 239. In this case, the House of Lords said that there is an implied obligation on a landlord to maintain

---

[6] Another extra marks point—not a crisis if you don't get it, though.

[7] Sets out the issue.

essential access and services to premises without which the premises would be unusable.

In *Quick v Taff Ely BC* **[1986] QB 809**, however, condensation caused by metal window frames was held to be outside **s 11**, as it was due to a design fault rather than to any lack of repair.

A tenant's remedies for breach of a repairing covenant are damages,[8] which might include the cost of temporary accommodation elsewhere, storage of furniture if necessary while the repairs are carried out, and cleaning and redecoration afterwards (*McGreal v Wake* **(1984) 1 EG 42**). Susie may also carry out the repairs herself and set off the cost against future rents (*Lee-Parker v Izzet* **[1971] 1 WLR 1688**), although she should first give notice to Frieland Ltd that she intends to do this. She may also sue Frieland Ltd for specific performance of the covenant, which extends to common parts of the building (**Landlord and Tenant Act 1985, s 17**). Under the **Environmental Protection Act 1990**,[9] a tenant of premises which are in such a bad state of repair as to make them 'prejudicial to health' or a nuisance may apply to a magistrates' court for an order to repair the premises, but it has been said that only reasonable orders should be made (*Southwark LBC v Ince* **(1989) 21 HLR 504**, dealing with noise abatement), and in view of the decision in *Quick*, it is unlikely that Susie would obtain such an order with regard to the windows.

As regards the disturbance from the use of part of the shop premises as a massage parlour, Susie would have had an action for breach of the landlord's implied covenant for quiet enjoyment of the premises if the user were by the landlord himself or the breach of the covenant was due to the lawful user by another tenant of the landlord's. The covenant does not extend to the illegal user of another tenant, however (*Sanderson v Berwick-upon-Tweed Corporation* **(1884) 13 QBD 347**), and such an action will probably not be available. She would, of course, have an action for nuisance in tort against Kingpin and Minnie.

[8] Easily missed point—extra marks if you get it.

[9] Another extra marks point. In practice, this might be the best route for a tenant.

➕ LOOKING FOR EXTRA MARKS?

■ Note the comments above which contain tips for extra marks. In practice there would be a number of routes to find a solution for the tenant—this answer aims to cover them all.

TAKING THINGS FURTHER

- Bridge, S, 'Leases—Contract, Property and Status', in L Tee (ed), *Land Law: Issues, Debates and Policy* (Willan 2002), pp 98–131.
- Bright, S, 'Leases, Exclusive Possession and Estates' (2000) 116 *LQR* 7.
- Bright, S and Gilbert, G, *Landlord and Tenant Law: The Nature of Tenancies* (OUP 1995).
  All three cover the nature of tenancies.
- Law Commission, *Landlord and Tenant: Privity of Contract and Estate*, Law Com No 174, 1988.
  A Law Commission paper on privity of contract and estate, which is a useful read.

Online Resources

For extra essay and problem questions on this topic, as well as advice on revision and exam technique, please visit the online resources.

Easements
and Profits

10

ARE YOU READY?

In order to attempt the questions in this chapter, you will need to have covered the following topics:

- types of easement (eg express and implied easements);
- the nature of an easement;
- the creation of easements;
- other rights, such as profits à prendre.

KEY DEBATES

Debate: the question of whether the categories of easement can be extended is a popular debate and the quotation 'the categories of easements are not frozen' reflects that.

Modern usages which can have enormous economic value (such as car parking) may be highly relevant in the determination of this legal question (*Re Ellenborough Park* [1956] Ch 131). The Supreme Court decision in *Regency Villas Title Ltd v Diamond Resorts (Europe) Ltd and others* [2018] UKSC 57 has breathed new oxygen into the debate. Exercise is not just recreation; it is positively good for you. The debate now is: is this a new form of easement or a new kind of property right?

Q

'A tendency in the past to freeze the categories of easements has been overtaken by the defrosting operation in *Re Ellenborough Park* [1955] 3 All ER 667' (*per* Russell LJ, ***Dowty Boulton Paul Ltd v Wolverhampton Corp (No 2)*** [1973] 2 All ER 491).

Critically discuss the extent to which you agree that the categories of easements should alter in line with societal needs.

!

CAUTION!

■ It is important in an essay question of this type to show both an understanding of the law and also the ability to analyse and critique the law. Do you agree that the categories of easements should be flexible in accordance with the needs of society? Whether you agree or not, you need to argue your case. The expectation of tutors is not that you will just display knowledge but that you can show the dangers and problems inherent in a change in the law and how that might affect cases in the future. To do this requires you to use the knowledge you have acquired and argue about it—that is what makes an excellent lawyer and rates a decent mark for an essay. So, reference the case law and the secondary authority in a question of this sort. There are, as might be expected, some new decisions in this area of law, which give you a handy reference point for your arguments. Remember that you can agree or disagree with the proposition—but you cannot sit out of the argument.

O

DIAGRAM ANSWER PLAN

Discuss the following:
- ■ issue: the nature and type of easements;
- ■ rule: rules for the creation of easements;
- ■ application: *Ellenborough Park, Regency Villas Ltd v Diamond Resorts (Europe) Ltd* [2018].
- ■ Provide a conclusion: the categories are not (and should not be) closed.

A

SUGGESTED ANSWER

Introduction

The issue relates to the extent to which new types of easements can be created. There has in the past been a reluctance amongst the judiciary to be creative in this area, especially where the nature of the easement might be to impose a positive obligation on the servient tenement. *Re Ellenborough Park* **[1955] 3 All ER 667** was an exception to this principle to the extent that it permitted a new right to wander over a neighbouring garden. But recent case law such as that exemplified in *Regency Villas Title Ltd v Diamond Resorts (Europe) Ltd* **[2018] UKSC 57** and *Coventry (t/a RDC Promotions) v Lawrence* **[2014] UKSC 13** has indicated some further movement in this area. In *Regency Villas*, the very modern context of timeshare property arose, and it was held that the timeshare owners of a number of flats and houses had the right to use facilities in a neighbouring leisure centre and gardens. These rights included the use of a swimming pool, a golf course, squash courts, tennis courts, and a range of other facilities. This represents a small but significant advance on the position in *Re Ellenborough Park* in that it extended the ambit of an easement to an activity which previously had been excluded as mere recreational use. A *ius spatiandi* ('the privilege of wandering at will over all and every part of another's land') (*International Tea Stores Co v Hobbs* **[1903] 2 Ch 165** at 172; *Re Ellenborough Park* **[1956] Ch 131** at 136)[1] has not previously been regarded as constituting an easement under English law (*Mounsey v Ismay* **159 ER 621; (1865) 3 Hurl & C 486**). This judicial approach actually goes back to the Roman period, where it was stated that there was no general right to wander around on another's land.[2]

The Characteristics of an Easement

There are four characteristics of an easement: the need for a dominant and servient tenement; the requirement that the right must accommodate the dominant land; the need for two different owners; and, the right to be capable of being the subject matter of a grant. In *Re Ellenborough Park* **[1956] Ch 131**, the owners were granted the right to walk around neighbouring land—a right of perambulation (Evershed MR at 140). This goes against the old principle that a right to wander was not recognised. Nevertheless, Evershed MR granted the right to wander around other than over a defined path and to have a picnic, although the right would not extend to walking over the formal flower beds or picking the flowers. Smith considers this right to wander at will as a substitute for having a garden.[3]

Baker[4] argues that the *Ellenborough* right differed from a *ius spatiandi* as it was a right with an objective purpose, which therefore means that it can benefit the dominant tenement (one of the key characteristics of an easement). Baker also argues, however, that a *ius spatiandi* should be recognised as it is in other jurisdictions.[5] Clearly, this is correct as the limitation of the right does not accord with modern practice. As Malcolm argues, a right to wander in a neighbouring cemetery which bordered the gardens of neighbouring properties

---

[1] Check out these pinpoint references to see what the judges said on this point.

[2] For extra points, you could reference here *Re Ellenborough Park* **[1956] Ch 131** at 142, where Evershed MR refers to G R Y Radcliffe, *Real Property Law* (2nd edn, Oxford University Press 1938) as follows: 'This principle is well illustrated by the Roman jurist Paul when he says that you cannot have a servitude giving you the right to wander about and picnic in another's land.'

[3] R Smith, *Property Law* (9th edn, Pearson 2017), p 515.

[4] A Baker, 'Recreational Privileges as Easements: Law and Policy' [2012] *Conv* 37, 44.

[5] For extra marks, cite *Dukart v District of Surrey* (1978) 86 DLR 609.

could equally be an easement, albeit there was no defined path and no right of access to the cemetery throughout the night.[6] There is no reason why this right could not be exercised without contemplating damage to the graves, gardens, or whatever the constituent parts of the claimed area are.

[6] R Malcolm, 'Rights of Perambulation', *Estates Gazette*, 31 October 1992 (issue 9243), p 131.

The Changing Nature of Easements

It is clear that new easements can be acknowledged by the courts. As Russell LJ said in *Dowty Boulton Paul Ltd v Wolverhampton Corp (No 2)* [1973] 2 All ER 491: 'A tendency in the past to freeze the categories of easements has been overtaken by the defrosting operation in *Re Ellenborough Park* [1955] 3 All ER 667'. And Lord St Leonards in *Dyce v Lady James Hay* (1852) 15 D (HL) 14 at 15, argued too that the law can accommodate itself to the changing circumstances of society. Nevertheless, the decision in *Re Ellenborough Park* has been considered controversial and there tend to be few examples of new easements developing, as noted by Reno.[7] Further, Gray[8] has argued that the conservatism of English judges is because of the negative impact on the marketability of land that such restrictions might have. So, cases where an easement has been refused have included a right to a view, a right to privacy (*Browne v Flower* [1911] 1 Ch 219), and a right to protection from the weather (*Phipps v Pears* [1965] 1 QB 76).

[7] R Reno, 'The Enforcement of Equitable Servitudes in Land: Part I' (1942) 28 *Virginia L Rev* 958.

[8] K Gray and S Gray, *Elements of Land Law* (5th edn, OUP 2009), p 616.

Despite this historical negative approach to the creation of new types of easement, there has been a significant indication of change in some recent case law, such as an easement allowing noise from a racetrack (*Coventry (t/a RDC Promotions) v Lawrence* [2014] UKSC 13). In this case, the Supreme Court held that there can be an easement to create noise enforceable against the owners of neighbouring properties and such a right can arise through prescription. As Malcolm argued, the courts are likely to be more reluctant to extend the categories of easements where the claim is based on long user rather than express grant, but clearly, this obstacle was overcome in *Coventry v Lawrence*. Dixon noted that some of the problems about establishing a right to make a noise over a period of time include variation in intensity and duration.[9] However, it seems that as long as there is no vagueness in the claimed right, then it is more likely to succeed, and Lees suggests that any practical problems are likely to be resolved by the courts.[10]

[9] M Dixon, 'The Sound of Silence' [2014] 78 *Conv* 79.

[10] E Lees, '*Lawrence v Fen Tigers*: Where Now for Nuisance?' [2014] 78 *Conv* 449, 452.

Of much modern significance is the Supreme Court decision in *Regency Villas*, where the issue of whether new easements can be recognised to reflect the changing needs of society is again raised. Here the issue of the recognition of sporting and recreational rights—not previously recognised—arose. Have the needs of society changed to such an extent that it has now become necessary to recognise these as capable of constituting property rights rather than mere personal rights?

Recreational or Sporting Easements

In *Regency Villas*, Lord Briggs, giving the majority decision in the Supreme Court, considered this critical point and concluded, rejecting the view expressed in *Mounsey v Ismay* **(1865) 3 H & C 486**, that physical exercise is now generally considered to be either desirable or essential and something more than mere recreation or amusement. He stated (**para 81**):

Whatever may have been the attitude in the past to 'mere recreation or amusement', recreational and sporting activity of the type exemplified by the facilities at Broome Park is so clearly a beneficial part of modern life that the common law should support structures which promote and encourage it, rather than treat it as devoid of practical utility or benefit.

This change in approach rests entirely on what was perceived as the need to reflect changes in society. This was not prevented by a right of the servient owner to charge or the possibility of the dominant owners bringing their own facilities to enable sport to be pursued. Even where the facilities such as the swimming pool and the golf course were more complex, this would not prevent their use being upheld as an easement—as McLeod argues, this is potentially akin to a new property right.[11]

[11] G McLeod, 'The Traditional Concept Hits the Bunker: Easements after Regency Villas Title Ltd v Diamond Resorts (Europe) Ltd' (2019) *Conv* 3, 250–73. See also R Malcolm, 'Rights of Perambulation', *Mainly for Students*, Estates Gazette, 31 October 1992 (issue 9243), p 131.

Conclusion

Provided that the general characteristics of an easement are met (ie it is clear, certain, and not too wide; it does not amount to a right of joint occupation or effectively oust the servient owner; and, it offers utility or benefit to the dominant tenement), then there should be no barrier to the extension of easements to meet the changing needs of society.

There is one difficulty, in addition to the problems about the imposition of positive obligations on servient owners which might not have been anticipated or agreed, which is that such burdens may tend to make land less marketable. The spurious easement of fencing (*Crow v Wood* [1971] **1 QB 77** and *Churston Golf Club v Haddock* [2019] EWCA Civ 544) supports that proposition. But overriding that, it must be right that the law can adapt to reflect the needs and practices of people and the way in which they live. This principle must be more important than the potential ability to sell or otherwise market land, which simply puts profits in the hands of one owner. Where a group of people or even just a single neighbour has an enjoyment of a right over a period of time such as for recreational purposes, then the modern approach should be to protect that activity as a proprietary right, regardless of the impact it might have on the potential for profit. The recreational or other right may act as a suppressant on the profitability of the land, but the converse is also true. Such a right itself can add value to the dominant land, as well as benefiting the human beneficiaries of that right in terms of the quality of their lives where it benefits or adds to the utility of their property.

⊕ **LOOKING FOR EXTRA MARKS**

There are a number of secondary sources on this topic, which is unsurprising given the transformational nature of the decision in **Regency Villas**. Consider, for example, the argument that this opens a Pandora's Box (C Bevan, 'Opening Pandora's Box? Recreation Pure and Simple: Easements in the Supreme Court Regency Villas Title Ltd v Diamond Resorts (Europe) Ltd [2018] UKSC 57; [2018] 3 WLR 1603' (2019) 1 *Conv* 55–70). There is also an interesting article by Bray on the Court of Appeal decision (J Bray, 'More Than Just a Walk in the Park: A New View on Recreational Easements' (2017) 6 *Conv* 418–39). The suggested answer touches on a number of these arguments, but for extra marks it could be further expanded. The conclusion could also be challenged in a dialectical manner with arguments given for both sides, unlike the suggested answer, which comes down firmly on one side. Further discussion of the dissenting opinion of Lord Carnwath (the one judge who dissented in **Regency Villas**) would also carry extra marks. You might also venture, if especially adventurous, into a discussion of the Court of Appeal decision on the spurious easement of fencing in **Churston Golf Club v Haddock** (briefly mentioned in the answer) as an example of a property right imposing a positive obligation, and compare it with the much more dramatic example of this new type of easement in **Regency Villas**.

Q **QUESTION** | **2**

In 2009, Miranda was the owner of a plot of freehold land. At one end of the plot, and adjoining the main road, stood a house and garden. In the middle of the plot there were tennis courts and a shed, and beyond that was a muddy wood which adjoined a lane. Miranda and her tennis partners often searched the wood for their lost balls.

In 2010, Miranda contracted to sell the house and garden to Silvia and permitted Silvia to go into immediate possession. Miranda (who had herself never used the shed) also allowed Silvia to store her diesel lawnmower in the shed. The subsequent conveyance to Silvia contained a reservation of a right of way from the main road across the garden to the tennis courts.

In 2011, Miranda conveyed the middle part of the plot (containing the tennis courts and the shed) to Ophelia, who began hiring out the tennis courts for club matches. Over the years, the frequency of such hirings has increased steadily. Miranda is concerned that the increased foraging for lost balls in the wood is damaging the rare plant species which grow there. Furthermore, whilst in the past visitors to the tennis courts have crossed the garden on foot, they have recently started to traverse it in minibuses and coaches. When Silvia complained to Ophelia last week, Ophelia demanded that Silvia remove her lawnmower from the shed.

Advise Miranda and Silvia.

DIAGRAM ANSWER PLAN

Identify the issues	■ The legal issues are (a) requirements for an easement; (b) the nature of an easement; (c) implied easement, reservation of easement, and intensification of use.

Relevant law	(a) *Wheeldon v Burrows* (1879); *Re Ellenborough Park* [1956]; and **Law of Property Act 1925 (LPA 1925), s 62**.
	(b) *Wright v Macadam* [1949]; *Copeland v Greenhalf* [1952]; and *Grigsby v Melville* [1972].
	(c) **LPA 1925, s 62** (*Wheeldon v Burrows* (1879); *Goldberg v Edwards* [1950]; and *Sovmots v Secretary of State* [1979]).

Apply the law	Discuss the following:
	(a) **Is there an easement to forage for lost balls?**
	■ Requirements for easement:
	● definite in scope (*Re Ellenborough Park*; *Mulvaney v Jackson* [2002])?
	■ Means of acquisition:
	● by implication under *Wheeldon v Burrows*?
	● by implication under **LPA, s 62**?
	● (note the effect of *Wood v Waddington* [2015] on prior diversity of occupation).
	(b) **Easement for storage of the lawnmower**
	■ Is this too extensive (*Wright v Macadam*; *Copeland v Greenhalf* [1952]; *Grigsby v Melville*)?
	■ Means of acquisition:
	● **LPA 1925, s. 62** (*Sovmots v Secretary of State*; *Goldberg v Edwards*);
	● implied easement under *Wheeldon v Burrows*?
	(c) **Right of way**
	■ Takes the benefit of right of way (**LPA 1925, s 62**).
	■ Scope of reservation:
	● construction against purchaser (**LPA 1925, s 65**) (*St Edmundsbury and Ipswich Diocesan Board v Clark* [1975]);
	● evidence from the physical nature of access (*White v Richards* (1998));
	■ Increase in intensity:
	● scope of the express easement is determined at the time of grant (*Jelbert v Davis* [1968]);
	● but easement is not lost through the excessive user (*Graham v Philcox* [1984]; *Wood v Warrington*).

Conclude	■ Advise Miranda and Silvia.

CAUTION!

- The problem involves separate aspects of the law of easements: whether certain rights can exist as easements; implied easements; whether the burden of an easement affects a person who takes a conveyance of the burdened land; and increase in intensity of user. The suggested answer tackles these matters as follows:

  - whether there can exist an easement to forage for balls; and, if so, whether, and by what means, such an easement was created;

  - whether there can exist an easement to store a lawnmower in a shed; and, if so, whether, and by what means, such an easement was created; and

  - the scope of an easement by reservation and increase in the intensity of its user.

- There have been some cases on the extent of easements. This has to be considered in relation to the way in which the easement is claimed, that is, by express or implied grant.

(A) SUGGESTED ANSWER

Miranda, as the owner of the wood, will be able to prevent the foraging for balls unless Ophelia and her visitors have a legal right to forage. As Miranda does not appear to have given a contractual licence for such purpose, such right, if one it be, can exist only as an easement. To be valid,[1] an easement must accommodate the dominant tenement; ie it must benefit it as a piece of land. The right claimed must not be merely a personal benefit to the owner; *Hill v Tupper* (1863) 2 H & C 121. As the benefited land comprises tennis courts, this will probably be satisfied. More difficult to surmount, however, is the requirement that the right claimed be of definite scope,[2] which thus excludes a mere right to wander at will over another's land (*ius spatiandi*). In *Re Ellenborough Park* [1956] Ch 131, the right to walk at will in a garden qualified as an easement because there were defined pathways: the visitors could not walk over the flowerbeds. In *Mulvaney v Jackson* [2002] EWCA Civ 1078, the right to use a backyard as a communal garden for recreational and amenity purposes was similarly confirmed, as was the right to use a swimming pool in *Regency Villas Title Ltd v Diamond Resorts (Europe) Ltd* [2017] EWCA Civ 238. A right to forage for lost balls may pose greater difficulties because there is no apparent restriction on the right claimed (since the balls could land anywhere). It is therefore unlikely that such a right could exist as an easement. If this is so, Miranda can sue the foragers in trespass, and she may be able to obtain injunctive relief to prevent future foraging.

[1] Definition of easement.

[2] Nature of easement.

If, however, such a right is held capable of existing as an easement,[3] it is necessary to determine if such easement was acquired in any of the ways recognised by the law. It might have been created impliedly. When Miranda owned the tennis courts, her foraging for lost balls may be considered to be the exercise of a quasi-easement over the wood for the benefit of the tennis courts. Unless Miranda excluded implied easements from the conveyance to Ophelia, the grant would have been effective to vest in Ophelia all those quasi-easements over the retained land which are continuous and apparent, necessary to the reasonable enjoyment of the land granted, and which were, at the time of the grant, used by the grantor for the benefit of the part granted (*Wheeldon v Burrows* (1879) 12 ChD 31; *Wood v Waddington* [2015] EWCA Civ 538). These are cumulative, not alternative, requirements: *Wheeler v J J Saunders Ltd* [1996] Ch 19 (CA). 'Continuous' means a right which does not require personal activity for its enjoyment. Strictly, this excluded a right of way, but such a right has been held to pass under this doctrine (*Borman v Griffith* [1930] 1 Ch 493). 'Apparent' means a right which is discoverable by inspection of the land. Since the wood is muddy, there may be evidence of the foragers' footprints, which would meet this requirement. The quasi-easement could pass to Ophelia under the **Law of Property Act (LPA) 1925, s 62**, despite the fact that, when Miranda herself foraged, she did so as owner of the wood, not through the exercise of a 'liberty' or 'privilege' (as established in *Long v Gowlett* [1923] 2 Ch 177). Prior diversity of occupation was not considered necessary in *Wood v Waddington* [2015] EWCA Civ 538.

Ophelia will not be able to prevent Silvia from continuing to store her lawnmower in the shed if Silvia has an easement to do so. The right

claimed as an easement[4] must not be so extensive as to amount to possession of any part of the servient tenement (*Copeland v Greenhalf* [1952] Ch 488). In *Grigsby v Melville* [1972] 1 WLR 1355 (affirmed [1974] 1 WLR 80), a claim to store bottles in a cellar failed because, on the facts, it amounted to a claim to exclusive user. If the owner is excluded from possession for short periods only, however, a right can be an easement (*Miller v Emcer Products Ltd* [1956] Ch 304—use of a lavatory; *London & Blenheim Estates Ltd v Ladbroke Retail Parks Ltd* [1994] 1 WLR 31—limited right to park a car). Similarly, provided it is limited in extent, a right of storage can also qualify (*Wright v Macadam* [1949] 2 KB 744—storage of coal in a shed). Whether Silvia's claim to store her lawnmower can comprise an easement will therefore depend upon the comparative sizes of the mower and the shed, and the manner of storage. If the mower fills the shed or otherwise prevents reasonable user by Ophelia, the claim will probably fail. If it succeeds, it will include the ancillary right of way across Ophelia's land in order to fetch and return the mower.

[5] Here comes the point about acquisition of the easement.

Even if the storage of the mower can comprise an easement, Silvia must still establish that such an easement was acquired.[5] When she went into possession of the house and garden between contract and completion, she had merely a licence from Miranda to use the shed for storing the mower, and such licence could have been withdrawn at any time. However, unless it provided otherwise, the conveyance would have passed to Silvia, as legal easements, all 'liberties' and 'privileges' at the time of the conveyance enjoyed with the land (**LPA 1925, s 62**). In *Wood v Waddington* **[2015] EWCA Civ 538**, it was said that diversity of occupation was not necessary where the exercise of the right claimed was continuous and apparent. The permission to store could thus be transformed, on the conveyance, into a legal easement (cf *Goldberg v Edwards* **[1950] Ch 247**).

[6] Deal here with the next method of acquiring the easement.

An alternative claim[6] to an easement of storage based on the doctrine of *Wheeldon v Burrows* is less likely to succeed. Although Miranda may be considered, before completion, to be exercising, through Silvia, a quasi-easement, the requirement that the right claimed be necessary for the reasonable enjoyment of the dominant tenement is unlikely to be satisfied: there are many other places where the mower could be stored, and Miranda herself never found it necessary to use the shed for this purpose.

[7] Deal now with how it binds successors in title.

[8] First unregistered title.

[9] Then registered title.

The burden[7] of any easement of storage will bind Ophelia, the present owner of the servient tenement: in land with unregistered title[8] because it is a legal interest; in land with registered title[9] because it is an overriding interest under the **Land Registration Act (LRA) 2002**. If Ophelia transfers her plot in the future, the easement will bind a purchaser for value as an overriding interest only if one of three criteria is satisfied: namely, if the purchaser has actual knowledge at the time of the disposition; if the easement would at that time have been obvious on a reasonably careful inspection of the land; or if it can be proved that the easement was exercised within the period of one year before the disposition was made: **LRA 2002, Schedule 3, para 3**.

[10] Next deal with the right of way and **s 62**.

[11] This is an express reservation—an important point.

[12] An extra point here—you can survive without it.

[13] Another extra point.

By virtue of **LPA 1925, s 62**,[10] Ophelia will take the benefit of the right of way. Miranda expressly reserved[11] a right of way over Silvia's garden. Therefore, whether Silvia can prevent large numbers of Ophelia's guests crossing her garden in motor vehicles depends upon the scope of such reservation. If the reservation does not specify whether the right is one to cross on foot only, or by some other means, it will be construed against the grantor. Before 1926, a reservation took effect by way of a re-grant and was thus construed against the purchaser.[12] After 1925, a reservation operates without any re-grant (**LPA 1925, s 65**). Nevertheless, there are *dicta* of the Court of Appeal[13] to the effect that a post-1925 reservation is also to be construed against the purchaser (*St Edmundsbury and Ipswich Diocesan Board v Clark (No. 2)* **[1975] 1 WLR 468**). Evidence relating to the physical nature of the access may give some indication of the easement's scope. In **White v Richards (1998) 68 P & CR 105**, the grant of the use of an unmade-up track 8 feet 10 inches wide 'with or without motor vehicles' was held not to extend to up to fourteen heavy lorries a day, and the Court of Appeal said that the extent of the user should be determined in the light of the physical characteristics of the track at the time of the grant. In the absence of any evidence, however, the reservation will be construed in favour of Ophelia; ie to include the use of motor vehicles.

Although there does not appear to have been any change in user of the right of way, it seems that there has been increased intensity of user.[14] In contrast to an easement acquired prescriptively (**British Railways Board v Glass [1965] 1 Ch 538**), the scope of an express easement is determined at the time of the grant (**Jelbert v Davis [1968] 1 WLR 589**). Silvia can therefore restrain any increase in intensity beyond what could have been contemplated at the time. Excessive user does not itself, however, cause the easement to be lost (**Graham v Philcox [1984] 1 QB 747**).

[14] This is the intensification-of-use point.

✚ LOOKING FOR EXTRA MARKS?

■ There are some flagged points in the suggested answer which are worth extra points. For instance, you are not told whether the title is registered or unregistered—so tackle both. Points about the pre-1925 situation would send your marks sky-high.

Ⓠ QUESTION 3

In 1967 Joe, the fee simple owner of Greenacre, agreed with one of his neighbours, Celia, that she might park her car from time to time on a corner of one of his fields near to her house.

In 1974, Joe erected a large greenhouse on the boundary of one of his fields and started to grow in it tomatoes for sale. In connection with this, and at about the same time, he put up a sign on the wall of a neighbouring cottage, which belonged to Harry, advertising the sale of fresh eggs and produce. Also in 1974, Joe installed a water butt to catch the rain from the greenhouse roof. When Joe was not about, Celia used to cross on to Joe's land to draw water from the butt in order to wash her car when it was parked on her own land.

In 1977, Harry leased his cottage to Tommy for a term of years which expired nine months ago. After the termination of this lease, Harry conveyed his cottage to William, who has now obtained planning permission to erect a house that, when built, will block direct sunlight to Joe's greenhouse. William is also objecting to the presence of Joe's sign on his cottage wall.

Celia has now concreted over the area of the field where she parks her car. Joe wishes to prevent any further user of this area for parking, and to stop Celia drawing water from his butt.

Advise Joe.

DIAGRAM ANSWER PLAN

Identify the issues	■ The legal issues are the nature of an easement and prescription.
Relevant law	■ This is *Moody v Steggles* (1879); *Re Ellenborough Park* [1956]; *Newman v Jones* (1982); *London & Blenheim Estates Ltd v Ladbroke Retail Parks Ltd* [1994]; and the **Prescription Act 1832**;.
Apply the law	Discuss the following: (a) **Is there an easement of parking?** ■ Criteria for easement (*Re Ellenborough Park*): ● right to park anywhere in the field could be an easement (*Newman v Jones*); ● but not if it is a particular space (exclusive possession) (*London & Blenheim Estates Ltd v Ladbroke Retail Parks Ltd*). ■ Creation? ● There is no prescription at common law (not enjoyed since 1189); ● **Prescription Act 1832, s 2** (forty years' actual user): – no written consent or agreement; – *nec vi, nec clam*; – 'next before action'. ● Lost modern grant? – twenty years' enjoyment *nec vi, nec clam*, and *nec precario*. (b) **Is there a right to draw water from the butt for the washing of the car?** ■ This is not a profit à prendre (not soil or produce thereof) (*Alfred F Beckett Ltd v Lyons* [1967]). ■ Is there an easement? ● does it accommodate a dominant tenement (*Re Ellenborough Park*)? ● or mere personal benefit to C (*Hill v Tupper* (1863))? ● even if it qualifies, secrecy precludes the claim based on prescription. (c) **Is there an easement of light to the greenhouse?** ■ What are the criteria for easement? ● An especially high degree of light can qualify (*Allen v Greenwood* [1980]). ■ Creation? ● **Prescription Act 1832, s 3** (twenty years' uninterrupted actual enjoyment): – no written consent or agreement; – letting to T does not stop the period running (*Simper v Foley* (1862)). (d) **Is there an easement for the sign?** ■ What are the criteria for easement? ● Does it accommodate a dominant tenement (*Moody v Steggles* (1879))? ■ Creation? ■ **Prescription Act 1832, s 2**: ● the twenty-year period begins against the fee simple owner, H; ● so can include the period when the land was leased to T (*Pugh v Savage* [1970]).
Conclude	■ Advise Joe.

> ❗ **CAUTION!**

- This question requires you to have a good knowledge of the acquisition of easements by long user, or (as it is technically called) prescription.

- You need to grasp how the three methods of prescription relate to each other to get to grips with this question.

> Ⓐ **SUGGESTED ANSWER**

[1] This is the point about the nature of an easement and whether new categories can emerge.

Joe will be unable to prevent Celia from parking her car in the corner of his field if she has acquired an easement to do so. The first issue,[1] whether a right to park a car in a specified parking bay can be an easement, remains a matter of some dispute. In the Scottish case of *Moncrieff v Jamieson* **[2008] 1 P & CR 21 (HL)**, Lord Scott thought that it could, because he considered the correct test to be whether the servient owner retains possession and control. He pointed out that the servient owner would still be able to build above or below a designated parking space, or place advertising hoardings on the walls. Lord Neuberger in the same case, however, was more cautious, and was not prepared to abandon the test established in *Copeland v Greenhalf* **[1952] Ch 488**. These were the only two members of their Lordships' House to comment on the English law on this point, and it therefore seems that the test remains that was laid down in *Copeland v Greenhalf*. This being so, there can be no easement of parking in a specified parking bay, since this would amount to a claim to exclusive possession and would thus deprive the servient owner of the reasonable use of that part of his land (*London & Blenheim Estates Ltd v Ladbrooke Retail Parks Ltd* **[1994] 1 WLR 31**). For the same reason, a right effectively to fill the parking area with vehicles cannot exist as an easement (*Batchelor v Marlow* **[2003] 1 WLR 764**; *Central Midlands Estates Ltd v Leicester Dyers Ltd* **[2003] 2 P & CR DG1**). However, a right to park a car anywhere within a larger area (*Newman v Jones*, **unreported, 22 March 1982**) or within any one of several parking bays (*Hair v Gilman* **(2000) 80 P & CR 108, CA**) is capable of being an easement and of accommodating the dominant tenement (*Re Ellenborough Park* **[1956] Ch 131**). More evidence is therefore needed in the problem to ascertain whether Celia's claim is one merely to park anywhere within a larger defined area in a corner of Joe's field, or in a particular space: the concreting suggests the latter. In any event, a mandatory injunction will be available to compel Celia to remove the concreting.

If Celia's right was to park anywhere within a defined area and was thus considered capable of existing as an easement, she would still

[2] Next point on the creation of easement.

need to establish that such an easement had been created.[2] As there

[3] Don't waste time considering other methods which cannot apply—go straight for the key issue.

[4] Get rid of this method—it can't apply for the reason given.

[5] First method, which may work.

[6] Next method.

[7] Extra marks for this one.

[8] Don't forget the personal benefit point—a no-no for an easement.

was no express grant, any such right could arise only[3] by prescription or by presumed grant. Like all the other possible easements in the problem, it could not arise by prescription at common law,[4] since it is easy to establish that it could not have been enjoyed since 1189 (*Bury v Pope* (1588) Cro Eliz 118).

Under the **Prescription Act 1832, s 2,**[5] where the claim to an easement (other than an easement of light) has been actually enjoyed without interruption for forty years, the right is deemed absolute and indefeasible unless it was enjoyed by written consent or agreement. The user must still, however, have been *nec vi* (not by force) and *nec clam* (nor by stealth) (*Gardner v Hodgson's Kingston Brewery Co Ltd* [1903] AC 229; *Smith v Brudenell-Bruce* [2002] 2 P & CR 4), which appears to have been the case here. Under general principles, even oral permission defeats a claim to an easement. The effect of **s 2** is that any permission given *during* the running of the forty-year period defeats the claim. If, however, permission is given only *before* that period, it will defeat the claim if it is written, but not if it is merely oral: *Gardner v Hodgson's Kingston Brewery Co Ltd*. There is no evidence of such consent here.

The user that Celia must establish is user 'next before action'. Thus, any rights she has under the statute are inchoate until recognised in court proceedings. If, therefore, Joe interrupts the user, and Celia acquiesces in it for a period of at least one year, Celia's inchoate rights will be lost (**Prescription Act 1832, s 4**).

If Joe were able so to destroy a claim under the statute, Celia might, as a last expedient, claim a presumed easement of parking under the doctrine of lost modern grant.[6] Twenty years' enjoyment *nec vi, nec clam, nec precario* (not by force, nor by stealth, nor by permission), which does not need to be next before action, raises a presumption that in the past there was a grant (since lost) (*Bryant v Foot* (1867) LR 2 QB 161). Even evidence that no such grant was made is ineffective to rebut the presumption (*Tehidy Minerals Ltd v Norman* [1971] 2 QB 528). In practice, Celia would probably claim an easement under both the **Prescription Act 1832** and the doctrine of lost modern grant.

Although a right to remove something from the land of another must generally fall within the category of profits à prendre, a right to draw water cannot be a profit because,[7] even though water collected in a butt is capable of ownership, water is not part of the soil or the produce of the soil (*Alfred F Beckett Ltd v Lyons* [1967] Ch 449). If the claim is therefore to rank as an incorporeal hereditament, it must be capable of comprising an easement. A right to take water to wash one's car would not appear to satisfy the requirements of *Re Ellenborough Park* [1956] Ch 131, since it seems not to accommodate the alleged dominant tenement, but merely to be a personal benefit[8] to the owner of the car (cf *Hill v Tupper* (1863) 2 H & C 121). In any event, Celia's apparent

[9] Another negative for Celia.

secrecy[9] (*clam*) in drawing the water will preclude her from claiming that any such alleged easement was acquired by prescription.

[10] And the next issue.

Joe[10] will be able to prevent the construction of the house in the way proposed if he can establish an easement of light to his greenhouse. A right to receive an especially high degree of light for growing plants in a greenhouse was held to comprise an easement in *Allen v Greenwood* **[1980] Ch 119**. Under the **Prescription Act 1832, s 3**, an easement of light can be acquired by twenty years' uninterrupted actual enjoyment (next before action), unless with written consent or agreement. In this instance, therefore, the user does not have to be as of right. For the same reason, the general requirement that acquisition must be by a fee simple owner against a fee simple owner does not apply to the acquisition of an easement of light under the statute. Thus, the time during which Harry's cottage is let to Tommy does not stop the period of twenty years from running (*Simper v Foley* **(1862) 2 J & H 555**). It would therefore appear that Joe could, by action, both establish the acquisition of an easement of light and also obtain an injunction to prevent William's building on his land so as to interfere with such easement.

[11] And the next one.

A right to have a signboard [11] affixed to the wall of another's house is capable of being an easement (*Moody v Steggles* **(1879) 12 ChD 261** (sign advertising a public house)). Although Joe's sign relates to his business, it will probably be held (as in *Moody v Steggles*) to accommodate the dominant tenement, in this case, Greenacre. Twenty years ago, Harry's cottage had been leased to Tommy. This will not, however, prevent the period of twenty years next before action required under the **Prescription Act 1832, s 2** from running, since Joe's sign had been affixed at a time when the fee simple owner (Harry) was in possession (*Pugh v Savage* **[1970] 2 QB 373**).

Joe may alternatively plead that he has acquired either or both the easement of light and the easement relating to his sign under the doctrine of lost modern grant. This is possible, since the period of twenty years' user that gives rise to the presumption may include a period during which the servient land was tenanted where (as here) there was initial user against a fee simple owner (*Pugh v Savage*).

+ LOOKING FOR EXTRA MARKS?

■ The profit à prendre point is one that many less well-prepared students may miss, so if you cover that one, then you are likely to be rewarded with extra marks. There is also a lot of case law, so capturing it all is going to be rewarded.

Q

In 2008, Clement and Bailey were the adjoining freehold owners of Nos 3 and 5 Shoreditch Lane, respectively. Clement had difficulty parking his car in the garage of No 3 without using the driveway of No 5. Following discussion between them, Clement and Bailey in November that year entered into a written contract (signed by each of them) whereby, in consideration of Clement's paying Bailey the sum of £5,000, Bailey agreed that Clement and his successors in title were to have a right in perpetuity to use the driveway of No 5 for the purpose of parking a motor vehicle in the garage of No 3.

Three months ago, Bailey sold and conveyed the freehold title of No 5 (which was at the time unregistered) to Stepney, who knew nothing of the agreement between Clement and Bailey. Stepney has now objected to Clement's use of the driveway of No 5.

(a) **Advise Clement.**

(b) **To what extent would your advice differ if the title to No 5 had been registered when Bailey had acquired it?**

(c) **To what extent would your advice in (a) and (b) differ if the agreement of 2008 had been oral only?**

!

CAUTION!

■ Easements can be either legal or equitable and students often fall into the trap of supposing an easement is equitable. Let's get this one nailed: equitable easements arise in somewhat narrow circumstances only. Part (a) of the question deals with an equitable easement arising from a valid contract. Part (b) deals with the position in registered land, where it is clear that the equitable easement needs to be protected by entry of a notice on the charges register of the burdened title. Part (c) raises the difficult issue of proprietary estoppel, and whether such a right is binding on a third-party purchaser.

◎ DIAGRAM ANSWER PLAN

Identify the issues	■ The legal issue is equitable easement in registered and unregistered title.
Relevant law	■ This is *Walsh v Lonsdale* (1882); the **Law of Property (Miscellaneous Provisions) Act 1989**; and the **Land Registration Act (LRA) 2002**.

Apply the law	Discuss the following:
	(a) **Unregistered title**
	    ■ Is this an equitable easement?
	        ● Is it a valid contract for easement (**Law of Property (Miscellaneous Provisions) Act (LP(MP)A) 1989, s 2**)?
	        ● If so, it creates equitable easement: *Walsh v Lonsdale*.
	    ■ Is it binding on the third party (S)?
	        ● It depends on registration as Class D(iii) land charge.
	(b) **Registered title**
	    ■ Equitable easement was created after **LRA 2002** came into force.
	    ■ It was binding on S if protected by notice at the time of transfer to S.
	    ■ You cannot argue overriding interest under **Schedule 3, para 2** (no actual occupation).
	(c) **Agreement is oral only**
	    ■ There is no valid contract to create an equitable easement (**LP(MP)A 1989, s 2**).
	    ■ But C might acquire rights by proprietary estoppel (on payment of the £5,000).
	    ■ If it is an unregistered title, it seems estoppel is proprietary interest, and whether it binds S depends on equitable doctrine of notice (*Ives v High* [1967]).
	    ■ If a registered title, estoppel binds S only if entered as a notice on the charges register (you cannot argue overriding interest under **Schedule 3, para 2**, since there is no actual occupation).

Conclude	■ Advise Clement.

[1] It is reasonable to make this assumption in this way.

[2] One of the ways in which an equitable easement arises.

(a) Assuming that the written agreement[1] satisfies the requirements of the **LP(MP)A 1989, s 2**, it is a valid contract to create a legal easement. A valid contract to grant a legal easement itself creates an equitable easement[2] according to the maxim that equity looks upon as done that which ought to be done (cf *McManus v Cooke* **(1887) 35 ChD 681** and the principle of *Walsh v Lonsdale* **(1882) 21 ChD 9**). It would therefore seem that, from the agreement made in 2007, Clement acquired an equitable easement to use the driveway for the purpose of parking his car in his own garage.

[3] Nice clear statement of the problem.

The difficulty for Clement, however, is that the servient land has since been conveyed to a third party, Stepney. The issue is therefore whether Clement's equitable easement is binding on Stepney.[3] If it is, Clement will be able, if necessary, to obtain an injunction to prevent Stepney from interfering with the exercise of such right.

As the title to No 5 was unregistered when it was conveyed to Stepney, it is important to ascertain whether the equitable easement was protected by registration against the name of Bailey (the estate owner at the time the easement was created) as a Class D(iii) land charge under the **Land Charges Act 1972 (LCA 1972), s 2(5)**, before the completion of Stepney's purchase. If it was so protected,[4] the easement is binding on Stepney. If it was not, it is void against Stepney if he was a purchaser of the legal estate for money or money's worth (**s 4(6)**).

[4] Deal with both possibilities.

(b) If the title to No 5 had already been registered when Bailey acquired it, then whether the easement is binding upon Stepney depends upon the principles of registered land. As the equitable easement was created after **LRA 2002** came into force (13 October 2003), it cannot be an overriding interest in its own right. Under that Act, the only easements created on or after that date that are capable of being overriding in their own right are legal easements, and even these can be overriding only in limited circumstances: **LRA 2002, Schedule 3, para 3**. It would be difficult to argue that Clement had an overriding interest for the purposes of **Schedule 3, para 2** of that Act, since his transient use of the driveway of No 5 could hardly amount to actual occupation. The equitable easement will be binding on Stepney, therefore, only if it was already protected by the entry of a notice on the charges register of No 5.

[5] Next issue.

(c) If the agreement entered into in 2008 had been oral,[5] it would not have satisfied the requirements for a valid contract for the creation of an interest in land under the **Law of Property (Miscellaneous Provisions) Act 1989, s 2**. This section requires (*inter alia*) a contract for the sale or other disposition of an interest in land to be made in writing incorporating all the terms. The oral agreement would not therefore have created an equitable easement. However, as Clement paid Bailey £5,000 under the void contract, the requirements for proprietary estoppel appear to be satisfied, in that Clement acted to his detriment in reliance upon Bailey's representation that Clement would have a right to use the driveway of No 5 in perpetuity. As **s 2(5)** of the **1989 Act** expressly states that the section does not apply to constructive trusts, but does not make any saving for estoppel, the estoppel may arise under a constructive trust:[6] *Yaxley v Gotts* **[2000] Ch 162 (CA)**.

[6] This is quite a tricky point—if you can work through it you will get extra marks.

If the title to No 5 had been unregistered when acquired by Bailey, there is some uncertainty whether an estoppel, being inchoate in nature, is capable of binding a third-party purchaser for value. In *E R Ives Investment Ltd v High* **[1967] 2 QB 379**, the Court of Appeal considered that rights arising by proprietary estoppel are outside the machinery of what is now **LCA 1972** and so bind a purchaser according to the equitable doctrine of notice. In the view of Lord Denning MR in that case, such a right arising by proprietary estoppel is not an 'equitable easement' within Class D(iii), since such a right was not one capable of being conveyed or created at law before 1926.

[7] This section is worth extra marks—it is a nice discussion of the merits.

Ives v High was controversial at the time,[7] since it seemed to be giving proprietary effect to a licence, and an argument was advanced that the decision rested more soundly on the alternative basis on which the Court of Appeal relied, namely the doctrine of mutual benefits and burdens: F R Crane, 'Estoppel Interests in Land' (1967) 31 *Conv* (NS) 332. Furthermore, in *United Bank of Kuwait plc v Sahib* **[1997] Ch 107**, Peter Gibson LJ explained *Ives v High* as turning on the joint application of the principles of mutual benefits and burdens and proprietary estoppel. His Lordship did not, however, refer to the slightly earlier decision of *Lloyds Bank plc v Carrick* **[1996] 4 All ER 630, 642**, where Morritt LJ, whilst not expressing a concluded view, thought that, in the light of *Ives v High*, it would be difficult to maintain that an equity by estoppel cannot bind a successor in title with notice.

On the authority, therefore, of *Ives v High*, the estoppel would be binding on Stepney unless he could establish the defence of *bona fide* purchaser for value of the legal estate without notice of the estoppel. The positioning of Clement's garage might put Stepney on notice that Clement has some rights to use No 5 as an access when parking his car, but this is a matter of evidence. Ironically, therefore, Clement might have rights binding on Stepney (through the equitable doctrine of notice) if the agreement is void for non-compliance with **s 2** of the **1989 Act**.

The uncertainty that exists in unregistered titles as to the proprietary status of an equity by estoppel before the court has awarded a remedy, no longer arises in registered titles, as the matter has been dealt with expressly in **LRA 2002**. Thus, if the title to No 5 had already been registered when acquired by Bailey, the equity by estoppel would have created a proprietary interest capable of binding successors in title from the time the equity arose: **LRA 2002, s 116**. The time the equity arose would have been the date Clement paid the £5,000. The equity could (and should) then have been protected by a notice in the charges register of Bailey's title. It is in the nature of informal agreements of this kind, however, that they tend not to be so protected. If such agreement was not so protected, it will not bind Stepney, as rights by estoppel are not overriding interests in their own right. It can also hardly be argued that Clement's equity by estoppel is protected as an overriding interest under **Schedule 3, para 2** of the **2002 Act**, since (as stated in the answer to part (b) mentioned earlier), Clement can scarcely be considered to be in actual occupation of that part of the drive of No 5 that he used in order to park on No 3.

LOOKING FOR EXTRA MARKS?

- Dealing with the merits of registered title in this context will earn extra marks. The point about estoppel arising is a tricky one, so if you can work your way through that (without losing your head) you will be rewarded. Likewise, the point about *Ives v High*. The discussion on this in the suggested answer is probably beyond the routine suggested answer, so if you manage to nail it then, again, extra marks must surely flow your way.

- Cover the options (if written/if oral) and so on.

TAKING THINGS FURTHER

- Law Commission, *Making Law Work: Easements, Covenants, and Profits à Prendre* (Law Com No 327, 2011), at para 3.123.

  Having three methods of prescription is unduly complex, and the doctrine of lost modern grant sticks out like a sore thumb in the context of registered land, where the equivalent would be a lost registration! In this report, the Law Commission recommended the replacement of the current methods of acquiring easements by prescription with a single method, applicable to all easements (so no longer distinguishing between easements of light and other easements, with a single period of prescription of twenty years (which would not have to be 'next before action')). This report contains, besides recommendations for reform, an excellent discussion of the current law.

■ Cash, A, 'Fencing Easements, Their True Character and How They Arise: *Churston Golf Club Ltd v Haddock Churston Golf Club Ltd v Haddock* [2019] EWCA Civ 544; [2019] 4 WLR 60' (2019) 3 *Conv*, 300–9.

Discusses the question of the positive easement of fencing.

■ Haley, M, 'Easements, Exclusionary Use and Elusive Principles: The Right to Park' [2008] *Conv* 244.

■ Xu, L, 'Easement of Car Parking: The Ouster Principle is Out but Problems May Aggravate' [2012] *Conv* 291.

Two articles looking at emerging categories of new easements.

There are also several articles and other readings listed in the comments to Question 1, which focus on the topical question of the extension of new types of easements.

Online Resources www.oup.com/uk/qanda/

For extra essay and problem questions on this topic, as well as advice on revision and exam technique, please visit the online resources.

11

Freehold Covenants

ARE YOU READY?

In order to attempt the questions in this chapter, you will need to have covered the following topics:

● the running of the burden and benefit of freehold covenants;
● the rule in *Tulk v Moxhay* (1848);
● assignment and annexation of freehold covenants;
● building schemes.

KEY DEBATES

Debate: annexation has caused much unnecessary difficulty.

It would have been simpler if equity had simply followed the law and treated the benefit as being annexed to the land in those cases in which it can pass at common law. However, at least in the past, it appeared that the equitable rules relating to annexation were different from, and (unfortunately) more technical than, the rules relating to annexation at common law (see *Rogers v Hosegood* [1900] 2 Ch 388 and *Re Ballard's Conveyance* [1937] 1 Ch 473). *Federated Homes Ltd v Mill Lodge Properties Ltd* [1980] 1 WLR 594 may have changed this, both by extending the scope of implied annexation in the **Law of Property Act (LPA) 1925, s 78**, and by casting doubt upon the correctness of *Re Ballard's Conveyance*. The decision in *Federated Homes* has also considerably reduced the importance of assignment.

Q

| | **QUESTION** | 1 |

In the summer of 1989, Pip was the fee simple owner of a plot of some 5,000 acres, the title to which was unregistered. The plot slopes gently from north to south. The southern half of the plot (called Fruitlands) comprises orchards; the northern half (called Homestead) comprises a dwelling-house and extensive gardens. In the autumn of 1989, Pip conveyed Fruitlands to Squeak. In the conveyance to him, Squeak covenanted with Pip 'for the benefit of Pip's adjoining land':

(a) to maintain the drainage ditches on Fruitlands in order to prevent the flooding of Homestead; and

(b) to use Fruitlands for agricultural purposes only.

As Fruitlands was not at the time in an area of compulsory registration of title, the second of these covenants was immediately registered against Squeak's name as a land charge, Class D(ii).

In 1995, Pip conveyed Homestead to Cherry. The following year, Squeak conveyed Fruitlands to Wilfred.

Wilfred has neglected to repair the drainage ditches on Fruitlands, with the result that Cherry's land is periodically flooded. Wilfred also intends to build a block of flats on part of Fruitlands.

Advise Cherry.

!

CAUTION!

■ You will find it useful to consider the benefit and burden separately. In the absence of any evidence in the problem of any assignment of the benefit, the only issue to consider on the benefit side is whether the benefit has been effectively annexed.

■ Most students will be able to point out that the burden of covenants cannot run at common law, whereas the burden of negative covenants is enforceable in equity against most persons coming to the land, provided the other requirements of equity are met. Don't forget, though, that the effect of the common law rule is that the original covenantor remains liable in damages for breaches of covenant which occur even after he has conveyed the burdened land. Although Cherry's bringing an action for damages against Squeak for breach of the covenant to maintain the drainage ditches does not itself ensure that those ditches are repaired, it may indirectly (through a chain of covenants) have this effect.

DIAGRAM ANSWER PLAN

Identify the issues	The legal issue is burden of positive and negative covenants.

Relevant law	This is *Tulk v Moxhay* (1848); **LPA 1925, ss 78 and 79**; and *Federated Homes* [1980].

Apply the law	**Discuss the following:**
	(a) **Drainage covenant** (*positive covenant*)
	 ■ The burden cannot run at common law or in equity.
	 ■ If the benefit runs at common law, C can sue S for damages. Requirements for running of benefit at common law are:
	  • annexation (**LPA 1925, s 78** and *Federated Homes*);
	  • is there a chain of indemnity covenants?
	(b) **Agricultural covenant** (negative covenant)
	 ■ Burden can run to W in equity if certain conditions are met (*Tulk v Moxhay*):
	  • The intention that the burden runs (**LPA 1925, s 79**).
	 ■ Does the benefit pass to C in equity:
	  • equitable annexation (**LPA 1925, s 78** and *Federated Homes*);
	  • annexation to each and every part (*Ballard* [1937]; *Federated Homes*)?
	 ■ If both benefit and burden run, C can obtain injunction against W.

Conclude	■ Advise Cherry.

A   SUGGESTED ANSWER

[1] Starting point—later you will refer back to this when dealing with liability at common law.

Neither Cherry nor Wilfred was an original party to the covenants[1] contained in the conveyance of 1989. If, therefore, Cherry is to obtain injunctive relief against Wilfred for breach of either covenant, she must establish both that she is entitled to the benefit of each covenant and that Wilfred is subject to the burden of each.

[2] Don't go straight into the rules in equity—deal first with the common law to show that it doesn't apply here.

The initial problem for Cherry is that, at common law,[2] the burden of a covenant does not run with the burdened land (*Austerberry v Corporation of Oldham* (1885) 29 ChD 750 (CA), affirmed by the House of Lords in *Rhone v Stephens* [1994] 2 AC 310). Neither covenant therefore binds Wilfred at common law. In equity,[3] the burden of a covenant can bind (*inter alia*) the covenantor's successor in

[3] Now go on to the position in equity.

title, but only if the covenant is negative in substance and the other requirements of the rule in *Tulk v Moxhay* (1848) 2 Ph 774 are satisfied. A positive covenant (ie one which requires the expenditure of money to prevent its being breached) cannot be enforced against such successor in equity. The covenant to maintain the drainage ditches is clearly a positive covenant, as it requires expenditure of money. Thus, regardless of whether she can show that the benefit of the covenant has passed to her, Cherry will not be able to compel Wilfred to maintain the ditches.

The corollary of the principle of *Austerberry v Corporation of Oldham* is that the original covenantor remains liable on a covenant at common law even after he has parted with the land. Cherry will therefore be able to sue Squeak for damages for breach of covenant (a) if she can show that she has acquired the benefit of such covenant at common law.

In order for the benefit of a covenant (whether positive or negative) to run with the land at common law (ie to be annexed to the land), the covenant must satisfy several requirements.[4] First, it must touch and concern the covenantee's land; evidence that the value or occupation of Homestead is improved by the restriction upon the user of Fruitlands will suffice. Second, both the covenantee and his successor in title must have a legal estate in such land; this is clearly the case here. Third, there must be an intention when the covenant is made that the benefit is to run with the land.

This third requirement has been the subject of much recent judicial analysis. **LPA 1925, s 78** deems a covenant relating to land of the covenantee to be made with the covenantee and (*inter alia*) his successors in title, which expression is deemed to include the owners and occupiers for the time being of the land of the covenantee intended to be benefited. It does not, therefore, matter that Squeak expressly covenanted with Pip alone, because Pip's successors in title are statutorily included: *Federated Homes v Mill Lodge Properties Ltd* [1980] 1 WLR 594. The section does not apply where the covenant makes it clear that the benefit is not annexed (*Roake v Chadha* [1984] 1 WLR 40), but no such exclusion is contained in the covenant entered into by Squeak. The Court of Appeal in the *Federated Homes* case left open, however, the question of whether the covenant must identify the benefited land by express words or by necessary implication, or whether it is sufficient if the identity of the benefited land can be gleaned from the document itself or from evidence outside the document. In the later *Crest Nicholson Residential (South) Ltd v McAllister* [2004] 2 EGLR 79, the Court of Appeal held that the former interpretation is the correct one. In the *Crest* case, it was held that the benefit of restrictive covenants had not been annexed by

[4] Now go on to list all three.

conveyances that did not identify the benefited land. A case where there had been sufficient identification was *Whitgift Homes Ltd v Stocks* **[2001] EWCA Civ 1732**, where the reference in the conveyances was to 'the Vendors' Estate at Croydon'. The expression 'for the benefit of Pip's adjoining land', which is similar to the descriptions used both in *Federated Homes* and in *Rogers v Hosegood* **[1900] 2 Ch 388**, is therefore sufficient to effect annexation.

Cherry can therefore sue Squeak, the original covenantor, for damages for breach of the covenant. If, as would be usual, Squeak obtained an indemnity covenant from Wilfred when he conveyed Fruitlands to Wilfred, Cherry's threat to sue Squeak for damages, which would in turn induce Squeak to sue Wilfred for damages, might be sufficient to induce Wilfred to repair the ditches. No such indirect method of enforcement will avail Cherry, however, if Squeak did not take an indemnity covenant, or if he is untraceable or bankrupt, or if he has died and his estate has been wound up.

Covenant (b), by contrast, is negative in substance, so Cherry may be able to obtain an injunction against Wilfred to prevent the building under the doctrine of *Tulk v Moxhay* **(1848) 2 Ph 774**. For this to occur, it must be shown that the original parties to the covenant intended that the burden of the covenant should run with the land of the covenantor. Although Squeak appears to have expressly covenanted on his own behalf only, the effect of **LPA 1925, s 79** is (subject to a contrary intention) to treat the covenant as being made by the covenantor on behalf of himself and (*inter alia*) his successors in title. If there were other covenants made by Squeak expressly on behalf of himself and his successors in title, it might be inferred that a covenant with him alone was not intended to bind successors (*Morrells Ltd v Oxford United Football Club Ltd* **[2001] Ch 459**). Assuming, however, that there is no such counter-indication, this requirement is also met. If covenant (b) satisfies these and the other requirements for *Tulk v Moxhay* **(1848) 2 Ph 774** (ie that it touches and concerns the land and was taken for the benefit of the covenantee's land), it will be binding upon Wilfred, since it was protected by registration as a land charge. Had the title to Fruitlands been registered,[5] the covenant would have been protected if it had been registered as a minor interest in the charges register of the title.

As Cherry must rely upon the rules in equity to pass the burden of the covenant, she will also have to establish that the benefit of covenant (b) has been passed to her in equity. Broadly, the requirements for equitable annexation are the same as those for annexation at common law, discussed earlier in Key Debates, except that in equity it suffices if the claimant has merely an equitable interest in the benefited land. In *Federated Homes*, the burdened land remained

[5] Extra mark here for getting this point.

in the ownership of the covenantor. Nevertheless, because the claimant sought an injunction, an equitable remedy, the case appears to have concerned annexation in equity. In any event, in *Roake v Chadha*, where there had been a change in the ownership of the burdened land, the judge proceeded on the basis that the principle in *Federated Homes* was equally applicable to annexation in equity. It is therefore likely that the benefit of covenant (b) has been annexed in equity.

An additional complexity in relation to equitable annexation was, however, added in *Re Ballard's Conveyance* [1937] 1 Ch 473, in which Clauson J held that if the benefit of the covenant were expressed to be for the benefit of the vendor's retained land, it would not be annexed to each part of it. Therefore, unless the covenant touched and concerned the whole land, there would be no annexation at all. Since Homestead presumably comprises some 2,500 acres, the absence of appropriate words of annexation to each and every part would appear to be fatal to Cherry.

[6] This is how to deal with a wobbly point.

However, Brightman LJ in *Federated Homes* cast doubt[6] on the soundness of the reasoning in *Ballard*, and considered it inconsistent with both *Williams v Unit Construction Co Ltd* (1951) 19 *Conv* 262 and *Smith and Snipe's Hall Farm v River Douglas Catchment Board* [1949] 2 KB 500 (although these both concerned annexation at common law). Brightman LJ's *dicta* are more sensible[7] and will probably be followed. It would therefore seem that the benefit of covenant (b) has been annexed in equity to Homestead, and is enforceable by Cherry, who will be able to prevent Wilfred from building.

[7] Take a view.

✚ LOOKING FOR EXTRA MARKS?

■ Most questions on covenants will involve the passing of the burden as well as the benefit, but for extra marks mention briefly (in no more than one sentence) that because it is necessary to show the passing of the burden, then the common law rules on the passing of the benefit are of no assistance, before proceeding to apply the rules in equity. There are some tips in the comments above which show you how to earn extra marks.

Ⓠ QUESTION | 2

In 1974 Clifford, the fee simple owner of Whiteacre, the title to which was unregistered, conveyed part of it to Arlington. In the conveyance, Arlington covenanted on behalf of himself and his successors in title with Clifford and with the other owners for the time being of land adjoining Whiteacre not to use the land thereby conveyed to him (*inter alia*) as a fish-and-chip shop. The conveyance

▶

⊙

expressly stated that the benefit of the covenant was not to pass to any subsequent owner of the benefited land except by assignment.

At the time of the conveyance from Clifford to Arlington, Buckingham was the fee simple owner of an adjacent plot, Blackacre. In 1980, Buckingham conveyed Blackacre to Ashley. This conveyance did not contain an express assignment of the benefit of Arlington's covenant; but in the negotiations preceding the conveyance to Ashley, Buckingham represented to Ashley that he would have the right to enforce the covenant.

In 1985, Arlington conveyed his part of Whiteacre to Lauderdale, who has recently expressed the intention of opening a fish-and-chip shop on that land. Ashley died last month. By his will, he gave all his property to Godolphin, whom he also appointed his executor.

Advise Godolphin if he can prevent Lauderdale from opening the fish-and-chip shop.

! CAUTION!

■ As in Question 1, both the benefited and the burdened land have been assigned. Since the covenant is negative in substance, the answer needs to state that the burden can be enforced against Lauderdale, the successor in title to the original covenantor, provided it was protected by registration.

■ This question is, however, primarily concerned with the passing of the benefit and whether the benefit of the covenant has passed to, and is enforceable by, Godolphin. This requires showing that the benefit of the covenant was acquired by Buckingham in the first place (explaining the impact of **LPA 1925, s 56**), and was then passed on from him to Ashley (by assignment), and then from Ashley to Godolphin (through operation of law). Annexation, it should be noted, is inapplicable, both because no benefited land is identified (***Crest Nicholson Residential (South) Ltd v McAllister* [2004] EWCA Civ 410**) and because it is, in any event, expressly excluded by the wording of the covenant, as it was in ***Roake v Chadha* [1984] 1 WLR 40**. Therefore, you should not spend too long on annexation: it is sufficient to show why annexation cannot be relied upon in this question.

DIAGRAM ANSWER PLAN

Identify the issues	■ The legal issue is the running of the benefit and burden in freehold covenants.
Relevant law	■ This is the rule in *Tulk v Moxhay* (1848).
Apply the law	**Discuss the following:** (a) **Is there passing of burden of negative covenant?** 　■ Requirements for running of burden in equity. 　■ Protection as a Class D(ii) land charge? (b) **Is there passing of benefit in equity to Ashley?** 　■ As original covenantee (**LPA 1925, s 56**)? 　■ As successor in title: 　　● annexation (**LPA 1925, s 78**) excluded; 　　● assignment (express or implied)? (c) **Is there passing of benefit in equity from Ashley to Godolphin?** 　■ Assignment by operation of law? 　■ Implied assignment?
Conclude	■ Advise Godolphin.

SUGGESTED ANSWER

¹ Set this out at the start—it clarifies the issues.

² Don't leave this unsaid.

If Godolphin is to succeed, he must establish[1] both that Lauderdale is subject to the burden of the covenant and that he has himself acquired, and is entitled to enforce, the benefit of the covenant (*Dano Ltd v 8th Earl of Cadogan* [2003] EWHC 239 (Ch)). As the burden of a covenant will never pass at common law[2] (*Rhone v Stephens* [1994] 2 AC 310), it will be necessary to consider the rules for the passing of the burden and the benefit in equity.

The Burden

³ First things first.

First, the burden.[3] Since the covenant in the problem is negative in substance, it may bind Lauderdale, as successor in title to the original covenantor, under the doctrine of *Tulk v Moxhay* (1848) 2 Ph 774. For this doctrine to operate, the covenantee (or his successors) must, both at the time of the covenant and subsequently, own nearby land for the protection of which the covenant was entered into—which is the case here. The restrictive covenant must also 'touch and concern' the dominant land, ie affect its mode of occupation or value. This requirement may also be satisfied, if, for example, it may be inferred that the covenant was taken in order to benefit Whiteacre and adjoining plots by protecting them from the smells emanating from a fish-and-chip shop. Evidence may therefore be needed to show whether Blackacre is in fact capable of benefiting from such covenant. It must also be shown that the burden was intended to run with the land: this is satisfied by Arlington's having covenanted on behalf of himself and his successors in title.

Even if these requirements are met, however, if Lauderdale was a purchaser of the legal estate for money or money's worth, he will still take free of the covenant unless it was registered against the name of the estate owner of the burdened land, Arlington, before the completion of his purchase, as a land charge, Class D(ii). This is the case even if, at that time, he knew of the covenant's existence (*Midland Bank Trust Co v Green* **[1981] AC 513**).

The Benefit

[4] And now deal with the benefit.

Second, the benefit.[4] If Godolphin has to show the passing of the burden of the covenant in equity and is to enforce the covenant by means of an injunction against Lauderdale, he must show that he has acquired the benefit of the covenant in equity. This requires him to establish that he acquired it as Ashley's executor, and that Ashley had in turn acquired it from Buckingham.

Buckingham was not named as a party to the 1974 conveyance; ie he was not an express covenantee. Nevertheless, by virtue of **LPA 1925, s 56**, a person may take (*inter alia*) the benefit of any covenant respecting land, despite not being named as a party to the conveyance. In effect, the section enables a person who could have been a party to the conveyance to be an original covenantee, provided that he can be identified. In *Re Ecclesiastical Commissioners for England's Conveyance* **[1936] Ch 430**, where the covenant was made (*inter alia*) for the benefit of the owners for the time being of land adjacent to that conveyed, it was held that such owners, being identifiable, could have enforced the covenant. It would therefore seem that, since he can be similarly identified from the wording of the covenant, Buckingham, as owner for the time being of land adjoining Whiteacre, could likewise have enforced the covenant made by Arlington.

Only owners for the time being can take the benefit of **LPA 1925, s 56**, and this therefore excludes Ashley, who acquired Blackacre only subsequently. It might be argued that the benefit passed to him through annexation under **LPA 1925, s 78(1)**, which deems that a covenant relating to any land of the covenantee to be made with the covenantee and (*inter alia*) his successors in title. For two reasons, however, such an argument will fail. First, although the point was left open in *Federated Homes v Mill Lodge Properties Ltd* **[1980] 1 WLR 594**, it has since been held that there can be statutory annexation under this section only where the benefited land is identifiable (as in *Federated Homes* itself), either expressly or by necessary implication, from the conveyance: *Crest Nicholson Residential (South) Ltd v McAllister* **[2004] 2 EGLR 79**. No benefited land is identifiable in this way in the conveyance from Clifford to Arlington. Second, it was held in *Roake v Chadha* **[1984] 1 WLR 40** that, whilst **s 78** does not permit the range of persons with whom the covenant is made to be reduced, statutory annexation can be excluded by the covenant itself. The wording of the covenant in the problem, expressly limiting the passing of the benefit to assignment, has this effect. Annexation is therefore excluded.

If, therefore, the benefit of the covenant passed to Ashley, this can only have been through assignment. The requirements for a valid assignment in equity are fivefold,[5] and were laid down by Romer LJ in *Miles v Easter* **[1933] Ch 611**, thus:

[5] Then lay them out—don't leave them unsaid.

(a) the covenant must have been taken for the benefit of land of the covenantee;

(b) the land must be indicated with reasonable certainty;

(c) the dominant land must be retained in whole or in part by the plaintiff; and

(d) be capable of benefiting from the covenant; and

(e) the assignment of the covenant and the conveyance of the land to which it relates must be contemporaneous.

[6] Now work through them—skim those which are clearly satisfied and deal in depth with those that aren't.

In the question, the first three requirements[6] of *Miles v Easter* appear to be satisfied. The fourth requirement is satisfied if the covenantee is thereby enabled to dispose of his land to advantage; ie if it increases the value of his land (*Miles v Easter* at 631). Assuming therefore (as discussed earlier) that the covenant 'touches and concerns' the benefited land, the fourth requirement is satisfied also.

Unless the assignment is contemporaneous with the conveyance—the fifth requirement—the benefit of the covenant is lost in equity. Thus, in the absence of an express assignment to Ashley, the fifth requirement is met only if a contemporaneous assignment can be implied. In *Miles v Easter* itself, there are conflicting *dicta*, both at first instance and in the Court of Appeal, regarding the need for the assignment to be (as in that case) express. Other authorities, however, suggest that the assignment may be implied; ie that it is enough that the vendor stated in the contract for the sale of the land, or represented to the purchaser in the negotiations preceding the sale, that the latter would have the right to enforce the covenant (*Renals v Cowlishaw* (1878) 9 ChD 125, at 129–31, and *White v Bijou Mansions* [1937] Ch 610, at 622). It would therefore appear from the facts of the problem that Ashley acquired the benefit of the covenant by implied assignment effected at the same time as the conveyance to Ashley.

[7] Last point.

The final issue[7] is therefore whether the benefit of the covenant has passed from Ashley to Godolphin. An express assignment by Ashley to Godolphin as his personal representative is obviously unnecessary. The benefit of the covenant is personal property of the deceased and will pass to his executor by operation of law (*Ives v Brown* [1919] 2 Ch 314; *Newton Abbot Cooperative Society Ltd v Williamson and Treadgold Ltd* [1952] Ch 286). After he has administered the estate, Godolphin will, in due course, no doubt execute a vesting assent of the retained portion of Whiteacre in favour of himself (*Re King's Will Trusts* [1964] Ch 542), together with an assignment of the benefit of the covenant. Even if not expressly assigned to himself as beneficiary, the benefit of the covenant would presumably be thereby assigned impliedly. Indeed, even in the absence of an assignment in the strict sense, the same result would ensue were he treated as retaining the benefit of the covenant as executor, since he would be holding it on a bare trust for himself as beneficiary (cf *Earl of Leicester v Wells-next-to-the-Sea UDC* [1973] Ch 110). Whatever his present capacity, therefore, Godolphin will be able to enforce the covenant.[8]

[8] A clear conclusion.

➕ LOOKING FOR EXTRA MARKS?

■ Setting out the burden and benefit separately helps to clarify and gain extra marks.

ⓠ QUESTION | 3

The requirements for a building scheme are merely indicia of an intention to create a community of interest with reciprocity of obligation. Where such intention is found, equity is willing to read the covenants in the light of the surrounding facts. A building scheme is therefore no more than a species of implied annexation, and the law relating to such schemes is purely evidential. The notion of reciprocity of rights and obligations is the only characteristic which a building scheme shares with the doctrine of mutual benefits and burdens laid down in *Halsall v Brizell* [1957] Ch 169.

Discuss.

⚠ CAUTION!

■ Make sure you address every matter with which the quotation in the question deals and don't be afraid to disagree with statements which you consider incorrect—and, of course, to explain why.

■ If a question asks you to discuss a quotation, do not simply write a general essay on the topic. You will obtain more marks if you address the specific points that the quotation raises.

■ In this question, the examiner is evidently trying to get you to discuss the juridical basis underlying building schemes and the quotation itself usefully provides a ready-made structure for your answer. The quotation comprises four sentences and it will be seen that each of them requires you to deal with a distinct point. The first invites you to consider whether the requirements for a building scheme are indeed no more than indications of an intention to create a community of interest. The second calls for a discussion of equity's approach to the construction of covenants once a building scheme has been found. The third effectively asks you to consider whether a building scheme is no more than a form of implied annexation. The last expects you to compare the principles underlying building schemes with the doctrine of mutual benefits and burdens. So, use a Point, Evidence, and Analysis (PEA) approach within each of these four elements.

⊙ DIAGRAM ANSWER PLAN

■ Consider traditional requirements for a building scheme (*Elliston v Reacher* [1908]).
■ Discuss equity's approach to construction of covenants in a scheme.
■ Discuss the building scheme as a form of implied annexation.
■ Make a comparison with doctrine of mutual benefits and burdens.

Ⓐ SUGGESTED ANSWER

[1] Establish the basics.

The classic requirements[1] for a building scheme (or scheme of development as it is sometimes known) were laid down by Parker J in *Elliston v Reacher* [1908] 2 Ch 374. The requirements are fivefold:

(a) the plaintiff and the defendant should have derived their titles from a common vendor;

(b) before the sale of the plots, the common vendor must have laid out his estate for sale in lots subject to restrictions intended to be imposed on all the lots;

(c) the restrictions were intended by the common vendor to be and were for the benefit of all the lots sold;

(d) the original purchasers must have bought their lots on the understanding that the restrictions were to enure for the benefit of the other lots; and

(e) (added in *Reid v Bickerstaff* [1909] 2 Ch 305) the geographical area to which the scheme extends must be clear.

In *Elliston v Reacher*, Parker J considered that, where all the points were established, 'the community of interest imports in equity the reciprocity of obligation which is in fact contemplated by each at the time of his own purchase'. Since this decision, the courts have tended to emphasise this broader element of reciprocity (see *Brunner v Greenslade* [1971] Ch 993 and *Jamaica Mutual Life Assurance Society v Hillsborough Ltd* [1989] 1 WLR 1101). They have therefore been less concerned to find that all five requirements have been met.[2] In *Baxter v Four Oaks Properties Ltd* [1965] Ch 816, for instance, Parker J's second requirement was not satisfied, but the court found an intention to create mutually binding covenants and held that this sufficed to create a scheme. Further, in *Re Dolphin's Conveyance* [1970] Ch 654, the court considered that both the first and second requirements were unnecessary. Nevertheless, an intention to create a community of interest with reciprocity of obligation is not in itself sufficient; the fifth requirement must always be met (*Lund v Taylor* (1975) 31 P & CR 167; *Jamaica Mutual Life*). The vendor may, however, retain the right to exempt part of his retained land from the stipulations (*Allen v Veranne Builders Ltd* [1988] (unreported)).

Where the requirements of a building scheme are met, the court simply treats the covenants as being mutually enforceable amongst the owners of the lots. This suggests that the basis for enforceability is something other than annexation or assignment—that building schemes create their own rights and obligations through the principle of reciprocity. Extrinsic evidence is admissible in order to show that the requirements, and the element of reciprocity, are present; such evidence could be of the parties' acts and statements before conveyance (which might include, for instance, details of sales advertisements), and even evidence from the common vendor's predecessor in title (*Kingsbury v LW Anderson Ltd* (1979) 40 P & CR 136).

It is sometimes contended that it is possible to achieve by a building scheme what cannot be achieved by annexation; ie the creation of reciprocal mutual rights amongst successive purchasers of lots. Even outside a building scheme, however, earlier purchasers can take the benefit of the covenants entered into by later purchasers if the covenants are expressed to be made, not merely with the common

[2] Then go on to consider some of the cases where this was demonstrated.

vendor for the benefit of his retained land, but also with existing owners of previously sold plots for the benefit of such plots (**LPA 1925, s 56**). By this means, the benefit of later purchasers' covenants is annexed to the land of earlier purchasers.

If, however, in the foregoing circumstances, a building scheme exists, earlier purchasers can enforce in equity the covenants entered into by later purchasers even if they are not made covenantees under **LPA 1925, s 56**. An earlier purchaser's equity could be treated as arising merely through the application of the principle of reciprocity. It could, alternatively, be treated as deriving from covenant. Under the latter analysis, where equity finds an intention to create mutually enforceable obligations, it will readily infer the intention to make earlier purchasers original covenantees of later purchasers' covenants and to annex the benefit to their land.

Implied annexation therefore means that, once there is sufficient evidence to show the existence of the scheme itself, extrinsic (or further extrinsic) evidence can be used to show that the covenants are annexed to the land. The older cases proceeded on this footing, and established that, where a building scheme exists, the court will construe the covenants with a view to ensuring that the benefit of each purchaser's covenant is annexed to the lots of all the others (*Spicer v Martin* **(1889) 14 App Cas 12 (HL)**). Similarly, in *Rogers v Hosegood* **[1900] 2 Ch 388**, both Farwell J (at first instance) and the Court of Appeal treated a building scheme as merely exemplifying the general rule that a deed is to be construed in the light of surrounding circumstances (see S J Bailey, 'The Benefit of a Restrictive Covenant' [1938] 6(3) *CLJ* 339–66, at 364).

Although implied annexation appears to explain the earlier decisions on building schemes, the importance attached in modern times to the underlying principle of reciprocity of obligations has made it more difficult to reconcile some recent cases[3] with any form of annexation. Thus, it has been held that, if two or more of the lots come into common ownership, the covenants are not destroyed, but will, upon severance, become once again enforceable amongst their owners inter se (*Brunner v Greenslade*; *Texaco Antilles Ltd v Kernochan* **[1973] AC 609, PC**). Furthermore, a Commonwealth court has expressed its preparedness to uphold a building scheme purely on the basis of intention, even if the conveyances contain not a single covenant (*Re Louis and the Conveyancing Act* **[1971] 1 NSWLR 164**).

Therefore, the law relating to building schemes appears to have outgrown its origins in the equitable rules pertaining to the construction of deeds.[4] In this respect, its development is not unlike that of the

[3] Here you are discussing the evolving approach on this issue.

[4] Showing knowledge here of the way the law is developing.

doctrine of mutual benefits and burdens. This doctrine also developed from a principle relating to deeds, namely that if a person is named as a party to a deed and takes a benefit under it with knowledge of the facts, he is bound by it, even though he does not execute it (*R v Houghton-le-Spring* (1819) 2 B & Ald 375). From this narrow basis, the law moved a long way so that, in *Tito v Waddell (No 2)* [1977] Ch 106, at 301–3, Megarry V-C was able to refer to the 'pure principle' of benefits and burdens, namely that a person who takes the benefit of a deed must also take it subject to the burdens it contains. In *Rhone v Stephens* [1994] 2 AC 310, however, the House of Lords retreated from such wide formulation, and stated that the doctrine can apply only where the benefits and burdens are reciprocal and not independent of each other; the benefit cannot therefore be the whole benefit taken under the deed. Even within such confines, however, the doctrine can result in a subsequent purchaser of land being bound by a covenant made by a predecessor in title (*Hopgood v Brown* [1955] 1 WLR 213).

⁵ Refer back to the quotation—it reminds you to keep within the ambit of the question.

⁶ Listing them gives you a good clear conclusion.

As the quotation states,⁵ the notion of reciprocity of obligations underpins both building schemes and the doctrine of mutual benefits and burdens, but there are considerable differences. First,⁶ a purchaser of a lot subject to a building scheme cannot escape from the obligations it imposes by choosing to forego the benefits it confers; whereas a purchaser who does not wish to take a benefit under a deed cannot be subjected to a reciprocal burden. Second, the only obligations that can be enforced in a building scheme are those which are negative or restrictive in nature; whereas, under the mutual benefits and burdens doctrine, even a positive obligation (such as the payment of a levy for the use of roads and sewers as in *Halsall v Brizell* itself) can be enforced. Third, the obligations imposed by a building scheme are probably enforceable against subsequent purchasers only if protected by registration as a land charge or by notice; whereas the burdens imposed by the doctrine of *Halsall v Brizell* are not, as such, registrable as land charges (*Hopgood v Brown*).

 LOOKING FOR EXTRA MARKS?

■ To answer this question, you must have a good knowledge of the case, but laying out your answer in the PEA fashion, where you make the point, then give evidence and analysis by discussing the cases, will help to convey your knowledge and earn extra marks.

TAKING THINGS FURTHER

■ Clark, P, 'The Benefit of Freehold Covenants' [2012] *Conv* 145.

■ O'Connor, P, 'Careful What You Wish For: Positive Freehold Covenants' [2011] *Conv* 191.
Both containing good discussions of the benefit aspect of the running of covenants.

■ Law Commission, *Making Land Work: Easements, Covenants and Profits à Prendre* (Law Com No 327, 2011).
A good exposition of the law.

Online Resources   www.oup.com/uk/qanda/

For extra essay and problem questions on this topic, as well as advice on revision and exam technique, please visit the online resources.

12 Mortgages

ARE YOU READY?

In order to attempt the questions in this chapter, you will need to have covered the following topics:

● creation of mortgages;

● clogs on the equity of redemption;

● the remedies of a mortgagee and protection of the mortgagor.

 KEY DEBATES

Debate: remedies of a mortgagee where the mortgagor defaults is an area of the law where, over recent years, the courts have had to consider entirely new social circumstances, with booms and slumps in property prices and what is known as 'negative equity', where the sale price of the house is not enough to cover the mortgage debt.

The debate rests on questions about whether the mortgagee owes a duty of care in equity to the mortgagor and any subsequent encumbrancer on the exercise of his powers. There are recent cases, too, in which the courts have interpreted the applicable legislation on sale more generously towards a mortgagor, recognising that even though a mortgagor has defaulted, his interest should not be entirely disregarded in granting a remedy to the mortgagee (*Cheltenham & Gloucester Building Society v Norgan* [1996] 1 WLR 343).

Q

(a) Discuss the ways in which a legal mortgage may now be created in registered land.

(b) David is the tenant of a fifty-year lease of a shop. Five years ago, he borrowed £20,000 from Quickslip Bank plc in order to expand his business, and the sum was secured by a legal charge on the leasehold property. Quickslip Bank plc has recently discovered that David has had financial problems, as a result of which he had become in arrears with his rent, and the landlord has forfeited the lease. The landlord says that he had no notice of the mortgage to Quickslip Bank plc, and that in any event, the mortgage would have been prohibited by the terms of the lease, which includes a covenant not to assign or sublet without first obtaining the landlord's consent in writing.

Advise Quickslip Bank plc.

!

CAUTION!

■ This two-parter is both essay and problem. Balance the time out between the two. The essay is relatively straightforward and quickly dealt with.

■ This may seem a very technical area—but in the commercial world these provisions are key and are well used.

◻

DIAGRAM ANSWER PLAN

(A)

- Give a brief background to the creation of mortgages.
- Discuss the impact of the **Land Registration Act (LRA) 2002**.
- Discuss the effect of creating charge.
- Consider the effect of registration and non-registration.
- Mention the 'registration gap'.

(B)

Identify the issues	▪ The legal issue is breach of covenant against assignment and subletting.
Relevant law	▪ This is the **Law of Property Act (LPA) 1925, s 146(4)**.
Apply the law	**Discuss the following:** ▪ There is a possible breach of covenant against assignment and subletting: • the effect of **LPA 1925, s 146(4)**; • the method of forfeiture; • relief from forfeiture in equity.
Conclude	▪ Advise Quickslip Bank Ltd.

SUGGESTED ANSWER

[1] Even though it is now some time since the Act was passed, the point should be made, as many mortgages will pre-date this Act.

[2] You could just say that mortgages must be made by legal charge, but displaying knowledge of the background is worth extra marks.

(a) Important changes to mortgages of registered land were introduced in **LRA 2002**.[1] Since the date that Act came into force (13 October 2003), a legal mortgage of registered land (whether freehold or leasehold) can be created *only* by legal charge: **LRA 2002, s 23(1)(a)**. However, although the method of mortgaging by demise can no longer be used, this makes little practical difference,[2] since even before the **2002 Act** came into force, mortgages were virtually always made by legal charge. If a registered proprietor were now to attempt to create a mortgage by demise, the registrar would simply reject the application for registration.

A charge does not transfer any legal estate to the mortgagee, but merely designates certain property as security for the debt. However, **LPA 1925, s 87(1)** gives to a mortgagee by way of legal charge 'the same protection, powers and remedies' as if he were a mortgagee by way of demise. His position is further strengthened by the inclusion of charge by deed by way of legal mortgage as a legal interest in **LPA 1925, s 1(2)**.

The charge takes effect as a *legal* charge only on registration: **LRA 2002, s 27(1), (2)(f)**. The chargee must therefore be entered in the register as the proprietor of the charge: **LRA 2002, Schedule 2, para 8**. Until registration, the charge takes effect only in equity, and so needs to be protected by a notice on the charges register.

Failure to register the legal charge leaves the chargee at risk of being subject to subsequently created legal estates and interests: *Barclays Bank plc v Zaroovabli* **[1997] Ch 321**. This is another instance of the registration gap, which will disappear when e-conveyancing is introduced,[3] so that the creation and registration of the legal charge will be simultaneous.

[3] We are still waiting for that part of the **LRA 2002** to be implemented.

(b) A legal charge of the leasehold property does not constitute a breach of a covenant against assignment or subletting, as it is not a disposal of the leasehold term.[4] Therefore, unless the covenant in the lease were more comprehensive and specifically mentioned charging, the execution of the legal charge to Quickslip Bank plc by David will not be a breach of this covenant.

[4] This is the key point, and leads to a relatively quick conclusion.

LPA 1925, s 146(4) states that, where the lessor is proceeding by action or otherwise to forfeit a lease for breach of covenant or for non-payment of rent, an underlessee, including an underlessee by way of mortgage, may apply to the court to have the lessee's estate vested in him upon such conditions as the court thinks fit. If the court makes such an order, a new lease is created between the lessor and the underlessee or mortgagee. Although Quickslip has a mortgage by way of legal charge, it has a right to apply under this subsection, because **LPA 1925, s 87(1)** gives a mortgagee by way of legal charge the same 'protection, powers and remedies' as a mortgagee by way of demise or subdemise[5] (*Grand Junction Ltd v Bates* **[1954] 2 QB 160**).

[5] And here is the main point of importance in the commercial world.

The problem does not state whether the landlord forfeited the lease pursuant to a court order or merely by taking peaceable re-entry. The method of forfeiture is, however, crucial to Quickslip, because it has a right to apply for relief under **LPA 1925, s 146(4)** only while the landlord is 'proceeding by action or otherwise' to forfeit the lease. Similar words are used in **s 146(2)**, which enables relief to be sought by the tenant. It has been held that, once a landlord has re-entered pursuant to a court order, he is no longer 'proceeding', so that the tenant's right to seek relief under **s 146(2)** is lost (*Rogers v Rice* **[1892] 2 Ch 170**). However, if the landlord re-enters peaceably without a court order, he can still be considered to be 'proceeding', and the tenant is not precluded from applying for relief (*Billson v Residential Apartments Ltd* **[1992] AC 494**). Given the similarity of the wording of the two subsections, the same principles probably[6] govern the right of a mortgagee to seek relief under **s 146(4)**.

[6] A probability here—so state it as such.

Where the forfeiture is made for non-payment of rent, other forms of relief may be available to the mortgagee. If the landlord has re-entered pursuant to an order of the High Court under the **Common Law Procedure Act 1852, s 210**, the mortgagee has six months after such entry to apply for relief. Such relief, if granted, takes the form of a new lease; but it will be granted only if the mortgagee pays all the arrears of rent, costs, and damages. At the end of six months, the right to apply for relief is barred.

The **1852 Act** applies, however, only if all the requirements of **s 210** are satisfied, and one such requirement is that the rent is six months or more in arrears. If, therefore, the arrears were less, the mortgagee's right to apply for relief derives from the equitable jurisdiction of the Court of Chancery, now exercisable by the High Court under the **Senior Courts Act 1981, s 38(1)**. Relief under this section will also be available if the landlord peaceably re-enters. The court will generally require an application to be made within six months of re-entry, but it may accept an application made slightly after such period (*Thatcher v C H Pearce & Sons (Contractors) Ltd* [1968] **1 WLR 748**, where the application was permitted even though made six months and four days after re-entry).

If the landlord has re-entered for non-payment of rent pursuant to an order of a county court, an underlessee (including a mortgagee) may apply for relief under the **County Courts Act 1984, s 138**. The application for relief must be made within six months of the re-entry (**s 138(9A)**). The High Court has no inherent jurisdiction to relieve a mortgagee whose application is made after the statutory period of six months (*United Dominion Trust Ltd v Shellpoint Trustees* [1993] **35 EG 121, CA**).

[7] Don't forget this point.

However, the problem contains one further twist,[7] as it would appear that the Quickslip Bank plc did not receive any notification of the landlord's forfeiture proceedings. A landlord seeking an order of forfeiture from the High Court is obliged (under the **Civil Procedure Rules**) to serve a copy of the proceedings upon any underlessee or mortgagee of whom it is aware. A parallel obligation applies if the landlord is proceeding in a county court. These rules do not help Quickslip if the landlord had not been notified of Quickslip's legal charge. If, however, the landlord had been notified, and nevertheless failed to serve a copy of the proceedings upon Quickslip, the latter may be able to apply for

[8] Note this is an equitable procedure, as the common law failed to contemplate this.

relief in equity[8] independently of statute (*Abbey National Building Society v Maybeech Ltd* [1985] **Ch 190**). Indeed, if the landlord deliberately refrained from notifying Quickslip, the latter might be able to claim relief even after six months of re-entry, on the ground that the landlord should not be permitted to use the statutory time limit as an engine of fraud. There is no direct authority to this effect,

[9] Display your knowledge of the potential weakness of this point.

however, and the status of *Maybeech* is not entirely free from doubt[9] (see *Smith v Metropolitan City Properties Ltd* [1986] **1 EGLR 52**).

Subject to the foregoing caveat, therefore, if the landlord in the problem has re-entered pursuant to an order of the court, Quickslip will be able to seek relief only if it applies within six months of the re-entry. If the landlord has re-entered peaceably without a court order, Quickslip will need to apply for relief within a reasonable time. In any event, relief will not be granted which would prejudice the interests of a third party, eg a *bona fide* purchaser for value of a legal estate without notice of the right to apply for relief (*Fuller v Judy Properties Ltd* [1992] 1 EGLR 75).

+ LOOKING FOR EXTRA MARKS?

■ Dealing with the authorities which are open to challenge in a careful and critical way will earn extra marks.

Q QUESTION | 2

Ten years ago, Quentin purchased a fifty-year lease of a market garden with the aid of a loan of £100,000 from Sunnyveg plc secured by a legal mortgage over the property. At that time, it was difficult to obtain finance, and Quentin agreed to pay interest at 10 per cent above the bank base rate.

The mortgage deed provides that the capital outstanding should be recalculated annually to align with the retail prices index, and that Quentin shall not redeem the mortgage for twenty-five years. Quentin further undertook in the mortgage deed that for the twenty-five years he would first offer to sell to Sunnyveg plc any asparagus produced by the market garden at the market price before selling it elsewhere.

Quentin has now obtained a more favourable offer of finance and would like to redeem the mortgage.

Advise him whether this might be possible, as to the terms of the mortgage generally, and whether the agreement relating to the asparagus crop is enforceable against him.

! CAUTION!

■ The equity of redemption and 'clogs on the equity' is one of the favoured areas of mortgages for examination questions. Make sure you know the different provisions which may be regarded as clogs on the equity. You should also be aware of the underlying principles which determine whether or not the court will be prepared to intervene—terms in the mortgage deed which are oppressive and unconscionable to the mortgagor.

DIAGRAM ANSWER PLAN

Identify the issues	■ The legal issue is clogs on the equity of redemption.
Relevant law	■ This is *Fairclough v Swan Brewery Ltd* [1912]; *Kreglinger v New Patagonia Meat & Cold Storage Co Ltd* [1914] and related case law; *Knightsbridge Estates Trust Ltd v Byrne* [1939]; *Cityland v Dabrah* [1968]; and the **Consumer Credit Act 1974**.
Apply the law	**Discuss the following:** ■ the equitable principle that equity will not allow a clog on the equity of redemption; ■ the effect of postponement of right to redeem; ■ unconscionability; ■ collateral advantage.
Conclude	■ Advise Quentin.

A SUGGESTED ANSWER

[1] Setting the scene.

Equity has traditionally protected the mortgagor[1] from the exploitation of his weaker position by an unscrupulous mortgagee. One of the ways in which this protection was effected was by the inviolability of the mortgagor's equity of redemption; this arises as soon as the legal date for redemption has passed.

Equity takes the view that the essential nature of a mortgage is a security for a loan, and that on repayment of the loan, the mortgagor is entitled to have back his property freed from all obligations arising under the mortgage. This requirement of freedom from any encumbrances imposed in a mortgage deed is expressed in the equitable principle that 'equity will not allow a clog on the equity of redemption'.

One possible clog on the equity would be an undue postponement of the right to redeem the mortgage. Any such postponement which renders the right to redeem illusory will be void. Thus, in *Fairclough v Swan Brewery Ltd* [1912] AC 565,[2] a clause which provided that a mortgage was redeemable only one month before the expiration of the mortgagor's lease, leaving the mortgagor with no property worth redeeming, was held to be void.

[2] This is case law, so you need to have good coverage of the cases.

Postponement, of itself, may not necessarily be bad, however. In *Knightsbridge Estates Trust Ltd v Byrne* [1939] Ch 441, Greene MR said that a postponement would not be bad unless it was in some way oppressive or unconscionable. In that case, a postponement of the right to redeem for forty years was upheld. The mortgagee had provided the mortgagor with finance at a time when credit was difficult to obtain. The parties were two large business associations and there was a reciprocal agreement that the mortgagee would not call in the loan for the period of postponement.

[3] Now go to the problem and apply the law.

In this case,[3] Quentin would still have twenty-five years of his lease left if he were to redeem after twenty-five years, so that the postponement would not appear to render the equity of redemption illusory as in *Fairclough*. However, Quentin does not appear to be a large commercial undertaking, as in *Knightsbridge Estates*, and there is no evidence of any reciprocal arrangement by Sunnyveg. It may therefore be possible for Quentin to obtain a declaration from the court that the postponement is oppressive, and therefore void.

As part of its protection of the equity of redemption, equity has been anxious to ensure that a mortgagor should not have to pay an excessive rate of interest. Thus, in *Cityland v Dabrah* [1968] Ch 166, a lump sum payment, which would have meant that the purchaser paid an interest rate of 57 per cent when spread over the period of the mortgage, was varied to give a rate of 7 per cent. This principle has been given statutory force with regard to certain qualifying mortgages within the **Consumer Credit Act 1974** if the terms of the mortgage are 'oppressive and unreasonable'. A rate of 10 per cent above the base rate might well be oppressive, and it might be possible to obtain an order varying it.

However, it will not necessarily be oppressive or unconscionable to link both capital and interest to a particular index. In *Multiservice Bookbinding Ltd v Marden* [1979] Ch 84, outstanding capital was recalculated according to the exchange rate with the Swiss franc which, after inflation and devaluation of sterling, more than doubled the original loan! As the provision was made to protect the mortgagee and was not intended to take advantage of the mortgagor, it was upheld. Further, in *Paragon Finance v Nash* [2002] 1 **WLR 685**, it was held that where a mortgagee is entitled to vary an interest rate, he does not have an unfettered discretion to do so. Nevertheless, where he raises it over and above the market rate to head off his own financial difficulties, that may be reasonable. It is probable therefore that the recalculation of capital outstanding on Quentin's loan will be valid.

[4] Here comes the point about collateral advantage.

The provision giving Sunnyveg a first refusal on any asparagus crop produced by Quentin for twenty-five years may be regarded as a collateral advantage[4] obtained from the transaction by Sunnyveg. Such an advantage continuing after the redemption of the mortgage would undoubtedly be void as repugnant to the equity of redemption, as the mortgagor is entitled to have back his property in an unencumbered state (*Noakes v Rice* [1902] AC 24). However, unless Quentin is able to redeem the mortgage before the period of twenty-five years specified in the mortgage has elapsed, this principle would not apply here, as the agreement is to subsist for twenty-five years (the duration of the mortgage) only. In *Biggs v Hodinott* [1898] 2 Ch 307, a mortgagor who agreed to buy only the mortgagee's beer for five years, and thereafter for as long as the loan was outstanding, and where the mortgagee agreed not to call in the loan for five years, was held to be bound by the agreement.

Collateral advantages were discussed by the House of Lords in *Kreglinger v New Patagonia Meat & Cold Storage Co Ltd* [1914] AC 25. In that case, part of the consideration for a loan by wool brokers to a meat-preserving company was a right of pre-emption on any sheepskins for five years. As in *Biggs v Hodinott*, there was a reciprocal agreement not to call in the loan for five years. The House of Lords felt that the rigid application of the doctrine of 'no clogs on the equity of redemption' was inappropriate to what was essentially a commercial contract between two business parties, and Lord Mersey referred to the doctrine as 'an unruly dog, which, if not securely chained to its own kennel, is prone to wander into places where it ought not to be'. More recently, Lord Phillips MR has said that the doctrine, like the appendix, no longer serves any useful purpose and should be excised: *Jones v Morgan* [2002] 1 EGLR 125, 136 (CA). In *Warnborough Ltd v Garmite Ltd* (2004) 1 P & CR D 18, the vendor of property left the purchase moneys outstanding on a mortgage he held, and the purchaser granted him an option to purchase the property. Jonathan Parker LJ, applying the *dictum* of Lord Haldane in *Kreglinger*, said that the option granted by the purchaser did no more than to raise the question as to whether the rule on 'clogs' applied but that, in each case, the court must look at the substance of the transaction to decide its true nature. In this case, the option could have been part of the sale and purchase transaction rather than the mortgage.

It is difficult to see that the asparagus agreement is in any way unconscionable or unfair[5] to Quentin, as it is merely a right of first refusal at market value. However, the arrangement does not appear to give any reciprocal rights to Quentin as in *Biggs* and *Kreglinger*, and so may be voidable.

In *Esso Petroleum v Harper's Garage* [1968] AC 269, the House of Lords held that any restrictions on trade[6] contained in a mortgage deed are also subject to the general common law rules as to restraint

[5] And here is the unconscionability point.

[6] This final point on the common law might be missed—so if you get it, it is worth extra marks.

of trade, so that an alternative way in which Quentin might be able to avoid this agreement is to show that it is excessive under the common law rules. As at common law, it is possible to sever the part of the mortgage agreement which is bad as an excessive restraint on trade (*Alec Lobb (Garages) Ltd v Total Oil Great Britain Ltd* [1985] 1 WLR 173).

➕ LOOKING FOR EXTRA MARKS?

■ A thorough examination of the cases will earn those marks and also, if you manage to get that final point on the common law position on restraint of trade, that will push the marks up too.

Ⓠ QUESTION | 3

Some years ago, when the property market was buoyant, Robin and Anne purchased the freehold of a desirable residence, Orchard Cottage, for £250,000 with the assistance of a loan of £175,000 from the Quickslip Bank, secured by a legal mortgage over the property. Robin unfortunately became redundant a year ago and he and Anne began to experience problems in keeping up the mortgage repayments. They obtained planning permission for two bungalows on plots which are part of the orchard, being part of the cottage grounds, hoping to ease their financial problems by selling these off.

They are now six months in arrears with the mortgage repayments and the bank is seeking immediate possession of the property in order to sell it. The agents instructed by the bank have prepared particulars of sale which do not mention the planning permission, although the bank has been told of it.

(a) Advise Robin and Anne of the bank's rights of possession and sale of the property.

(b) How would your advice differ, if at all, in the following circumstances:

■ The bank has already contracted to sell the property to Cuthbert, but Robin and Anne have since received a higher offer for the property from Denis, and intend to contract to sell to him.

❗ CAUTION!

■ This question concerns the remedies of a mortgagee where the mortgagor defaults. It is an area of the law where the courts have had to deal with the social context of 'booms' and 'busts' in property prices and the problems of 'negative equity' (where the price of the property is not sufficient to cover the mortgage debt). So, watch out for recent case law on this.

DIAGRAM ANSWER PLAN

Identify the issues	■ The legal issues are: (a) mortgagee's rights; and (b) priorities.
Relevant law	This is: ■ (a) **Administration of Justice Act (AJA) 1970, s 36; AJA 1973, s 8; LPA 1925, s 101;** ■ (b) **LPA 1925, s 91(2).**
Apply the law	■ (a) Consider the legal mortgagee's right to possession; the mortgagor's default; the power to suspend the order for a 'reasonable time'; the exercise of the mortgagee's statutory power of sale; the duty to take reasonable care. ■ (b) Consider the priority between mortgagee and third party.
Conclude	■ Advise Robin and Anne.

SUGGESTED ANSWER

[1] State the basic common law position.

[2] A nice quote if you can remember it in the exam room.

[3] And then state the practice point—remember that mortgages operate in the real world.

(a) Unless there is a provision in the mortgage deed to the contrary, a legal mortgagee has a common law right[1] to possession of the mortgaged property 'before the ink is dry on the mortgage deed'[2] (*per* Harman J in *Four-Maids Ltd v Dudley Marshall (Properties) Ltd* **[1957] Ch 317**). This is because the mortgagee has a legal lease of the property, or, if he has a legal charge, he has all the same rights as if he had a legal lease (**LPA 1925, s 87(1)**).

In practice,[3] a mortgage deed will often provide that the mortgagee's right of possession shall arise only on the mortgagor's default. The courts may be reluctant to limit this to a default on the mortgage repayments, however, and in *Western Bank Ltd v Schindler* **[1977] Ch 1** (where the mortgage had been defectively drafted), it was held that the mortgagee still had a right to possession where he had no other rights. In that case, the mortgagor had not defaulted on the mortgage repayments, as no repayment was due until a life policy matured, thereby providing the capital and interest to repay the loan. The mortgagor had defaulted on the payments due under the life policy. Although the power of sale was not exercisable, it was held that the mortgagee had a right of possession. Buckley LJ said, 'It is a common law right which is an incident of his estate in the land. It should not, in my opinion, be lightly treated as abrogated or restricted.' It was held (Goff LJ dissenting) that **AJA 1970, s 36** still applied to allow the court to postpone possession for a limited period.

If the mortgaged property is a dwelling-house, as in this question, then, where a mortgagee brings an action in which he claims possession, his right to possession will be restricted by **AJA 1970, s. 36** and by **AJA 1973, s 8**. It would seem that **s 36** is operable only where court proceedings for possession take place (*Ropaigealach v Barclays Bank plc* [2000] QB 263). So, the mortgagee's right to possession could be exercised by peaceable entry without the assis-

4 An additional point worth extra marks.

tance of the court. This is regulated by **s 6(1)** of the **Criminal Law Act 1977**, which would prevent the use of threatening behaviour or force.[4] But a right of peaceable possession of unoccupied premises without a court order is possible. **Section 36** is only triggered where the mortgagee of a dwelling-house 'brings an action in which he claims possession'. However, as it would seem that Robin and Anne are in occupation, the bank is likely to seek a court order for possession, thus bringing into play the effect of **s 36**. If, however, the bank was to sell the property and it was the purchaser who brought an action for possession, Robin and Anne would not be able to rely on **s 36**, as the action would have been brought by someone other than the mortgagee. In *Horsham Properties Group Ltd v Clark* [2008] EWHC 2327 (Ch), the court rejected an argument that the purchaser's possession action breached the mortgagor's right to peaceable enjoyment of her possessions under Article 1 of the **First Protocol**

5 Contrary to popular opinion, the human rights provisions don't change everything.

to the European Convention on Human Rights.[5]

If it is the bank that brings an action for possession, **s 36(2)** of the **1970 Act** gives the court a discretion to suspend an order for possession if it appears to the court that the mortgagor is likely to be able to pay off any sums due within a reasonable period. If the prospect of such repayment is merely speculative, the court is unlikely to exercise its discretion. In *Bristol and West plc v Dace* [1998] EWCA Civ 1468 (CA), the court refused to exercise its discretion where the mortgagor was resting his hopes of repayment on the prospect of winning a legal action against his neighbour and then selling the property. Robin and Anne's plans to sell the building plots would have to be considered in the light of this. It may be that, on the facts, this is not considered speculative but a real method of repayment.

Section 8(1) of the **1973 Act** provides that the court may treat as sums due such instalments of the mortgage as the mortgagor would have been expected to pay by the date of the hearing and may effectively ignore any provision in the mortgage deed, making the whole of the mortgage debt due on default on any one instalment.

Section 36, however, gives the court power only to suspend an order for possession for 'such period or periods as the court thinks reasonable'. Such suspension must be for a specified time and cannot be an indefinite adjournment (*Royal Trust of Canada v Markham* **[1975] 1 WLR 1411**). The ground for the suspension is that the mortgagor is likely to make good any defaults or remedy any other breach of obligation in the mortgage deed, within a reasonable time. In *Realkredit Danmark v Brookfield House Ltd* **[1999] EWCA Civ 630**, the Court of Appeal held that the size of the arrears and the defendant's inability to pay were relevant factors for the judge to have taken into account in granting a possession order.

The courts had always regarded a 'reasonable time' as anything between two and four years, and the guidance on **s 36(2)** in the *Supreme Court Practice* referred to 'at least two years'. However, in *Cheltenham & Gloucester Building Society v Norgan* **[1996] 1 WLR 343**,[6] Waite LJ said, 'the court should take as its starting point the full term of the mortgage' and ask 'would it be possible for the mortgagor to maintain payment-off of the arrears by instalments over that period?' This effectively puts lenders in a position of having to show why a lesser period should be adopted, instead of the borrower having to persuade the court that he could catch up on payments within a set period of between two and four years. Evans LJ, who gave a concurring judgment, suggested eight questions which the county court judges should ask in deciding whether or not to exercise this discretion. These include such matters as how the arrears accumulated, whether the borrower's difficulties are temporary, the type and terms of the mortgage, how much remains owing, and any factors affecting the security which should influence the period of repayment.

In *Norgan*, the security was valued at a sum of £100,000 in excess of the debt and so was a very adequate security. In this question, the amount of security is not as great proportionately as in *Norgan*, which may justify a lesser period than the whole of the mortgage term.

Even if Robin and Anne are not able to persuade the court to reschedule their repayments over a very much longer period, they may be able to persuade the court that they have every possibility of paying off the arrears by selling the plots with planning permissions, and the court might then be prepared to exercise its discretion in their favour.

In *Target Home Loans Ltd v Clothier & Clothier* **(1992) 25 HLR 48**, the Court of Appeal used the power to suspend a possession order under the **1970** and **1973 Acts** for four months to enable the mortgagor to sell the property while in possession. It was accepted that this would be likely to realise a higher sale price than if the mortgagee repossessed and then sold a vacant property. It is possible therefore that Robin and Anne may be able to achieve a stay of any possession

[6] Here starts your discussion of the cases.

order on the ground that they themselves are trying to sell the property and have a realistic chance of doing so.

The case of *Clothier* was considered, however, in *National & Provincial Building Society v Lloyd* **[1996] 1 All ER 630**, where Neill LJ (referring to the judgment of Waite LJ in *Norgan*) said that the court must be even-handed between the mortgagor and the mortgagee. In *Lloyd*, the court refused to suspend a possession order on the mortgagor's claim to be able to sell parts of the property (two barns) to pay off only part of the debt. It was said that there was no reason why the mortgagee should have to accept piecemeal sales of parts of the property from time to time.

In practice, a mortgagee will usually seek possession only in order to sell the mortgaged property with vacant possession. A mortgagee who seeks to occupy the property is strictly accountable to the mortgagor for profits which *might* have been made, as well as for those which were *actually* made, and therefore is not in a very happy position (*White v City of London Brewery Co* **(1889) 42 ChD 237**, where the mortgagee of a public house was liable to the mortgagor for the difference in rent which he might have received if he had let it as a free house and not as a 'tied' house).

The mortgagee's statutory power of sale is contained in the **LPA 1925, s 101**, and applies to all mortgages made by deed, unless there is a contrary intention stated. It only *arises*, however, when the mortgage moneys have become due; that is, when the legal date for redemption has passed. It only becomes *exercisable* under one of the three circumstances set out in **LPA 1925, s 103**. These are that the mortgagee has demanded repayment of the capital outstanding and the mortgagor has defaulted for three months, that the mortgagor is two months in arrears with interest payments under the mortgage, or that the mortgagor is in breach of some other covenant in the mortgage deed, such as a covenant against letting the property. The legal date for redemption is usually inserted, quite unrealistically, into a mortgage deed as six months after the date of the mortgage. This is not because anyone imagines for a moment that the mortgagor will be able to repay the whole of the loan and interest at that time, but so that the remedy of sale is available to a mortgagee fairly early on. Assuming that the legal date for redemption in their mortgage deed has passed, as Robin and Anne are six months in arrears with the interest payments, the power of sale has become exercisable.

If the title to Orchard Cottage had been registered, any limitations on the chargee's powers of sale (such as a postponement of the legal date for redemption) should have been entered as restrictions on the freehold title. By virtue of **LRA 2002, s 52(1)**, the chargee of a registered charge has the power of sale of a legal mortgagee subject only to entries on the register. This provision seems to be intended to protect a purchaser against the risk that the property is transferred to him before the power of sale has arisen.

In exercising a power of sale, a mortgagee must take reasonable care to obtain a proper market price for the property. In *Cuckmere Brick Co v Mutual Finance Ltd* [1971] Ch 949,[7] the mortgagee instructed estate agents to sell. The estate agents were told that planning permission had been obtained for thirty-five houses, but were not informed that planning permission had also been obtained for a hundred flats. The auction advertisements therefore mentioned only the houses. The mortgagor drew the mortgagee's attention to this and requested a postponement of sale to allow the property to be correctly advertised. Evidence was given that housing developments are very different from flat developments, the latter involving a larger initial outlay but yielding higher profits. Developers involved in flat developments would not bother to attend an auction of land for housing development. The estate agents received a surveyor's letter indicating that the valuation of the land with planning permission for flats might be approximately double (£70,000) the valuation with planning permission for houses only (£35,000). The mortgagor wrote to the mortgagee on the question of valuation. The auction nevertheless went ahead. It was held that the mortgagee had not taken reasonable care to obtain the market value of the property and was liable to the mortgagor in damages for the difference between this and the price actually obtained. Such a claim by the mortgagor must be brought within six years (*Raja v Lloyds TSB Bank plc* (2001) Lloyd's Rep Bank 113).

Although it was suggested in *Standard Chartered Bank Ltd v Walker* [1982] 1 WLR 1410 (CA) that the duty owed by mortgagees in exercising the power of sale is one in the tort of negligence, this was doubted by the Privy Council in *Downsview Nominees Ltd v First City Corp. Ltd* [1993] AC 295, which preferred the view that the duty to obtain a proper market price is a duty in equity. The significance of the duty existing only in equity is that it is narrower in scope than the duty of care in negligence. Thus, it does not include any duty on the mortgagee to take steps to improve the value of the property, such as by obtaining planning permission, carrying out improvements, or letting: *Silven Properties Ltd v Royal Bank of Scotland* [2004] 1 WLR 997. There are also equitable duties of good faith and due diligence in relation to any dealings with capital moneys: *Medforth v Blake* [1999] 3 WLR 922 (CA), stating the duties of a receiver, which in this context were held in the *Silven* case to be identical to those of a mortgagee. It is now clear that the equitable duty extends to the mortgagor and anyone else interested in the equity of redemption,

[7] Some detailed facts follow—you might omit this if time is pressing, but it does help to explain the situation and display knowledge.

including later mortgagees and (as held in *Barclays Bank plc v Kingston* **[2006] EWHC 533 (QB)**) the mortgagor's guarantor.

Nevertheless, if Robin and Anne remind both the bank and the agents of the planning permissions, which will obviously increase the market price of the property, it might be questionable whether the bank will have acted in good faith if the sale then goes ahead without mention of this. They would have an action for equitable compensation against the bank, which must also be liable for any negligence of the agents instructed by it.

(b) The fact that Robin and Anne have received a higher offer for the property might suggest that the bank has not complied with its duty to take reasonable care to obtain the 'true market value' at the date of the sale: *Cuckmere Brick Co Ltd v Mutual Finance Ltd* **[1971] Ch 949**. Whether the bank has complied with this duty would therefore be a matter of evidence.[8]

It might appear from *Cuckmere Brick* that the Lords Justices were referring to a duty of care in tort; but (as discussed in part (a) earlier)[9] later cases, notably *Downsview Nominees Ltd v First City Corp Ltd* **[1993] AC 295**, have clarified that it is only a duty of care in equity. The practical significance of this in the problem is that there is no wider duty, for example, to sell at the best time from the mortgagor's point of view. Thus, in *China & South Sea Bank Ltd v Tan Soon Gin* **[1991] 1 AC 536**, the Privy Council held that a mortgagee is under no duty to delay exercising the power of sale until market conditions are more favourable. Robin and Anne cannot therefore argue that the bank is in breach of its equitable duty merely because the market value of the house has risen since the bank entered into the contract for sale.

The mortgagor's equity of redemption is extinguished when the mortgagee, in the exercise of its power of sale, enters into a valid contract for sale of the mortgaged property: see the judgment of Millett LJ in *National & Provincial BS v Ahmed* **[1995] 2 EGLR 127**. A contract of sale by the mortgagors, Robin and Anne, cannot put their purchaser, Denis, into a stronger position vis-à-vis the mortgagee than they are in themselves. Therefore, even if Denis were to protect his estate contract by entry of a C(iv) land charge (if the title to Orchard Cottage is unregistered) or by a notice in the charges register (if the title is registered) before Cuthbert had taken similar steps to protect his own estate contract, the bank's sale and subsequent conveyance or transfer to Cuthbert would be unaffected: *Duke v Robson* **[1973] 1 WLR 267**. Therefore, assuming that the power of sale has arisen, upon the bank's contracting to sell to Cuthbert, Robin and Anne's equity of redemption is replaced merely by an equitable interest in the property. Any contract of sale by Robin and Anne to Denis would therefore be merely a sale of such equitable interest. This equitable

[8] It is often difficult to deal with evidence rather than law in the exam context. But that is what this area of law entails.

[9] Don't repeat stuff—cross reference.

interest would then be statutorily overreached on the subsequent conveyance or transfer by the mortgagee (**LPA 1925, s 2(1)(iii)**) and become instead an equitable interest in any surplus remaining after the bank has applied the sale moneys in accordance with **LPA 1925, s 105**. Under that section, the bank would hold such surplus in trust for Denis (as the person entitled to the mortgaged property).

✚ LOOKING FOR EXTRA MARKS?

■ The detailed discussion of the cases helps to explain the context here and is worth extra marks. This is an area where points of evidence and shades of difference on the facts do matter.

↗ TAKING THINGS FURTHER

■ Brown S, 'Consumer Credit Relationships—Protection, Self-Interest/Reliance and Dilemmas in the Fight against Unfairness: The Unfair Credit Relationship Test and the Underlying Rationale of Consumer Credit Law' (2016) 36(2) *Legal Stud* 230–57.
Discusses the power relationship between mortgagee and mortgagor.

■ Clarke, A and Kohler, P, *Property Law, Commentary and Materials* (CUP 2005), Chapter 18.
An excellent discussion of security interests.

■ Howell, J, 'Land and Human Rights' [1999] *Conv* 287.
*A discussion on whether the right of a mortgagee to immediate possession of the land (amongst other matters) is compatible with the **European Convention on Human Rights**.*

Online Resources   www.oup.com/uk/qanda/

For extra essay and problem questions on this topic, as well as advice on revision and exam technique, please visit the online resources.

Skills for Success in Coursework Assessments

13

First Word

● It cannot be emphasised enough how important it is to write well. Lawyers are wordsmiths. Words are our tools and we must use them precisely to convey what we mean. Writing well is an essential requirement and if you have been pulled up about this in formative coursework, or, if you know that this is not your strong point, then do something about it. It may be that your university offers classes for writing skills. If it does, go to them. Practise writing and make sure you learn basic grammar from an English grammar book. You will be marked on whether you have made clear what you are arguing, and that comes from good writing skills.

● In coursework this is even more important than in exams because, as you have time to get it right, that will be the expectation. In the heat of the exam room there is leeway for some infelicities of style—not so in coursework.

Planning

● You have time to plan your coursework assignment, and that is time well spent. Coursework is about research and here is an opportunity to demonstrate your research skills. But how good are they? Before you get to this point you need to ensure that you have grasped how to use the law databases and the printed word. Much of research nowadays can be done online, but do not assume that everything is available online. While what is produced today is (almost) always put online immediately as well as being in print, that does not apply to historical material. For instance, *The Conveyancer and Property Lawyer* is not available online before the 1980s, and there may be important articles which you need to use from that era.

● Next, are you actually competent at using the databases? Ensure you go to the sessions arranged by your library for learning how to use these databases. They are all a bit different and can be idiosyncratic. You may also find that some of the journals you are used to finding in one place are no longer available there. That is for commercial reasons—publishers negotiate with the online databases and can pull out of one set and join another. If you can't find a journal article in one place, then hunt around and usually there is an invaluable person who can help you—the law librarian. Make their acquaintance.

- Having done the hard work of learning research skills, use them. Read all the primary (cases, statutes, etc) and secondary material (books, journal articles, policy documents, guidance, Law Commission reports, etc) you have been given and go a bit further for that first-class answer.

- Take notes as you read the points that link back to your coursework question. Your note should consist of the following:

  - citation (book, article, etc);

  - page number where you read the key point you want to use;

  - any verbatim quotation in quotation marks;

  - any argument, point, or dispute, etc on which you wish to rely.

You think you will remember these key things—but you won't. It is also the way to avoid an allegation of plagiarism (more on that later).

- As you do this reading (your research), start to develop your argument for the assignment. If you are asked to critique something, for example the status of overriding interests, then address this question as you read through the material. Build your coursework from your research.

- Write a plan for your coursework. If it is an essay, then you have an argument to make. Think of it as a thread which needs to link all the points you are going to make. For example, if the question asks you to consider whether the rules for adverse possession fairly balance the interests of the parties, then think through what your answer is going to be. Do you agree that the rules do achieve this or not? Or do you think there are some points either way? Set out your points so that each sets out to answer the question. Keep the thread going to the end.

- If it is a problem question, then list the issues and jot down in your plan all the cases etc. that are relevant, then the secondary material. If asked to advise, decide what your advice is going to be and ensure your conclusion deals with that.

Read, Research, then Reference

- Most Law Schools use OSCOLA (the Oxford Standard Citation of Legal Sources). Download and print a copy of it and keep it beside you as you do your research. In your notes write down the OSCOLA-proof citation. You only need to do it once—do it at the start. A few Law Schools use the Harvard system of referencing, so check before you start which is the preferred method.

- Make sure you reference any statement, opinion, argument, or statistic that you give. It is about giving credit where it is due and about enabling a reader to go and check for themselves what that author said. For example, 'as Lady Hale states, . . . '. Then in your footnote to this, put the source of this reference (in the correct OSCOLA (or Harvard) format). It is a good-news story for you, as it shows you have been going about your research in a diligent and profitable manner. Your feedback will mention that there has been good research undertaken. You will be rewarded for reading, researching, and referencing.

- If you are going to quote verbatim, then use the appropriate punctuation marks and cite (it is called pinpointing) the exact page numbers where that quote is to be found.

Practical Points

- Keep within your word limit.

- Footnotes and a bibliography must be included and done in OSCOLA (or Harvard) fashion. Note that (rather irritatingly) OSCOLA has different rules for footnotes and bibliography. Read OSCOLA and follow the rules.

- Proofread not once, but twice. Once when you have just finished; then go away for a few days, and then proofread again. On each occasion proofread twice—once for sense (does that sentence/paragraph make sense; is that sentence too long?), the second time for typographical errors. Even if you use a spellchecker, still go back and make sure it has chosen the correct word.

Last Word

- Enjoy the research involved and the writing, and most of all making the argument. It is what being a lawyer is all about.

COURSEWORK QUESTION

Critically[1] examine the extent to which the decision in *R (Newhaven Port and Properties Ltd) v East Sussex County Council*[2] [2015] UKSC 7 is effective in governing the ability of people to use land which appears[3] to be available for the public.

[1] Usual suspect—this requires a critical analysis of this decision not a description.
[2] Reading the case is not optional here.
[3] Really the key point—in the UK, we assume we can use the beach freely—but what is it that entitles us to do so? What is the nature of PROPERTY?

ANSWER POINTERS

1. <u>Refer to the two decisions of the UKSC</u> which consider the meaning of the phrase 'as of right' in the **Commons Act 2006, s 15(4)(a)**: *R (Barkas) v North Yorkshire County Council & another* [2014] UKSC 31 and *R (Newhaven Port and Properties Ltd) v East Sussex County Council & another* [2015] UKSC 7.

2. <u>Describe the effect of s 15 of the 2006 Act</u> (any person may apply to register land as a town or village green where a significant number of local people have enjoyed lawful sports and pastimes on that land 'as of right' for a period of at least twenty years). In particular, deal with the meaning of 'as of right' in **s 15(4)**. Discuss prescriptive acquisition (mention *R v Oxfordshire County Council, ex p Sunningwell Parish Council* [2000] 1 AC 335 at 349) and show how in *Barkas* and *Newhaven*, the Supreme Court applies the rules of acquisitive description by an analogy which derives from the use of the words 'as of right' in

s 15(4) of the **2006 Act**. It followed that the County Council's refusal to register the field as a village green under **s 15** of the **2006 Act** had been correctly upheld by the courts below, and the appeal was dismissed.

3. **Deal with the following three issues** (*Newhaven*, para 25):
   - whether the public enjoyed an implied licence to use the foreshore and therefore the use was not 'as of right';
   - whether the public enjoyed an implied licence to use the beach, by virtue of Byelaws permitting and regulating access to the harbour, including the beach, so that use of the beach was 'by right' and not 'as of right';
   - whether, in any event, **s 15** of the **2006 Act** cannot be interpreted so as to enable registration of land as a town or village green if such registration is incompatible with some other statutory function to which the land is to be put.

4. **Critical analysis**: here you need to get to grips with the key issue. Beaches in the UK appear to be freely available to the public. But what is the nature of the property right which we have to use them? Reference articles such as: Jill Robbie, 'Finding Common Ground: R (on the application of Newhaven Port and Properties Ltd) v East Sussex CC', (2016) 6 *Conv* 487–96, which is a case comment. For a different slant, which looks at 'wild law', see Helena Howe, 'Making Wild Law Work—the Role of "Connection with Nature" and Education in Developing an Ecocentric Property Law' (2017) 29(1) *J Env L* 19–45.

5. **Conclusion**: Critique the conclusion of the case noting that:
   - the user was by permission in the light of the byelaws;
   - in any event, the **2006 Act** cannot operate by reason of incompatibility with the statutory basis on which Newhaven's predecessors acquired the land, and the statutory purposes for which they held, and now Newhaven, holds, that land.

 Online Resources   www.oup.com/uk/qanda/

Go online for extra essay and problem questions and a podcast with advice on revision and exam technique.

Index